East Hampton: A History and Guide

East Hampton: A History and Guide

JASON EPSTEIN AND ELIZABETH BARLOW

Foreword by Everett T. Rattray

Illustrated by Ralph Carpentier

*A Selective Guide to
Living Well in East Hampton
by Irene Silverman*

Medway Press, Inc.
Wainscott and Sag Harbor

First Edition

Typography and design by Walter Bernard
Maps by Marvin Kuhn

Library of Congress Cataloging in
Publication Data
Epstein, Jason. Barlow, Elizabeth.
  East Hampton.
  Includes index.
  1. East Hampton, N. Y.—History.
  2. East Hampton, N. Y.—Description—
    Tours. II. Title.
F129.E13E67   974.7'25   75–5694
ISBN 0–915458–00–4

ACKNOWLEDGMENTS

Without the generous help of many long-time residents of East Hampton the authors could not have written this book. The writings of the late Jeannette Edwards Rattray were an important resource. Everett Rattray was kind enough to read the manuscript, as was Carleton Kelsey, and their great knowledge of the town saved us from many errors and improved our understanding on many points. Dorothy King, who supervises the Pennypacker Long Island Collection at the East Hampton Free Library, was always helpful, as was Jean Young of the John Jermain Memorial Library.

Dr. Larry McCormick of Southampton College shared his geological knowledge with us, and Sam Hammill and his colleagues at the Collins-Dutot partnership, who were hired as consultants by the Group for America's South Fork, provided valuable information on East Hampton's ecology. The late Fred Schmid of the Morton Wildlife Refuge was an entertaining and instructive field guide, and Richard Plunkett of the National Audubon Society offered some useful notes on birds.

A special pleasure has been our conversations with various descendants of the town's first settlers and early residents. Robert David Lion Gardiner was extremely generous with his time and knowledge; Raymond Osborn, David Osborn, and Amy Osborn Bassford of Wainscott have given us their recollections of that village; Asa Miller provided a lengthy and useful account of life in the Springs; and Ency Beyer has shared her knowledge of Sag Harbor.

Others who, like the authors, were not born here but have adopted the town and appropriated its past, were also helpful. Hilda Lindley helped us on our trips to Indian Field in Montauk, and Otto Fenn shared his intimate knowledge of Sag Harbor architecture. The authors also wish to thank Joseph Markowski, Jr., for the use of valuable documents in his possession and for his knowledgeable appreciation of the Whaler's Church. Phyllis Reed provided valuable assistance in compiling the section on services and shopping. As always, the authors take full responsibility for whatever errors and omissions remain in the text.

Contents

East Hampton is a good many things. Its very name is Hydra-headed, for East Hampton is a Town with a capital T. It would be a township in other parts of the nation; but within the Town there is also the incorporated village of East Hampton with a mayor and other civic trappings. East Hampton, the village, is a famous resort. Amagansett, another resort, is also a part of East Hampton, the Town, and exists without its own government. Ask a native of Sag Harbor, another incorporated village, about East Hampton, and he will assume you are speaking of East Hampton, the village, and likely enough embark upon a dissertation on social climbing, even though he may live in that portion of Sag Harbor which is a border province of East Hampton, the Town.

And there we have reason enough for a guide to East Hampton. From Montauk Point to the west side of Wainscott Pond, the Town's geography is fraught with confusion, its nuances only sketchily charted. Some have called East Hampton a state of mind; if anything, it is a state of many minds. A skilled ear can still detect the difference between the dialect of the Springs and that of Wainscott, and the adjoining town of Southampton is in another country.

These are reasons for a guide, and some of the reasons for a history. But East Hampton has had three good histories already, plus an abundance of shorter works describing this or that aspect of the Town's past. Why another history?

Our definition of history changes constantly, hence the need for new histories, fresh retrackings over old and difficult ground. David Gardiner's *Chronicles of East Hampton* was not enough for Henry Hedges; he had to write his *History of East Hampton Town*. Judge Hedges's work did not satisfy Jeannette Edwards Rattray, and her *East Hampton History and Genealogies* is whetting the curiosity of another generation.

What we have here is not new history; there is only one history of East Hampton Town, the one we are living today and the one our grandparents lived. There are only different ways of looking at this history. The narrator has his or her point of view just as surely in 1975 as did Nathaniel Prime a century and three-quarters ago when he wrote his excellent history of Long Island and dwelt long upon its ecclesiastical background; he was a minister, and this was to be expected. Prime was writing for his day, as were his successors for theirs.

If we have learned anything, at last and perhaps too late, it is the interdependence of all things in nature. Today's history recognizes this chain of life, and this book, unlike earlier histories and guides to this area, includes a careful look at the geology, botany, and climate of the South Fork. This is natural history; part of this volume is social history, as well. One of the authors has pondered long the question of Sag Harbor's sudden decline as a whaling port around 1850. The answer probably rests as much upon human, social factors as upon economics—the gold rush, for instance—or geology and geography, which combined to bring Nantucket down.

We cannot know what went on in the mind of a Montauk dying of measles, childhood nuisance turned plague in a population lacking in developed resistance, or in the minds of his survivors as they put their marks upon some paper passing title to their lands when title was a concept unknown to them. Nor can any history of the Revolution, or a reading of documents and letters, tell us exactly how it felt to live at that time and in this place. The best we can hope for is the history which through known fact and speculation, stated or inspired in the reader, leads that reader to a general sense of its subject.

Evocations, in history as in music, can be fine experiences. Such an experience is a journey, of a day or a week or a lifetime, through the ancient communities of the South Fork of the East End of Long Island, armed with some sense of what has happened here, when, and why. Such a sense of the past and guide to the present is in your hands.

Everett T. Rattray
editor, East Hampton *Star*

That East Hampton is of great historical interest can hardly have gone unnoticed by anyone who has spent time here. Relics of its rich and varied past are to be seen everywhere, from Montauk's Indian Field to the Victorian mansions of Sag Harbor and from the mills of East Hampton Village to the town's ancient burying grounds.

One purpose of this book, therefore, is to present this history, in so far as it can be determined from the available records. The first section is devoted to such a survey. It is intended for the armchair visitor or resident. However, the book is also meant to be a sightseer's guide. In another section the authors have attempted to explain the significance of this or that house or bit of landscape as each may be interesting from a historical, architectural, economic, or even geological point of view. A final section aims to remind the resident and acquaint the visitor with the necessary or amusing services available in the town. The authors have tried to be comprehensive, but they cannot pretend to have been exhaustive. They went where their curiosity and experience led them. Their omissions reflect their own limitations and not those of whatever topics they may have overlooked.

In the historical sections, nevertheless, the reader may find himself overwhelmed with detail, as the authors themselves were when they got into their subject. Nearly everything in the town—whether the houses, the churches, the streets, or even the trees and beaches—has its history, and soon one's imagination begins to populate the place with ancestral shapes and voices. The authors hope that before long the reader will find, as they themselves did, that these details of the past enlarge their appreciation of the town and reveal a dimension of East Hampton whose existence they suspected, but whose richness may have been unfamiliar to them.

More than that of most American towns, East Hampton's past remains a vital part of its present life. Though the modern town flourishes as a resort and as a fishing and agricultural center, an incalculable part of its energy comes from a continuing involvement with its origins, whether among its farmers whose ancestors, in some cases, worked the same farms three centuries ago, or its fishermen, some of whose techniques are not much changed since Indian times, or from its continuing and often stimulating struggles with the pros and cons of modern development, struggles which, as the reader will see, are as old as the town itself.

Jason Epstein and Elizabeth Barlow
East Hampton, April 28, 1975

A History of East Hampton

Overleaf:
Main Street, East
Hampton, shortly
after the erection of
the famous land
mark church in
1717.

THE FIRST SETTLERS

Of the original nine settlers who founded the town that would eventually be called East Hampton, six came from Lynn, Massachusetts. They were English and so they built their village in the New England style rather than in the Dutch style that prevailed in western Long Island; and for many years they maintained strong social and economic ties with the New England colonies. In 1657, nine years after the original settlement, they associated themselves formally with the colony of Connecticut at Hartford for purposes of counsel and defense; and, even though East Hampton was later incorporated into the colony of New York, the settlement continued to resemble the towns of New England in attitude and appearance.

Why these farmers, who had only recently come to Lynn from their homes in England, decided to move on to the hazardous new settlement in the Long Island wilderness is not entirely clear. Probably the English governors encouraged the settlement in order to forestall the Dutch, who also had their eyes on eastern Long Island. As for the settlers themselves, undoubtedly they were impressed by the large tracts of treeless plains they found on their arrival and by the abundance of fish and game in the adjacent woods and waters. Many of them had come originally from an area around Maidstone, an important agricultural town and port in Kent on the Medway some ten miles upriver from the North Sea. Their farming skills and their knowledge of the sea and ships fitted well with the natural advantages offered by eastern Long Island, and before long they prospered.

Along with their skills, they brought with them a long tradition of political and religious rebelliousness. Three centuries earlier many of their Kentish ancestors had joined Wat Tyler and Jack Straw in the popular uprising against Richard II, and in 1635 Archbishop Laud complained to Charles I that "there were yet very many refractory persons to the government of the Church of England about Maidstone."

Nor was it only in matters of politics and religion that the citizens of Maidstone, and the future settlers of East Hampton, were troublesome to the authorities. In 1524 a royal decree forbade them the use of hops in the brewing of beer because hops tended to "make people melancholy." Yet they persisted in growing this "wicked weed" until James II was finally obliged to legalize what he could no longer suppress. Maidstone is still a hop growing and brewing center.

Though Maidstone and the area around it were greatly troubled by successive outbreaks of plague in the early seventeenth century, the major reason for the immigration to the colonies must have been the continuing religious and political strife that dominated English history in the first half of the century. With the important exception of Lion Gardiner, the original settlers were Puritan opponents of the king and the established Church.

In addition to their stern morality they also had strong ideas on the subject of individual rights. Kent was unusual among English counties in that much of its land was in freehold; that is, it belonged to the men who farmed it and was not leased by them from the nobility or the crown as was commonly the case elsewhere in England. Thus the Kentish settlers of eastern Long Island cherished the concept of private property. From these facts emerges the character of the founders of East Hampton: they were independent in their habits of drink, their manner of worship, and their attitude toward property.

In 1648 a party of Dutchmen had come to Southampton, which had been settled eight years earlier, to buy land from the Montauk Indians. Thanks probably to the close relationship between Lion Gardiner and Wyandanch, the Montauk chief,

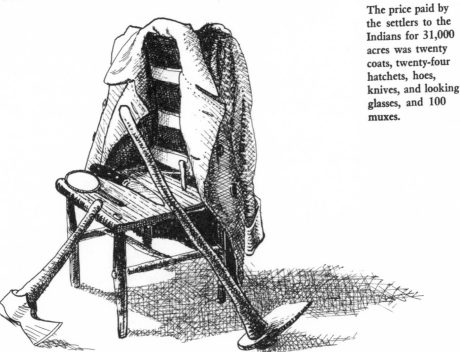

The price paid by the settlers to the Indians for 31,000 acres was twenty coats, twenty-four hatchets, hoes, knives, and looking glasses, and 100 muxes.

17

the English succeeded in preventing this transaction and on April 29, 1648, bought some 31,000 acres themselves from the Montauks. Thus the town of East Hampton was founded, though for the first fourteen years of its history its Kentish settlers called it Maidstone, as the settlers to their west called their settlements North Sea and Riverhead, which are also Kentish names. The purchase was made by Theophilus Eaton, governor of the New Haven colony, and Edward Hopkins, governor of the Connecticut colony, and it extended from the eastern boundary of Southampton to Hither Hills or Nominicks, in Montauk, which is approximately at the western edge of the present Hither Hills State Park. The price paid to the Indians was twenty coats, twenty-four each of hatchets, hoes, knives, and looking glasses, and 100 muxes, which were tools that the Indians used to drill the clam and periwinkle shells they then strung together as wampum, a product the Montauks exported as tribute to other more powerful Algonquian tribes throughout the northeast.

In 1651 the two governors deeded this land to the residents of East Hampton for the sum of £30 4s. 6p. Between 1658 and 1686 some 10,000 additional acres were purchased at Montauk to be held in common by the freeholders of East Hampton and to be used as summer pasture for their herds of cattle and sheep and horses.

In 1664 the Dutch surrendered New Netherlands to the British. Thereafter Long Island became part of the vast holdings of James, duke of York (later James II). Reluctantly the New England settlers of East Hampton severed their ties with Hartford and New Haven, and became part of the district of Yorkshire in the Province of New York. Yet as late as 1703 Lord Cornbury complained that "the people of the East End of Long Island are not very willing to be persuaded to believe that they belong to this province. They are full of New England principles. They chose rather to trade with the people of Boston, Connecticut and Rhode Island than with the people of New York."

The first inhabitants built their cottages in what is now the southern end of Main Street on either side of a marsh which was later excavated to become Town Pond. It was here that the community watered its livestock. The first town dwellings were hardly more than rude shelters, cellars dug in the ground, the walls covered with timber, and roofed with thatch. But within a few years the settlers had begun to erect the typical New England salt-box house, some twenty-five feet high in front, sloping to about eight feet at the rear. The sides and roofs were protected by shingles some three feet long, made of

cedar or cypress and all but indestructible. The interiors were dominated by huge fireplaces made of local brick; the ceilings were plastered with a compound of ground clam shells and cow hair. The settlers used seaweed and corncobs for insulation, traces of which are still found as the old houses are remodeled, and they framed their diamond-paned dormer windows in red cedar. They wainscotted their interior walls to the height of the windows and painted them blue. Their floors were made of white pine, and in their large attics they dried apples, corn, and fish. The Mulford house and the Payne house ("Home Sweet Home") survive on the south side of Main Street behind Town Pond as examples of this architecture.

At Baiting Hollow the settlers collected their cattle and fed or "baited" them before driving them to pasture at Montauk.

As in other New England colonial towns, the settlers did not build their houses around a square or in a compound, but rather in lines on either side of a single, long street. The great width of East Hampton's Main Street is a relic not of pretensions to grandeur on the part of the settlers but of the fact that they used this street less as a thoroughfare than as an extension of the village green, as a commons where sheep and cattle were gathered from the farmyards along its length to be driven to pasture in Montauk. Main Street was also used as a farmyard by people whose property abutted it—so much so that in 1654 an ordinance declared that "every man shall clear the highway in the street six foot from the pales all movables as namely carts, ploughs, wood stones or anything that is annoyance to the traveller either by night or day." Twelve

19

In 1654 John Scott appeared on Long Island, where he worked intermittently as a blacksmith and a privateer patrolling the Sound to discourage invasions by the belligerent Rhode Island Indians.

An aggressive entrepreneur, Scott was soon plying back and forth across the Sound as a coastal shipper. He was involved in whaling and the fur trade, rising to the status of a freeman of Southampton, which he represented as town attorney in the incessant boundary disputes between that town and East Hampton. Soon he had bought up by his estimation "near one third of Long Island" from the Indians.

In 1660, when Charles II acceded to the English throne, Whitehall was besieged with petitioners for the reissuance of colonial charters; each colony was trying to enlarge its previous claims. Scott set sail for London aboard the *Oak Tree* in October with £60 worth of curiosities to buy influence at court and a catechism authored by Southampton minister Abraham Pierson from which he had removed the original title page, attributing the approval of the translation to the well-known Algonquian linguist Thomas Stanton. Scott had counterfeited another leaf bearing the words: "Examined by that experienced gentleman (in the Indian language) Captain John Scott." He was twenty-eight at the time, "a proper handsome person" after he had outfitted himself with silk clothes and a light-colored curling wig, and he was able to make an impression at court and gain the king's ear. He wanted nothing less than that Long Island be made the fourteenth North American colony with himself as governor. To bolster his suit with the restored crown, Scott retailed stories of how as a child he had been caught cutting the harnesses of the Roundhead cavalry; this, he said, was why he was shipped to New England as a bound boy.

Upon his return in 1662, Scott laid claim to part of Montauk. In this he was probably acting as attorney for his fellow townsmen of Southampton who wanted pasturage rights to the lush grasslands on Montauk.* An entry in the East Hampton town records of that November states that a committee of townsmen including the minister Thomas James and Lion Gardiner "shall go to Southampton the next day to compound a difference between us and Captain John Scott, Esq. and Mr. John Ogden about Meantaquit [i.e., Montauk]."

The East Hampton delegation was in a difficult spot in dealing with Scott, who was doing nothing to dispel rumors that a patent grant from the king to him was imminent. In fact, he soon went back to England to urge his case along. However, upon his second return he put forth the interesting information that neither Southampton nor East Hampton need pay the taxes demanded of

* During the competitive period when new settlements were vying with each other in appropriating lands from the Indians there was much finagling which was given the barest guise of legitimacy according to the tenets of English common law. For instance, Lion Gardiner had his name and that of his son David put on record as the guardians of Wiamcambone, Wyandanch's son and presumably his heir during the brief period the young man outlived his father—an obvious attempt to bolster East Hampton's claim to Montauk. Not surprisingly, John Scott, with Southampton's interest in mind, did the same thing.

them by Connecticut, the magistracy under which they had thereto-
fore been governed, since Long Island "had another lord, viz. the
Duke of York to whom the soil was given by the King."

Scott continued to buy up more land, and, when Wyandanch's
widow died and his daughter, Quashawam, became the new sunk
squaw, Scott had an entry recorded in the Southampton town
records stating that "the sunk squaw Quashawam doth desire
and impower irrevocably her ancient and great friend John Scott"
to examine all Indian land deeds and to sue for all lands bought and
not paid for (Montauk fell into this category) and to sell all lands
not already sold. During that year—1663—Lion Gardiner died of
a heart attack, and East Hampton lost its foremost counselor on
Indian affairs. Relations between Southampton and East Hampton
became increasingly strained as Scott continued to press his claim
to lands on Montauk.

Scott was instrumental in organizing a "Combination" which
appointed him president until the duke of York or the king could
establish a government on Long Island. With 150 armed men he
advanced on Brooklyn and the other Dutch-governed towns of
Long Island. There he hoisted the British ensign and made speeches
in which he promised his listeners that under the English crown
they would enjoy a greater measure of self-government than under
the autocratic rule of Peter Stuyvesant. Stuyvesant was sufficiently
impressed by this rabble-rousing to sign a treaty with Scott stating
that the Dutch would not molest the English on Long Island.

But Connecticut Governor John Winthrop, who wanted all of
Long Island under his authority, was not impressed. He sent
deputies to Long Island with a warrant for Scott's arrest. Scott was
taken to Hartford, convicted of sedition and nine other offenses
including "gross and notorious profanation of God's Holy day,"
fined £250, and put into prison. He managed to escape just in time
to lead a small cavalry force to New Amsterdam where he tagged
along in Richard Nicolls's capture of the city in 1664 in the name
of the duke of York.

Although Long Island became part of the royal colony of
New York as Scott had insisted it would, he did not enjoy the
fruits of this victory, for it turned out he preferred the role of
populist to that of loyalist and of leader to that of subordinate in
the new regime formed under Nicolls. The people of Southampton
and East Hampton were enraged that under the Duke's Laws, as
the new provisions for governing Long Island were called, there
would be no free elections and taxes would be imposed without
their consent. Scott, who had gone around advertising the coming
of free elections and self-government in the Dutch towns and their
continuance in the largely autonomous English towns, took loud
exception to the Duke's Laws. His leadership of the disgruntled
Southampton faction lost him the favor of Governor Nicolls who,
in league with John Winthrop, found a pretext for confiscating his
considerable property and issued a warrant for his arrest. Scott
thereupon fled to Barbados, departing Long Island forever, leaving
his wife, children, and aged mother behind.

years later property owners were ordered to fence their land along Main Street.

Soon after the settlement was established the townsmen built a network of roads through the surrounding wilderness. Merchant Howell cleared Merchants Path, which led from Poxabogue to Northwest where the town maintained its port until Sag Harbor was settled in 1730. Along Baiting Hollow Road the settlers collected their cattle and fed or "baited" them, before driving them on to pasture at Montauk. Other roads were cleared to the salt meadows at Accabonac and Napeague and to the grazing lands at Wainscott and Montauk. Thus the tiny settlement spread out within a few years to pretty much its present boundaries. There was a bounty on wolves that infested the forests, and pits were dug to trap these animals. Since the Indian dogs were actually only half-tame wolves and the town's livestock was its most valuable property, the town passed an ordinance forbidding the sale to Indians of "any dog or bitch young or ould."

At first the settlers sent their grain to a mill in Southampton on the back of a bullock which they owned collectively. In 1653 they built a gristmill of their own at Northwest Harbor, and soon thereafter they built sawmills and additional gristmills in the village itself. These first mills were turned by horses or bullocks, but eventually they were replaced by windmills, most of which were "petticoat" or "smock" mills, so called because of the shape of their rotating caps which could be turned to catch a favorable wind. In the historical museum at Maidstone there is a model of such a mill, much like those built in East Hampton, except that the entire English mill turns on a post supported by brick piers, whereas only the caps of the surviving East Hampton mills turned. (Between 1770 and 1823 there was such a post mill in Amagansett.) Although the Gardiners owned their windmill, as a rule mills were owned by syndicates of townsmen.

Since skilled craftsmen were forbidden under strict British laws from emigrating from England, the first settlers had to send to Southold for a weaver, to Huntington for a blacksmith, and to Wethersfield in Connecticut for a carpenter. But within a short time the town became self-sufficient and even prosperous. Its inhabitants learned from the Indians how to plant and fertilize corn by burying a menhaden in each hill and how to dry the corn and pound it into samp, a product that is still sold in the town. So much did samp become the staple of the East Hampton diet that mariners lost in an autumn fog used to say they could find the Long Island shore by listening to the rhythmic pounding of the samp mortars. At first goats

The Indians taught the settlers how to plant and fertilize corn by burying a menhaden in each hill.

and sheep were imported from Connecticut, which the settlers called "the Main," and when these herds were established and pastures were cleared the settlers sent for cows and horses. Later they raised swine.

By the time the port of Sag Harbor was established in 1730 East Hampton was able to export to the West Indies and other markets hides, beef, tallow, pork, hoops, staves, cattle, horses, shoes, grain, and salt fish. By the end of the American Revolution Sag Harbor cleared more shipping for foreign trade than New York City and became the state's leading customs port. Whales contributed greatly to the town's prosperity, and shipments of sperm, oil, and whalebone were a source of much of the town's capital. In 1702 Abigail Baker, who married Daniel Hedges in that year, counted thirteen of these creatures dead on the beach in a single day as she rode from East Hampton to Bridgehampton.

Thirty-five years after the original settlement Thomas Osborn owned twenty acres of land, eight oxen, thirty-three cows, two horses, nine swine, and forty-eight sheep valued at £280 1s. 6p. William Mulford owned sixteen acres, two oxen, fifteen cows, no horses, nine swine, and forty-eight sheep, valued at £106 3s. 4p. That year all property held in the town was worth £9,075 6s. 8p. By 1687 East Hampton's population consisted of 223 males, 218 females, 26 male servants, 9 female servants, 11 male slaves, 14 female slaves, and 98 men capable of bearing arms. In the preceding seven years there had been 28 marriages, 116 births, 198 christenings, and 57 burials. East Hampton men lived long lives. Joshua Garlick lived to be 100. Jeremiah Conklin died at seventy-eight; Robert Dayton at eighty-four; Thomas Osborn at ninety. Stephen Hedges lived just six months short of 100 years.

By the beginning of the eighteenth century the population included two surveyors, three coopers, a plasterer, a glover, a hatter, a brickmaker, a glazier, two tailors, a blacksmith, two merchants, four ecclesiastics, a bartender, twelve carpenters, fifty-five shoemakers called cordwainers because they used cordovan leather, twenty-six weavers, and three "gentlemen."

At mid-century the first of three successive generations of the Dominy family had begun making the furniture and clocks for which they are famous in their shop at the north end of Main Street near Hook Mill. A descendant of the Dominy family is currently the plumber in the village of Wainscott.

As East Hampton has grown it has retained much of its prosperity, though it has lost the industrial activity suggested by its fifty-five shoemakers and twenty-six weavers. Today its economy is based largely on tourism, agriculture, and fishing.

LION GARDINER

The early history of the town was dominated by Lion Gardiner, the original proprietor of Gardiners Island, an area of some 3,400 acres, approximately three and one half miles off the north shore of the town. It was on this island that his wife Mary gave birth to a daughter, Elizabeth, the first English child born in the colony of New York. Gardiner, whose descendants remain in possession of the island to this day, had been sent to the colonies by the Lords Say and Brook to build a fort at the mouth of the Connecticut River. The original plan had been for lords and gentlemen and "divers other great persons in England," including John Hampden and Oliver Cromwell, among others, to establish a colony here. But Charles I correctly doubted the loyalty of these would-be colonists and forbade the settlement. The fort, however, remained as a defense against the Dutch, whose settlement had already extended as far as Stamford, and the powerful Pequots who occupied the banks of the Connecticut and Mystic rivers and with whom the English settlers of Massachusetts had recently provoked hostilities. For years these Pequots had demanded and were able to exact tribute from the Montauks and the other tribes of eastern Long Island so that the Indian name for Long Island came to be Paumanok, or land of tribute.

But in 1637 the British, under Gardiner, formed an alliance with Uncas, the Mohawk sachem, and together they destroyed the Pequots. To prove their usefulness to their new allies, the Mohawks murdered Sassacus, the hapless Pequot sachem, who

The first Manor House of
GARDINER'S ISLAND
ANNO *1639*

25

had fled to them for protection, and delivered his head to the English. According to Cotton Mather it was a "sweet sacrifice." Years later a descendant of Lion Gardiner wrote that the English "seemed to relish Indian blood as well as they loved wampum and land." It was as a result of this bloody victory that Gardiner met the great sachem Wyandanch, the leader of the Montauks. Three days after the English victory Wyandanch arrived at Saybrook from Long Island and asked whether the English planned to treat all Indians as they had treated the Pequots. "No," Gardiner replied, "but only such Indians as have killed Englishmen." Wyandanch indicated his peaceful intentions and put his tribe under the protection of the British. He proposed that "if we may have peace and trade with you we will give you tribute as we did the Pequots." Thus the Montauks made themselves dependent on the British settlers for protection from the more powerful New England tribes and became, in effect, Lion Gardiner's subjects. The tribute that the Montauks had once paid to the Pequots they now paid to the English.

Soon thereafter Gardiner purchased his island from Wyandanch and in 1639 took possession of it. By authority of Charles I he became its lord, and he and his heirs exercised feudal prerogatives over their domain until March 7, 1788, when the state of New York annexed the island to the town of East Hampton. Lion Gardiner had the instincts of a diplomat, and it was through his friendly mediation with the Indian Wyandanch that in the years before his death in 1663 he arranged the transfer of much eastern Long Island real estate to the settlers without feud or bloodshed.

THE INDIANS

To call these Indians Montauks, or Montauketts as they were sometimes called, is, in a strict sense, inaccurate, for as Roger Williams said of the Indians of Rhode Island, "They had no name to difference themselves from strangers, except what they take from their place of residence." The place of residence of the Indians whom the settlers called Montauks was according to the deed of 1648 Meunticutt Highland, a stockaded fort atop a hill overlooking Fort Pond Bay. The name itself, which may bear very little relationship to the word the Indians themselves used (the Dutch understood the word to be Mirrachtuala, Mirrachtaulecky, or Matowacs), may mean hilly land, or a place from which one looks out, or, according to other sources, it may simply mean "at the fort."

Poggatacut was the sachem of the Manhasset Indians of Shelter Island at the time of the English settlement of East Hampton. According to tradition, he was the older brother of Wyandanch, although it is not certain whether this term implied blood kinship or merely a friendly relationship between the leaders of two allied tribes. Poggatacut was the leader of the loose federation of Long Island tribes at the time the settlers arrived in East Hampton; not until his death in 1653 did this authority pass to Wyandanch. His name appears on a deed confirming Lion Gardiner's purchase of Gardiners Island for "ten coats of trading cloth."

Poggatacut,
Sachem of
Shelter Island

Wyandanch consulted him before joining the English side in the Pequot War; and Poggatacut must have counseled the participation of the Long Island Indians in the battle that annihilated their ancient enemies and supposedly bought them the protection of the English. To ensure this protection the Long Island Indians began sending to the authorities in Hartford the wampum they had formerly manufactured as tribute to their mainland overlords.

There is evidence that Poggatacut was less sanguine than Wyandanch about the alliance with the white man. Not trusting the English to the extent Wyandanch did, he applied to Hartford for a certificate spelling out the relationship of the English to the Long Island Indians. The commissioners of the United Colonies of New England deliberated and subtly replied that good behavior on the part of the Indians would be rewarded with freedom from molestation by the English. This was not quite the same as protection, and yet the English continued to accept the Long Island Indians' wampum payments.

Poggatacut eventually acceded to the inevitable colonization and subjugation of Long Island by the English. Before his death he deeded his tribal stronghold, Shelter Island, to Nathaniel Sylvester, an English trader from Barbados. Poggatacut's passing came to symbolize to the Montauks and other local tribes a watershed in their transformation from lords of the land to wards of the town. For generations, Indians passing along the highway between East Hampton and Shelter Island (present Route 114) would stop and reverently clear away leaves and debris littering Sachem's Hole, the spot where pallbearers rested the great old chief's body on their trip to the Indian burial ground in East Hampton. A roadside marker today points out the site to passing motorists.

Long before the English arrived, the Dutch called the area along the north shore of the town, adjoining Gardiners Bay, Crommegouw or "Crooked Country," probably because of its indented shoreline, though one historian has suggested, whimsically, that the Dutch may also have had in mind the many pirates who infested the area. They found the area "a fair and fertile land, inhabited by Indians, where the greater part of the wampum was made, for which furs are traded." The Indians, who were apparently numerous at this time, lived a settled and abundant life, in spite of their oppression by the Pequots. According to a legendary account, they were said to be as numerous as the blades of grass, and Governor Winthrop said that their canoes held as many as eighty people. Often these Montauks would travel to the shores of Connecticut and as far as Boston and New York to visit related tribes, but by the time of the English settlement the tribe was already in decline, the result of successive epidemics of smallpox, measles and other European diseases to which the Indians had no natural immunity.

"It is to be admired how strangely they have decreased by the Hand of God, since the English came to settle," wrote David Denton, an English pamphleteer who in 1670 was trying to encourage the English to settle in eastern Long Island as a further deterrent to the Dutch. "A Divine Hand makes way for them, by removing or cutting off the Indians either by wars one with the other or by some raging mortal disease." Yet if the tribe was in decline at the time of Denton's pamphlet, it was still intact. The Indians still lived in their dome-shaped tents covered with straw which they moved from corn field to hunting camp to fishing station across the Montauk hills or along the shores of Gardiners Bay according to the season. A traveler who visited the Indians a few years after Denton wrote described them as "stately and well-proportioned in Symmetry," which he attributed to their use of cradle boards in infancy. They had swarthy skin and long, lank, black hair, and to protect themselves from sunburn and cold they rubbed their bodies with "oil of Fishes, the fat of Eagles, and the grease of Rackoons."

Had they wished, even in their diminished situation these Indians could have destroyed the English settlement in the 1640s. That they didn't was a consequence of their fear of the mainland Indians and their dependence, accordingly, upon the settlers for protection. In the written agreements between Wyandanch and Lion Gardiner, Wyandanch's mark is not the traditional X but a pair of stick figures—two men, equals—shaking hands. To his credit, Gardiner always treated Wyan-

The Indian Sampson Occum was born in Mohegan near New London, Connecticut, in 1723. By his account he was "brought up in Heathenism" until about the age of sixteen when he was converted to Christianity by the Southold evangelist James Davenport. When he was twenty he went to Lebanon, Connecticut, where Davenport's brother-in-law Eleazar Wheelock agreed to undertake the novel experiment of educating an Indian along with the English scholars under his tuition. Occum lived with Wheelock for four years until poor eyesight forced him to discontinue his studies. On a fishing expedition with some Mohegan friends to Long Island, he visited the Montauks and was invited by them to keep school there. Occum agreed and in November, 1749, he settled on Montauk where he remained for twelve years, during which time he married Mary Fowler, an Indian woman.

Pasting an alphabet on small chips of cedar, Occum taught his pupils to recognize letters. He also held religious services, cultivating the seeds of Christianity that itinerant white evangelists had previously planted. For undertaking this missionary work he was granted fifteen pounds per annum by the Society for the Propagation of the Gospel in New England, a small stipend even in those days, especially compared to the four or five times greater allowances given to white missionaries, a discrepancy which cost Occum much hardship and bitterness.

To support his growing family Occum said he "Bound old Books for Easthampton People, Made wooden Spoons and Ladles, Stocked guns, & worked on Cedar to make Pails, Piggins and Churns, etc." Some of the books he bound can be seen today in the East Hampton library.

Eventually he was examined by Wheelock and other New England divines, and, upon their recommendation, on August 29, 1759, he was ordained by the Reverend Mr. Buell of East Hampton, who characterized him as "the glory of the Indian nation."

Outwardly the life style of the Montauks remained similar to that of their ancestors; Occum and his family lived in a wigwam which they rotated between Indian Field and the Hither Hills wood where they got their winter firewood. But the tribal ways were already practically extinct. To the benefit of future historians Occum set down a record of the ancient customs and practices as they were recounted to him by the older members of the tribe. In this little document one senses a nostalgia for the ampler life of the Indian ancestors who "used to make great dances or frolicks" when a child was named or held powwows during which "sometimes they would run into the water; sometimes into the fire; and at other times run up to the top of high trees and tumble down headlong to the ground, yet receive no hurt by all these." Of the powwow he commented, "I don't see for my part, why it is not as true as the English or other nation's witchcraft."

Throughout his life Occum remained the very prototype of the white Indian, converting other Indians to Christianity and teaching them to read and write. Following the years spent on Montauk he

conducted a ministry in his native Mohegan. In 1765 he was sent to England by his old mentor and father-figure Eleazar Wheelock. As a curiosity there he attracted much attention and was hugely successful in garnering subscriptions which Wheelock then misapplied by establishing not an Indian school but Dartmouth College.

Impoverished and disillusioned, Occum lapsed into occasional drunkenness, and for this his fellow churchmen condemned him as an apostate. But he was still an effective leader among his people. Retreating at last from white society in 1775, he led a group of young Indians from the coastal New England tribes along with thirteen Montauks into the wilderness of upstate New York to establish a colony among the Oneida Indians. They called their settlement Brotherton. Occum died and was buried at Brotherton in 1792. Eventually, as white communities were established in the area, the Indians on this reservation were persuaded to resettle near Green Bay, Wisconsin, where various Montauk descendants still live today.

Sampson Occum's Description of the Ancient Tribal Practices of the Montauks

A Montauk Indian before the settlers arrived.

Sir,

1. I shall begin with their marriages. They had four ways of marrying. The first is, as soon as the children are born, or presently after they are born, parents made matches for their children. The father of a male child goes to the parents of a girl, and takes with him a skin or two, such as they wore before the English came, and since they have had blankets, takes a blanket and some other presents, and delivers them to the parents of the girl, and then he will relate his business to them, and when he has done, the other party will manifest their thankfulness, if they agree in the matter; but if not, they will say nothing, but return the things, and the man must carry them elsewhere. But where there is agreement, they will proceed to accomplish the marriage. They prefix a time, and both parties will make preparations. The parents of the boy prepare cloathing, ornaments, and other presents; and the other prepare a great feast; and the relations of both parties generally join in making these preparations, and when the appointed time comes, the parents of the girl and their relations bundle up their preparations, and will call as many guests as they please. The other party also gets in readiness with their company, and all things being ready on both sides, the parents of the girl take up their child, and march with their company to the man's house, and they go in boldly without any compliments, and deliver their child to the man and his wife, and they receive their daughter in law with all imaginable joy, and the mother will suckle the young couple, the one at one breast, and the other to the other breast, and both mothers will take their turns in suckling the couple; and if the children are weaned, they must eat out of one dish; and in the mean time the whole company is devouring the feast, and after the feast they will distribute the presents one to another, and this being ended they have completed the marriage; and every

one returns to their wigwawms, and the couple that are just married are kept at their parents' houses till they are grown up, and if they see fit to live together they will; if not, the parents can't make them to live together, but they will choose other companions for themselves.

2. Parents stay till their children are grown up, and then will proceed in the same manner in marrying their children, as the former; but if the father be dead, the mother will undertake for her son; if both father and mother are dead, some near relation will undertake. There is no material difference between this and the other just mentioned. Many times the couple that are to be married never see one another till the very minute they are join'd in wedlock; in this the young man is seated in a high bench in a wigwam, and the young woman is led by the hand, by her father or by some near relation, to the young man, and set her down by him, and immediately a dish of victuals is brought and set before them, and they eat together, &c.

3. Young people and others are allowed to choose companions for themselves. When a young couple conclude to have each other, they acquaint their parents of it, or near relations; and they assist them in it, they generally make a feast &c. Sometimes the couple themselves make a small feast, and so call few neighbours to eat and drink with them.

4. The couple that are to live together make no noise about it; but the woman makes few cakes baked in ashes, and puts them in a basket and carries them to the man, and sets them down before him, and if they have been free together he is obliged to receive what is set before him, and to live together; but small provocations use to part them, and [they] marry others.

As for the Powaws, they say they get their art from dreams; and one has told me they get their art from the devil, but then partly by dreams or night visions, and partly by the devil's immediate appearance to them by various shapes; sometimes in the shape of one creature, sometimes in another, sometimes by a voice, &c. and their poisoning one another, and taking out poison, they say is no imaginary thing, but real. I have heard some say, that have been poisoned, it puts them into great pain, and when a powaw takes out the poison they have found immediate relief; at other times they feel no manner of pain, but feel strangely by degrees, till they are senseless, and then they will run mad. Sometimes they would run into the water; sometimes into the fire; and at other times run up to the top of high trees and tumble down headlong to the ground, yet receive no hurt by all these. And I don't see for my part, why it is not as true, as the English or other nation's witchcraft, but is a great mystery of darkness, &c.

. . . and after.

danch with dignity; at the same time he never lost an opportunity to enrich himself and the English settlement at the Indians' expense.

The destruction of the Pequots did not make Long Island safe for colonization; rather it elevated to power the aggressive Niantic chieftain Ninigret who, with his colleague Miantonomah of the Narragansett tribe, soon began to plan an uprising against the English settlers. In 1642 Miantonomah crossed the Sound and proposed to the Montauks that "we must be one as they are. Otherwise we shall be all gone shortly, for you know our fathers had plenty of deer and skins, our woods and plains were full of deer and turkeys and our coves of fish and fowl. But the English cut down the grass with their scythes and with their axes felled the trees. Their cows and horses eat up the grass and their hogs spoil our clam beds and we shall all be starved. Therefore stand not in your own light but resolve with us to act like men. Let us fall upon the English at an appointed time."

The plan was for fifty Narragansetts to join thirty Indians from Block Island, a hundred Shinnecocks, and a hundred Montauks, and at a given signal fall upon the whites and kill them. But Wyandanch revealed the plan to Gardiner, who alerted the magistracy in Connecticut, and so, according to

Gardiner, "the plot failed and the plotter, next spring after, died as Ahab died at Ramoth Gilead." Ahab, it will be recalled, was the king of Israel who had incurred the Lord's wrath for having plotted the death of his neighbor and then appropriating his garden. After he died in battle, the dogs licked his blood, as the angry Lord had said.

Relations thereafter between the Montauks and the mainland Indians deteriorated further while the Montauks came to depend still more upon the settlers for protection and trade. In August, 1653, Ninigret attacked the Montauks by surprise at night, killed two sachems and some thirty braves, and carried into captivity several women including Wyandanch's daughter Quashawam or Heather Flower. According to legend Ninigret's raid occurred on the night of Quashawam's wedding (hence the absence of a lookout), and as Quashawam was being carried off she witnessed the murder of her young groom. Whatever may actually have happened, Quashawam remained a captive while her father, with the help of his friend Gardiner, tried to get her back.

Uncas, the Mohegan chieftain, offered to attack Ninigret if the Montauks paid 700 fathoms of wampum. The wampum makers went to work overtime. Seven hundred fathoms of wampum comprised over 50,000 drilled beads, and besides this

An Indian village of the 1680s at Montauk. Third House was later erected near this site.

enormous bribe to Uncas, Wyandanch was sending untold sums of shell money to Ninigret. By September the matter was still not settled, and Quashawam and the other Montauk women languished in captivity until, at last, Gardiner supplemented Wyandanch's wampum with additional ransom raised from his own estate. Quashawam was finally restored to her father, and in gratitude Wyandanch made a present to Gardiner of the land that has since become the town of Smithtown. A remnant of this grant in the village of Bay Shore remains in the possession of the Gardiner family, where Robert David Lion Gardiner, who currently shares a lifetime tenancy of Gardiners Island with his sister Alexandra Gardiner Creel, has built a shopping center.

Hostilities between the Narragansetts and the Montauks continued until in 1658-59 nearly two thirds of the surviving Montauks died of an epidemic, probably smallpox. Wyandanch himself died in 1659. According to a descendant of Lion Gardiner, he had been poisoned. His nineteen-year-old son succeeded him as sachem, but ruled under the joint guardianship of his mother, the so-called sunk squaw, and Lion Gardiner. He died of smallpox in 1662.

In the midst of these calamities the tribe moved to East Hampton where the survivors set up an encampment at the eastern end of Town Pond between Gardiner's house and the house of Thomas James, East Hampton's first minister. In gratitude for this hospitality Wyandanch agreed to give "one half of all the whales or other great fish cast upon the beach from Napeague eastward to the end of the island" to James and the other half to Gardiner, a most generous gift considering the great value of whale oil at that time.

Thereafter the Montauks were likely to appear in the town records not as members of a sovereign tribe but in connection with regulations governing the sale of alcohol or the prevention of smallpox or the prohibition of firearms. John Scott, an English adventurer, described the Montauks at this time as "morose, dull, shrinking and [ill] humored." They had, he said, "a great sense of the injuries they sustained from the Europeans. They are strict computers of wrongs . . . but such people as have purchased their lands fairly have lived with them in peace and enjoyed a quiet neighborhood."

Within fifty years of the death of Wyandanch even the Indian language had begun to disappear. Lion Gardiner's grandson John was probably the last white man in the town to speak the tongue; he was a great fancier of Indian women and according to his descendant, the present Robert Gardiner, the father of numerous Montauk half-breeds. By the time of

John's death in 1738 the Indians were conversing in English, and they signed their contracts not with such names as Poniuts or Sassakatako, but as Tom and Will or as Hannibal and Pharaoh, reflecting the white man's interest in classical antiquity. In 1798 John's grandson, another John Lyon Gardiner, wrote that "there are now only four or five who speak the Indian language. . . . The language is low and soft when compared to that of the five nations . . . in a few years more it will be gone forever." Josiah Beman, a Montauk who converted to Christianity and preached the doctrine of universal salvation, died in 1815. He composed this epitaph for his tombstone:

> *Here Josiah Beman lies*
> *And nobody laughs and nobody cries.*
> *Where he's gone and how he fares*
> *Nobody knows and nobody cares.*

As much might have been said for the Montauks generally.

One of the few who did care was Lyman Beecher, the father of Harriet Beecher Stowe and East Hampton's minister at the time that Beman was offering his doctrine of universal salvation to anyone who would listen. "My spirit was greatly stirred," Beecher wrote, "at the treatment of the Indians by unprincipled persons who sold them rum. One man would go down to Montauk with his barrel of whisky in a wagon to the Indians to get them tipsy and bring them in debt. He would get all their corn and bring it back in his wagon. In fact he stripped them. Then in winter they must come up twenty miles, buy their own corn and pack it home on their shoulders or starve. I swore a deep oath to God that it should not be so. I didn't set up for a reformer, but I saw a rattlesnake in my path and I smote it."

But it was too late. By 1830 the Indians at Montauk had dwindled to five or six families. They had lost their farm land. No one any longer wanted wampum, and the surviving Montauks were reduced to weaving baskets and making brooms. Some worked as menials in East Hampton households. The fortunate ones went to sea on whaling ships.

In 1879 Arthur Benson, a land speculator from Brooklyn who gave his name to Bensonhurst, bought the former Indian lands at Montauk with the idea of developing them as fishing and hunting grounds for wealthy sportsmen. He may also have anticipated that Montauk might soon become a transatlantic port of entry. He rid himself of the few remaining Indians by pensioning them off at eighty dollars per year or by providing them small property grants in East Hampton.

Stephen Talkhouse delivers the mail.

That summer when some of these Indians tried to return to Montauk the town constables chased them off as trespassers.

The year Benson acquired Montauk a tall, hawk-nosed Indian named Stephen Pharaoh, more commonly known as Stephen Talkhouse, died. A whaler and a Civil War veteran, Talkhouse was often hired as the town messenger, walking many miles a day to collect and deliver mail when the Long Island Railroad terminated at Bridgehampton. His pedestrian abilities attracted the attention of P. T. Barnum, who took him to New York and advertised him in his circus as "King of the Montauks." Talkhouse is buried beneath the only in-scribed tombstone in the little Indian cemetery beside the former Indian lands at Montauk. The other Indians buried there lie nameless, their graves marked by rough boulders.

LOCAL GOVERNMENT

From the beginning the town of East Hampton governed itself. The town meeting was held monthly or every three weeks or "on the first wet day when all are to appear there at the beat of the drum." Attendance was obligatory for all free males and whoever failed to vote by "holding up his hands" was fined sixpence.

The East Hampton town meeting, like the town meetings of New England, evolved from the rebellious spirit of English Puritanism, the same spirit that was foreshadowed in Wat Tyler's uprising and was soon to cost Charles I his head, and that would eventually inspire the American Revolution. Though in the decades before the Revolution the people of East Hampton grudgingly suffered their English governors and reluctantly paid their royal taxes, they functioned for the most part as an independent political unit, cut off from New York City and even from Southampton by a wilderness, and depend-ent largely on themselves for their day-to-day government.

The town meeting elected all officers, constituted all courts, tried important cases, heard all appeals, ordered lands allotted, chose the minister and schoolteacher and fixed their salaries, ordered the church built, admitted or excluded settlers, ratified or annulled sales of land, assigned to committees their duties, made police regulations, built the prison, appointed the whale watch, and imposed fines for absence from the meeting, for failing to vote, and for disorderly conduct. The meeting also fenced the public lands, chose the military officers, fixed a time for burning the woods, expelled vagabonds, and provided for highways.

On many occasions the town meeting voted to petition the royal governors for the redress of grievances, particularly those having to do with taxation. Most annoying to the townspeople was the crown's decision to declare the whale a royal fish and tax the fourteenth part of it (some sources say a tenth). In 1716 Samuel Mulford, a distinguished citizen of the town, traveled to London to urge Parliament to repeal this obnoxious tax. Though at first he was ignored, he soon found himself celebrated in the capital when it was discovered by a journalist that he had sewn fishhooks into his pockets to discourage the pickpockets who mingled with the crowds waiting to be heard at Westminster. As a result of his celebrity he was brought before Parliament, spoke eloquently, and the tax was repealed. He returned to East Hampton a great hero and was known thereafter as "Fishhook" Mulford.

CRIME AND PUNISHMENT

In 1653, when the settlement was only five years old, the town meeting sentenced Goody Edwards to pay a fine of three pounds or stand for one hour with a cleft stick upon her tongue for having said that her husband had brought her "to a place where there was neither gospel nor magistracy." Goody Edwards was evidently a quick-tempered woman, for what had angered her was nothing more than her chagrin when she was unable to produce a fine English petticoat which she had boasted of owning. When the constable came to impose her punishment she kicked him, according to the town records, "and broke his shin." When her husband then advised her "to take her punishment patiently," she threatened to kill him.

The next year the town records reveal that

> *Daniel Fairfield a servant of Joshua Garlick, Fulke Davis, John Davis and John Hand, Jr., were brought before the three townsmen—John Mulford, Thomas Baker and John Hand— on a charge of masturbation, and, after extended examination and serious debate and consultation with their Saybrook neighbors, the townsmen, not deeming the offense worthy of loss of life or limb, determine that Fulke Davis shall be placed in the pillory and receive corporal punishment, and John Davis and Daniel Fairfield shall be publicly whipped, which was done, and was witnessed by the three townsmen.*

How John Hand, the townsman, was able to absolve his son John Hand, Jr., is not mentioned.

The indentured servant Daniel Fairfield remained a prob-

lem for the town. According to the record of December 19, 1655, "Mr. James [the minister] declareth against Daniel Fairfield for acting filthiness with his maid and attempting dalliance with his daughter." A jury found that "Daniel is guilty of the act with the one and of dalliance with the other." The record for March 3, 1656, orders that "when Daniel Fairfield's time is expired in May next with Goody Mulford that whosoever shall afterward [employ] him shall be bound in a bond of £20 for his good behavior."

In 1657, five years after six witches had been tried and executed in Maidstone, Kent, but a full generation before the Salem scandals, the little town was rocked by its first and only witchcraft case. Lion Gardiner's fifteen-year-old daughter Elizabeth, who had married the merchant Arthur Howell, fell ill, perhaps of pueperal fever, following the birth of a daughter. On her deathbed she became possessed of the notion that she had been bewitched. Several persons testified under oath to that effect, including Samuel Parsons who said he had heard Elizabeth say to her husband Arthur, "Love, I am very ill of my head and fear I shall have the fever." Whereupon she went to bed, according to Parsons, and, after suckling her child, "screeched out several times together very grievously . . . a witch, a witch; now you are come to torture me because I spoke two or three words against you." Lion Gardiner was called to his daughter's bedside, and while he was with her she cried out again and said that there was a black thing at the foot of her bed. Her husband had to restrain her as she struck out violently while raging against the "witch." Parsons also testified that he came again as the girl lay senseless with Goody Simons in the bed beside her, and that he and Arthur Howell both heard "a noise on the side of the bed as if something had scratched very hard."

Suspicion soon centered on Goodwife Garlick, once a servingwoman on Gardiners Island and the wife of the carpenter Joshua Garlick. Goody Simons testified that while she was nursing Elizabeth she had heard the girl say that Goody Garlick was "a double-tongued woman, and she asked saying, 'You did not see her last night stand by the bedside ready to pull me in pieces, and she pricked me with pins?'" Mary Gardiner, the girl's mother, herself not well, struggled to her "Bettie's" bedside. According to Mrs. Gardiner, Elizabeth "cried and cried, and she said, 'Mother, I am bewitched,' and I, not regarding it, said, 'You are asleep or have dreamed,' and she told me that she was not asleep, and I asked her who she saw, and she said, 'Goody Garlick in the further corner and a black thing at the hither corner, both at the foot of the bed,' and then I charged her that she should not tell her husband nor no living soul, and I said, 'Your husband will tell.' "

The town was in an uproar. Goody Edwards testified that Goody Garlick had been a wet nurse to some of the village babies and that these unfortunate children had subsequently sickened and died. Goody Birdsell said that the child of Goody Davis, a fellow servingwoman on Gardiners Island and the wife of one of the convicted masturbators, died as soon as Goody Garlick had held it in her arms, and Goody Davis corroborated this, adding that Goody Garlick was "a naughty woman." Lion Gardiner, trying to counter these attacks, set the record straight about Goody Davis's baby. He said that the child had died because Goody Davis had starved it by becoming wet nurse to an Indian child "for lucre of a little wampum."

The talebearers were not to be denied. Goody Birdsell and Goody Edwards both testified under oath that they had seen a pin being taken out of Elizabeth's mouth. At this point Joshua Garlick, on his wife's behalf, entered a defamation action against Goody Davis. To resolve the controversy the town meeting on March 19, 1657, ordered that "Thomas Baker and John Hand is to go unto Connecticut . . . to carry up Goodwife Garlick that she be delivered up unto the Authority there for the trial of the cause of witchcraft which she is suspected for." She was charged with the evil eye, "with causing the sickness of infants and the death of cattle, the torments of prickling pain and the blasts of atmosphere by droughts and unseasonable frosts on growing corn." Through the intervention of Lion Gardiner she was acquitted at Hartford, much to the relief of subsequent East Hampton historians.

Instead of hanging her, the magistrates fined Joshua Garlick £30 on his wife's account. The child of Lion Gardiner's unfortunate Elizabeth—her name was Elizabeth, too—was raised by her father Arthur Howell. She became the town heiress with her mother's carefully preserved trousseau of fine clothes bequeathed to her by her grandparents and livestock branded with her initials given to her by her father.

Punishment, however, remained an important part of the town meeting's business. Indians guilty of digging for ground nuts (Jerusalem artichokes) on land occupied by the English were put in the stocks and, if the offense were repeated, publicly whipped. In 1727 the meeting appointed R. Syme to be common whipper and paid three shillings for each person he whipped. (Evidently there had been an inflation. A century and a half earlier, William Simmonds had been paid only

fourpense a person by the Assizes at Maidstone for "whypping and sendyinge certain rogges out of the towne.")

And occasionally lynch law prevailed. Shortly after the Revolution Ebenezer Dayton, a Connecticut peddler "who had been in the habit of supplying the East End with gewgaws and nick-nacks," arrived in town infected with measles. When he insisted on appearing in church to advertise his presence, the indignant townsmen began muttering threats, and, before he could get out of town, a group of young men seized him, rode him on a rail through the village, and ducked him in Town Pond. It was reported that nearly 100 people caught the measles, although no one knew whether the sufferers had contacted the disease in church or at the disgraceful proceedings at the pond. The peddler apparently took the case to court where he was represented by Aaron Burr and was awarded $1,000 damages, collected from the defendants.

But if the town enforced its own laws rigorously, it did not necessarily obey those imposed by the English governors. In the early years of the settlement East Hampton's harbors served as havens for pirates, many of whom had begun their careers as privateers, seizing the ships of England's enemies under letters of marque issued by the crown. By 1699 Governor Bellomont described eastern Long Island as a "great receptacle for pirates," and tried to suppress them. "The people [of the East End]," he said, "have many of them, been pirates themselves and to be sure are all affected to the trade; but besides that they are so lawless and desperate a people that I can get no honest man to go and collect the excise among them and watch their trade. I hear that thirty pirates have come lately into the East End," Bellomont complained to London, "and have a great deal of money with them."

THE REVOLUTION

In two armed sloops and thirteen whaleboats Lt. Colonel Meigs returns to Connecticut after his successful raid on Sag Harbor, the only military action to occur in East Hampton during the Revolution.

On April 29, 1775, the East Hampton town meeting "being greatly alarmed at the avowed design of the Ministry to raise a revenue in America and shocked by the bloody scene now going on in Massachusetts Bay, do in the most solemn manner, resolve never to become enslaved and do associate under all the ties of religion, honor and love to our country, to adopt whatever may be recommended by the Continental Congress." The petition was signed by every eligible citizen.

With the defeat of Washington's forces in the Battle of Long Island on August 2, 1776, all of Long Island fell into the hands of the British. The British fleet, having evacuated Boston Harbor, took up positions in Gardiners Bay, and a British headquarters was established in Southampton under Lord Tryon. By the middle of September Long Wharf at Sag Harbor was crowded with refugees preparing to flee with their possessions across the Sound to Connecticut. So hasty was the exodus that according to tradition bread mixed in East Hampton that morning was baked in Connecticut by evening.

The British imposed an oath of allegiance to which the Americans grimly acceded, since the alternative was death. The prudent Colonel Abraham Gardiner himself administered the oath at bayonet point to his reluctant friends Colonels David Mulford and Josiah Hedges, though later all three of them became refugees in Connecticut. There remains an account, perhaps legendary, of a townsman named Bennett who, when a British officer instructed him in the oath, repeated the officer's instructions. The officer then explained further, whereupon Bennett repeated the explanation, pretending idiocy. Finally the officer denounced Bennett's stupidity, to which Bennett replied by repeating the denunciation. The resulting laughter put an end to the proceeding and, according to tradition, the British made little effort thereafter to secure the allegiance or subdue the spirit of the Americans. On the other hand, they did not hesitate to confiscate the crops and commandeer the farm animals of the townspeople.

Though relations with the British army remained poor throughout the seven years of the occupation, the town seemed less reluctant to entertain the fleet. At least once, and perhaps more often, British naval officers dined at Colonel Gardiner's house and were entertained by the young ladies of the town. Though such familiarity with the enemy might seem treacherous in retrospect, in fact it must have been dictated by simple

The Redoubtable Jedediah Conkling and the Infamous Major Cockrane

Of the British officers who oppressed the Americans, the most notorious was Major Cockrane from Edinburgh, billeted in Sag Harbor. Not only did he take provisions and livestock at will, he butchered the farmers' oxen and administered countless floggings, often with his own hand. One night a British ship carrying supplies came ashore in a storm. Cockrane called upon the local farmers to come to Abraham's Landing with their teams and carry the cargo away to Southampton. The farmers reluctantly arrived, and soon each had carried away his share of barrels. But at the end an extra barrel remained. Jedediah Conkling of Amagansett, a small man but a courageous one according to his contemporaries, was about to depart with his loaded wagon when the Major called him back and ordered him to take the extra barrel. Conkling refused. Cockrane repeated his order and Conkling refused once more. Cockrane then drew his sword and threatened to kill the farmer, but Conkling by this time had climbed to the top of his wagon and, waving his long ox goad, said to the officer, "Damn you, Cockrane, strike straight or you'll never strike another man." At this point Major Cockrane, preferring a stalemate to a test of arms, replaced his sword and Conkling departed, leaving the barrel on the beach.

Later that night at Nathaniel Huntting's tavern Cockrane said that the Amagansett farmer was the bravest man he' had ever met and requested the favor of a drink with him. Conkling grittily declined, swearing to the Major, "I'll see you burned in hell first."

Cockrane was no less brutal to his own troops and was "known to stamp with the heel of his boot on the toes of his men on parade till they could wring the blood from their stockings." He stabled his horses in the church at Bridgehampton and fired at anyone he chose. He pulled old Aaron Isaacs's wig off his bald head, called him a turncoat, and threw the wig into the fire.

caution on the part of the Gardiners, who have always put the security of their island above other considerations. Gardiners were to serve on both sides not only in the War of 1812 but in the Civil War as well.

Nor were the Gardiners unique in their prudence. When Amy Mulford asked her father Ezekiel, a staunch patriot, whether she should accept an invitation to a dance aboard an English ship, her father said, "Go. We are all English gentlemen, although we may think differently on various matters. ... You must accept their invitation affably and enjoy all the pleasures of the occasion with confidence in their loyalty to chivalry, also your father's willingness to entrust his daughter to such enemies." Amy took her father's advice, which proved to be correct. Not only did she suffer no disgrace, she returned home with the present of enough calico to make a dress.

The Reverend Samuel Buell, although a patriot, was also a man who enjoyed the pleasures of the chase. Once when he arrived late for the hunt Lord Percy became impatient and out of temper. Upon the clergyman's arrival and polite inquiry as to what regiment Percy commanded, Percy, intending to insult Buell, snarled, "A legion of devils just from hell!" Whereupon Buell bowed and replied, "I suppose I have the honor to address Beelzebub, the prince of devils."

The war years were generally miserable for the Long Islanders. What crops the British didn't plunder the American forces in Connecticut requisitioned. Industry languished, families were separated, and poverty settled on what had once been a pleasant and prosperous land.

The only military action of importance to occur in East Hampton was the raid of Lt. Col. Jonathan Meigs, who embarked from New Haven on May 22, 1777, in thirteen whaleboats to attack the British garrison at Sag Harbor. Under the protection of two armed sloops he crossed the Sound on May 23 and arrived at Southold at 6:00 P.M. Taking about 170 men with him in the whaleboats, he landed at midnight at the south end of Long Beach about two miles from the village. Two hours later a detachment of his men seized the British officers at James Howell's tavern and captured the British garrison adjacent to the present Whaler's Church on Union Street. A second detachment went to Long Wharf and destroyed twelve brigs and sloops, 120 tons of hay, corn, and oats, twelve hogsheads of rum, and various other provisions. Six of the enemy were killed and ninety taken prisoner. Meigs was back on the Connecticut shore by 1:00 P.M. the following day without a single casualty. Such a raid could hardly have succeeded without the complicity of the local population.

43

RURAL PROSPERITY

With the end of the war the residents of East Hampton resumed their lives as independent citizens, replenishing their herds of cattle and sheep, restoring their increasingly productive fields, destroying the privet hedgerows that marked their boundaries on the theory that these handsome plants were poisonous, and venturing still further out to sea in search of whales and trade. In 1784 Clinton Academy, the first chartered academy or secondary school in the state (the second was Erasmus Hall in Brooklyn, chartered three years later), was built in East Hampton and was to play an important part in attracting visitors from New York City and elsewhere to the area. The academy building still stands on the north side of Main Street, next to the offices of the East Hampton *Star,* where it serves as a museum of local history.

East Hampton's minister Samuel Buell, together with eleven other townsmen, raised £934 to build the school. Among the contributors were Nathaniel Gardiner, the son of Colonel Abraham Gardiner, and Aaron Isaacs, an immigrant Jewish peddler from Germany and the future grandfather of the poet John Howard Payne who would soon become famous as the author of "Home Sweet Home." The academy, which was named for George Clinton, New York's governor at the time, was opened on January 1, 1785. Two years later it received its first certificate of incorporation from the Regents of the University of the State of New York, and Governor Clinton presented it with a bell.

William Payne, the poet's father, taught English and writing, and young men came as boarders from as far away as New York City to prepare themselves for college. The school also accepted local children among its eighty students. At the height of its fame in 1815 its enrollment was 156. After the Civil War it declined as other schools were founded throughout Long Island. Eventually the academy became a center for the town's social and cultural life. For a while it served as the office of the East Hampton *Star* and later as the library until the present library was built in 1912.

In 1790 an act of Congress provided for the establishment of two customs districts in the state of New York, the first at Sag Harbor, the second at New York City, the less important of the two ports in foreign trade at the time. As early as 1760 the Gardiners had two large brigs in regular commerce with the Caribbean while New York City was still using small schooners and sloops. According to local historians, Martha

Clinton Academy in the 1790s, the first chartered academy in the state of New York.

Washington donated a sprig of boxwood to the Dering family, who were the proprietors of the new customs house, and this sprig may have been the ancestor of the many fine boxwoods that continue to grow in the village, though a more likely source is Sylvester Manor on Shelter Island, the original home of the Derings.

The history of East Hampton between the Revolution and the Civil War was one of slow growth and a more or less stable, largely self-sufficient economy. The inhabitants of the town tended to be inbred and reclusive. The town meeting concerned itself with the grazing lands at Montauk and with such matters as paying Henry Dominy £8 to build a schoolhouse at Northwest and providing £12 to build another school at Wainscott. In October 12, 1801, it voted to paint the meeting house a light red or peach "bloe." Two years later it voted to erect guideposts on the road to Sag Harbor. In 1810 it agreed "to get a box made in the gallery with a lock on it for Mr. Dimon to put his Psalm Book and pitch pipe in."

The more daring of the townsmen went to sea in search of whales or became investors in such ventures. The rest raised sheep and cattle and farmed the rich soil, often abusing it so that many of the original clearings were soon exhausted and new ones had to be opened. By the end of the eighteenth century nearly all the land now under cultivation had been cleared. Most of the original woodlands were cut for firewood and left bare. In 1806, according to a Boston geographer, the population consisted of 1,549 "inhabitants" and 886 slaves, the latter figure perhaps an exaggeration, though the Gardiners at the time kept some 200 slaves on their island, while the black population of Suffolk County itself was 13 percent of the total in 1790. By the 1830s most of these were to be freed and given the land called Freetown on North Main Street near the junction of the Springs and Three Mile Harbor roads.

The number of "inhabitants" was to increase by barely a thousand until the growth of the summer colony in the 1870s. Stability and conservative traditionalism were the hallmarks of the town, leading one mid-nineteenth-century observer to remark, "The steady habits and rigid morals of primitive Puritanism are probably retained here in greater purity than in any other part of the new world." J. Madison Huntting, who kept a journal in the 1840s and 1850s, noted on February 15, 1843, that "this day, according to the predictions of the Israelite, is the day when the dissolution of the world is to take place. But nothing at present has occurred to the natural eye in the heavens above or the earth beneath. Everything assumes the same appearance." Timothy Dwight, the president of Yale, visiting East Hampton in 1811, wrote: "A traveller is forcibly struck with a sense of stillness, and sequestration from the world. Every place seems to him a retirement. Noise and bustle clamor at such distance that the din is not heard."

This is not to suggest that life in East Hampton was uniformly dull. There were beached whales and shipwrecks, great storms, the annual cattle drives on and off Montauk each spring and fall, and, particularly after the Great Awakening in 1741, religious revivals to enliven the long winter months. Before the Revolution the town magistrates had found it necessary to fine several persons for incontinence and fornication. Nevertheless, Dwight sanguinely believed that provinciality bred virtue: "The insular situation of the inhabitants," he wrote, "while it has precluded them from many motives of improvement has also preserved them from many sources of corruption." John Lyon Gardiner, on the other hand, disagreed. "The licentiousness that prevailed during the [Revolution]," he said, "has had a tendency of making the people more lax in their morals and more profane perhaps." He noted a dangerous tendency toward secularism among certain townsmen who followed Voltaire and Tom Paine.

According to tradition Martha Washington gave a sprig of boxwood to the Dering family, the first proprietors of Sag Harbor's Customs House in 1790.

According to the great East Hampton preacher Lyman Beecher, "infidelity had gained a foothold" in the town. "An infidel club had been organized—not very large in point of numbers, but composed of men of talent, education and indefatigable zeal." Another historian spoke of the club's "frequent *soirees,* in which they endeavoured to sharpen up the spear of *ridicule*" and stated that "even boys in the street were heard retailing such wonderful arguments against the Bible as the following: that 'it was impossible for a whale to swallow Jonah, since it had been ascertained [in the case of these East Hampton boys by direct experience] that the throat of a whale is not bigger than a *junk bottle*.' " But "I always preached right to the conscience," Beecher wrote to Roxanna, his bride to be, "every sermon with my eye on the gun to hit somebody," and the religious differences in the town were soon healed.

A great diversion was General Training, when the militia would display its skills on East Hampton's Main Street. Here the people would watch the drills and "luxuriate on oranges and peanuts and ginger snaps and molasses candy and boiled cider, beer and ginger pop." According to a contemporary observer, General Training was an occasion not only for "martial music, the display of banners, the vestured uniforms, the mounted officers, the array of numbers, the exhibition of armor," but for "bargains and peddlars and auctions." One auctioneer, a New Englander, was "the most rapid, musical, sonorous talker conceivable. He opened his mouth and words streamed in endless and unceasing volleys. He would hold up wooden combs and cry 'Combs! combs! combs! Here's two dozen wooden combs! What'll you give me for 'em? Ah! Sixpence ha'penny. Going for sixpence ha'penny. Combs enough for the whole neighborhood. Combs enough to shingle a meeting house. All going for sixpence ha'penny.'" Next came suspenders, "Suspenders long enough for any man, short enough for any girl; let in and taken out like an old woman's conscience! How much will you give me for this pair of suspenders? Oh dear! If my grandfather knew I was selling goods at this rate he would get down on his knees and cry like a child." Such were the pleasures of life in East Hampton before the Civil War and the gradual discovery of the town by summer visitors from New York.

WHALING

Sag Harbor, however, which was settled in 1730, was a different, less provincial matter. With the end of the Revolution it became a busy and cosmopolitan port whose ships carried the goods produced in the hinterland to all parts of the world and whose whalers returned with cargoes of sperm, whale oil, and bone used respectively to make candles and soap, as lamp fuel and for corset stays, frames for umbrellas, hoop skirts, and various tools.

Whaling on eastern Long Island began with the Indians long before the white settlers arrived, and in the original deed of 1648 the Indians were promised the "fynnes and Tails of all such whales as shall be cast up on the beach." They found these parts a delicacy, used them in their religious sacrifices, and were willing to risk their lives in pursuit of them when they could not find adequate supplies on the beach.

Once established, the town of East Hampton immediately claimed ownership of all whales fortuitously cast up along the beach. To inject order into the scramble for such prizes, an ordinance was passed decreeing that the finder of a beached whale should receive a reward: if "first tidings" were carried by an Indian, he was to receive five shillings; if the discovery was made by an Englishman, he was to have "a piece of whale three feet broad." Another ordinance divided the entire male population of the town into two whale-cutting teams; overseers were appointed to supervise the men who carved up the drift whales, and those who wouldn't do their part were fined five shillings. It was further decreed that the gentlemen of the town, "Mr. James and Mr. Gardiner, shall give a quart of licker a piece to the cutters of every whale and be free from cutting." The tails and fins of the whales were reserved for the Indians, being of no worth to the English except as a means to promote interracial harmony.

Like the Indians before them the settlers appointed whale watches on the beaches at Wainscott and Amagansett. What they were looking for was the Atlantic right whale, so called because the great quantity of oil and whalebone or "baleen"

When a whale was sighted off Wainscott beach, the whale watch climbed to the top of a pole and alerted the townspeople. Soon the whale horns were heard throughout the village, and everyone ran to the beach to join the chase or watch it.

that it supplied made it the "right" whale to capture. These watches consisted of wigwams framed of oak saplings that had been sharpened and set into the sand, tied together with twigs and thatched with rye straw. The door faced south, toward the ocean, and at the top of the wigwam an elliptical opening served as a chimney. Nearby stood the stage pole, a tree some thirty or more feet high, set in the sand and with its limbs intact to make it easier to climb. When a whale was sighted a watchman would climb to the top of the tree and wave his coat, which the townsmen called "making a weft." Soon the whale horns blew along the shore, the cry "whale off" went up, the whalers came running to the whaleboats, and the dangerous chase was on.

By the 1660s four companies had been formed to sail along the coast as far south as Roanoke for as long as eight months in search of whales. One of these companies was owned by Jacobus Schellinger, the ancestor of Amagansett's present well driller. In 1664 Schellinger, a Dutchman, had immigrated to East Hampton from Staten Island after his farm and home had been destroyed by the British and Indians and his opportunities to participate in the colonial trade with Holland had been ended with the fall of New Amsterdam. Schellinger could have moved back to Holland where one of his brothers was a successful artist, another a surgeon, and a third a silk merchant. But he chose a more intrepid course. Earlier than the English, the Dutch had interested themselves in whaling, and Schellinger hoped to recoup his fortunes by becoming proficient in the "whale design." He brought his family with him to East Hampton, including his teen-aged stepson James Loper. Young Loper, working with Schellinger, became so able a whaler that in 1672 he was offered ten acres and a third of every catch if he would teach the Nantucket fishermen the techniques of whaling. He settled instead in East Hampton, and in the summer months when he was not chasing whales he was a cordwainer.

The whaling business must have prospered, for when James Loper married Elizabeth Howell, the child of Elizabeth Gardiner Howell, he was able to settle upon her £100 (a sort of reverse dowry, an unusual gesture for that period). Three years later he purchased an Indian girl named Beck, a captive from King Philip's War, to be her servant. Loper's seafaring was not confined to whale hunting; he became an exporter of horses to Barbados and ran small vessels probably out of Northwest Harbor to the West Indies, bringing back molasses, rum, sugar, Spanish gold, and logs.

But it was the Indians from whom the settlers had learned

Harpoon and lance

50

the techniques of the "whale design" in the first place, and for as long as whaling was an industry in America Indians shipped aboard the whaling vessels. In the early days of the East Hampton whale fishery, ships owned by Schellinger & Co. and by Thomas James, the East Hampton preacher, as well as by other entrepreneurs, were manned exclusively by Indian crews. These crews typically received half the blubber and bone as pay for their services, but competition for native whalers was so intense that companies soon tried to outbid each other with gunpowder, liquor, and other inducements until Southampton, in an effort to keep the Indians faithful to a single master, finally passed a law declaring that they could not be paid more than one cloth coat for each whale. In 1708 the Encouragement of Whaling Act provided that Indians could not be sued, arrested, or given strong drink during the whaling season which lasted from November 1 to April 15.

By 1687 there were seven whaling companies in the two towns and in that year they landed 2,148 barrels of oil. The following year a boundary was established after much dispute between Southampton and East Hampton. It extended from

Cutting out the whale. The Indians took the tail and fins. The townsmen took the rest.

51

In the 1840s the streets of Sag Harbor were crowded with Fijians, Sandwich Islanders, Kanakas, Portuguese, Chinese, Malays, Africans, Montauks, and Shinnecocks. In 1845 a fire devastated this area.

the western edge of the village of Wainscott, along the present Town Line Road, to a point just east of Hog Neck or Hoggonock, now North Haven, on the bay. At this northern end of the boundary the whaling sloops from the two towns would land their catches and "try them out," that is, render the whale blubber of its oil by boiling it down in large black iron kettles called "try pots." Some of these may still be seen as ornaments on East Hampton lawns as well as on the grounds of the Whaling Museum in Sag Harbor.

It was here, in 1730, at the northern end of this boundary, that the village now known as Sag Harbor was settled. It took its name from its proximity to the Southampton village of Sagaponack, or Sagg as it was then called (from sagabon, a large ground nut, *Apios tuberosa*). In 1753 it was agreed by the Southampton town meeting that Samuel Russell should build a wharf at Sag Harbor. This wharf, with a small tryworks, was built at the foot of the present North Haven bridge. A second wharf and larger tryworks were built in 1761 at the foot of what is now Main Street just west of where the present Long Wharf now stands. The boundary of 1688, which places that part of Sag Harbor to the east of Division Street in the town of East Hampton and the rest in the town of Southampton, bisects this wharf. A century and a half ago a tavern run by one Peter French stood at the foot of the wharf and straddled the town line. Patrons said that they ordered their liquor in one town and drank in the other.

In 1760 the first ships of what was to become the Sag Harbor whaling fleet went to sea but did not venture south of 36° north latitude. These were the sloops *Good Luck, Dolphin,* and *Success,* owned by Joseph Conkling and John Foster. They were followed in 1785 by the bark *Hope,* the first Sag Harbor whaler to be fitted with its own tryworks. The ship was owned by the Gardiners and proved to be a failure. In the same year Stephen Howell and Benjamin Huntting fitted out the brig *Lucy* for a voyage to the coast of Brazil. It returned with a profitable cargo of 360 barrels of oil and the growth of Sag Harbor as a major whaling port had begun. By 1839 Sag Harbor, with thirty-one ships in its fleet, had become the third largest whaling port in the world after New Bedford with 169 ships and Nantucket with seventy-seven.

In 1791 the Long Island *Herald,* the first newspaper on Long Island, was established in Sag Harbor under its editor, David Frothingham. Its first issue carried advertisements for a lost dog, a tailor, a school for young ladies, and a weekly packet boat for New London. Frothingham, whose house still stands on the west side of Main Street, was a supporter of

The try-pots were set up in pairs on brick or masonry foundations on the decks of whaleships.

Aaron Burr. With Burr's help he eventually became editor of the New York *Argus* where he was charged with libel by Burr's enemy, Alexander Hamilton. He was convicted, sentenced, and disappeared. By 1798 the first troupe of traveling performers had come to Sag Harbor and a year later a waxworks was exhibited.

When Timothy Dwight visited Sag Harbor in 1804 he noted that an "exceedingly good harbor allured the inhabitants to this unpleasant place; not unpleasant from want of prospect, but because it furnishes unpleasant streets and walks, and is unfriendly to every kind of vegetation," a result of the fact that the village had been built in a marsh which was gradually filled in as the inhabitants leveled first Turkey Hill, then Meeting House Hill that rose from the wetlands. Hampton and Burke streets were a swamp, Division Street impassable. In the year of his visit Dwight counted 120 houses in the village, "the principal part of which are on a winding street, terminating at the shore." Main Street was crossed by a swamp; nevertheless the population at the time had grown to 1,168.

The War of 1812 temporarily halted the whaling industry as the elegant British officer Captain "Kiss Me" Hardy anchored his fleet in Gardiners Bay. Hardy had been Nelson's flag captain at Trafalgar. When the great British admiral died in Hardy's arms his dying words became the flag captain's sobriquet. Inevitably "Kiss Me" became a favorite guest at Gardiners Island.

The purpose of the British fleet was to blockade the approaches to New York City by way of Long Island Sound. Presumably Hardy had no intention of invading or occupying eastern Long Island, but instead must have wanted to propitiate its population so as to carry on his blockade with as little interference as possible. Nevertheless, Sag Harbor turned itself into a garrison in 1812. There was a redoubt on Turkey Hill, just behind the present American Hotel, another at Bluff Point, and a third on Derings Hill near the present Catholic church. Some earthworks stood just to the west of the wharf, and for years thereafter this area was known as the North Battery. An arsenal built in 1810 at the corner of Church and Union streets supplied these various emplacements.

According to a contemporary diarist, "Many and many times both day and night an alarm would be sounded that the British were coming and the women and children would be taken off into the oak timber to stay until the cannon balls fired from the port at the wharf drove off the raiders." Yet the British appear to have attempted a landing only once, and this

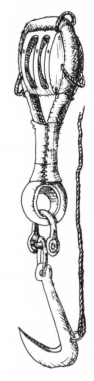

A blubber hook was used by whalemen to lift the blubber from the whale carcass.

was easily repelled by the Americans. Even on this occasion it is unlikely that the British had meant to capture the town, but simply to punish it for having harbored Joshua Penny. Penny was an intrepid patriot who, having invented a primitive torpedo, attempted repeatedly to mine the hulls of the British fleet. So much did Penny's efforts alarm Admiral Hardy that he ordered the bottom of his flagship the *Ramillies* to be swept every few hours. Penny was eventually betrayed by a Tory spy, arrested, put in irons, and fed on bread and water for the duration of the war.

With the war over, the Sag Harbor whaler *Argonaut* under Captain Eliphalet Halsey, a collateral ancestor of the American admiral who served in World War II, rounded Cape Horn in 1817 and became the first ship from this port to enter the Pacific. A year and eight months later it returned with 1,700 barrels of sperm oil.

Though a fire in 1817 destroyed much of the port, the damage was soon repaired. In the following year there were 150 buildings in the village, chiefly at the north end of Main Street and along Bay Street as well as on the wharf itself. By 1845, at the height of the whaling industry, the population reached 3,600, a figure it was never to attain again.

By 1819 a Sag Harbor whaler approached the coast of Japan. Nine years later there was a Sag Harbor whaler off Zanzibar. In 1848 Captain Royce of the Sag Harbor bark *Superior* passed through the Bering Strait into the Arctic Ocean and found the waters thick with bowhead whales, while three years earlier Captain Mercator Cooper reached the Japanese mainland. Having rescued some stranded Japanese sailors he approached the port of Jeddo where he was treated politely but ordered not to land at the risk of displeasing the emperor. The charts he made at the time were used eight years later by Commodore Perry.

By the 1840s Sag Harbor's shipowners, several of them descended from the original East Hampton families, had invested $1,500,000 in 12,522 tons of shipping. They employed 1,000 seamen, and along Main and Bay streets were some eighty businesses, including coopers, pump makers, ship chandlers, warehouses, oil cellars, riggers, masons, tailors, boat builders, and, at the cove at the foot of Glover Street, Samuel L'Hommedieu's ropewalk. For a typical voyage a Sag Harbor whaler might require of the local merchants sixty barrels of pork, sixty of beef, twenty-four of flour, 8,000 pounds of bread, 2,500 pounds of pilot bread, 4,000 pounds of ham and shoulders, 300 pounds of cheese, 700 pounds of butter, seven barrels of vinegar, three barrels of dried apples, three bags of coffee, 500

gallons of molasses, 300 pounds of codfish, and sixteen pounds of pepper, to say nothing of 2,000 empty barrels, ten dozen shoes, forty spruce poles, 500 pounds of tarred rope, 150 harpoons, and a half dozen penholders.

A cedar-planked whaleboat approaches a whale. The harpooner is in position at the bow. The mate, or boat-header, is at the stern.

According to the Sag Harbor historian H. D. Sleight, the ships would arrive "battered and weatherbeaten. . . . They were hove down to be sheathed and recoppered. Riggers, carpenters, masons, coopers, caulkers, iron workers found ropes and spars to be replaced, timbers and planks to be removed, tryworks to be set up, casks to be stowed, seams to be pitched and caulked and gear to be replaced. Painters swarmed over the hull and grocers and warehouse clerks and supercargoes ran to and fro taking orders and delivering provisions." By 1827 a pumping station had been built near the corner of Division and Bay streets, and pipes ran down to the wharf to supply the whale ships with fresh water.

The profit from a successful voyage could be huge, but the risks were huge too. Hundreds of Sag Harbor men were lost at sea, many of them hardly out of their teens. In Sag Harbor's Oakland Cemetery on Jermain Avenue the memorial stones tell of captains still in their late twenties or early thirties who died at sea, many of them East Hampton farm boys who came of age as boat steerers or harpooners; that is, as oarsmen who sat closest to the bow of the fragile whaleboat. When the boat was within a few fathoms of the whale the boat steerer would drop his oar, spring to his feet, and launch his harpoon. He would then change places with the boat header or steersman at the stern and assume the delicate task of keeping the plunging whaleboat from capsizing as the stricken whale dashed this way and that to rid itself of the harpoon. Meanwhile the boat header, now standing in the bow, would plunge his lance into the harpooned whale until it either died or escaped.

When a returning ship was sighted approaching the entrance to the port at Cedar Point lighthouse, the whole town would turn out. A signal went up on Jason Beebe's mill on Suffolk Street just south of Jefferson Street. The American flag was raised on the lighthouse at Cedar Point, and the proud owners in their tail coats and plug hats would board a sloop to meet their vessel as it stood off Barcelona Neck, probably named for its resemblance to the entrance to the Spanish port. By the time the ship had made fast, the wharf was jammed with villagers.

The streets of Sag Harbor were filled in these years with Fijians, Sandwich Islanders, Kanakas, Portuguese, Chinese, Malays, Montauks, and Shinnecocks. Queequeg, the pagan harpooner in Melville's *Moby Dick*, came to America in a Sag Harbor whaler. (So did the Marquis de Lafayette and later Andrew Carnegie.) Whalebone, which was not, in fact, the whale's skeleton but the flexible, sievelike teeth of the right whale, was piled high at the foot of the wharf and along Bay Street awaiting a rise in the market. Taverns abounded, then as now, and a red-light district stood near the present Noyac Road. Drunken sailors were locked up in a ship that sat in an anchorage, called Indian Jail, east of Hog Neck, adjacent to a point which was then called Sullen or Sulk's Neck. Melville's Queequeg had come to Sag Harbor hoping to improve himself and his fellow pagans by learning the ways of Christians; "But, alas! the practices of whalemen soon convinced him that even Christians could be both miserable and wicked; infinitely more so than all his father's heathens. Arrived at last in old Sag Harbor; and seeing what the sailors did there; and then going on to Nantucket, and seeing how they spent their wages in *that* place also, poor Queequeg gave it up for lost. Thought he, it's a wicked world in all meridians. I'll die a pagan."

One of the more famous Sag Harbor inebriates of this period, though not himself a sailor, was Jason Hoopete, an old Montauk Indian. When he entered the village, his long hair flowing in the wind, children would shout, "Here comes

Jason" and then run for cover for fear that he might return to savagery. By the time he passed the cooper's shop the workmen would put down their tools and begin to beat out a rhythm with their barrel staves. With Jason in the center, they formed a circle and danced to the roaring clatter of the staves. When they were done and the Indian and the coopers had shaken hands all around, Jason would move on to Smith's on the Dock where, according to the recollection of a late resident of the village, "fire water was to be had and a vast longing to be appeased."

Among the East Hampton families whose members entered the whaling industry as owners or captains were the Hunttings, the Howells, the Mulfords, the Hedges, the Paynes, the Piersons, the Hands, and the Osborns. James Fenimore Cooper, who married the daughter of a local family, lived in Sag Harbor from 1819 to 1823 where he invested unprofitably in various whaling ventures. He also began his career as a novelist here with the books *Precaution* and *The Sea Lions*. Natty Bumppo, the intrepid hero of his *Leatherstocking Tales,* is said to have been inspired by Captain David Hand of Sag Harbor, a descendant of one of the original East Hampton settlers.

Hand had fought heroically in the Revolution, both on land and sea. He was captured five times, and on one such occasion, after he had been impressed aboard a British merchantman, said, "All I ask now is to begin at the taffrail and fight the whole ship's crew forward and die like a man." He was later imprisoned at Halifax but escaped and made his way on foot through the wilderness to Sag Harbor, where he had a long and distinguished life. He married five times and died in 1840 at the age of eighty-four.

A whaling bark. Filled oil barrels are stacked in the hold. Bundles of staves are stored in the bow and made into barrels as needed. The tryworks are aft of the foremast. The captain's cabin is in the after part of the ship. The crew's quarters are forward.

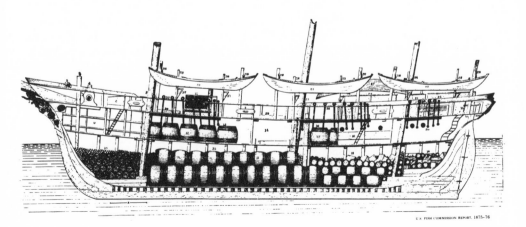

U.S. FISH COMMISSION REPORT, 1875-76

The Amistad Incident

On an August day in 1839 an event occurred, involving two Sag Harbor men, that was to arouse the entire country.

The men were Captain Henry Green, a Sag Harbor whaler, and his friend Peletiah Fordham, who kept Sag Harbor's foremost tavern, just west of the foot of Long Wharf. On the day in question they were hunting along the edge of Fort Pond Bay in Montauk when a small boat came ashore manned entirely by blacks. They had come from a long, low black schooner anchored in the bay. It was called the *Amistad*. Their leader, an African named Cinque, stepped ashore, introduced himself to the two men, and proposed that Captain Green pilot the *Amistad* to Sierra Leone. As the negotiations progressed Green noticed that a United States revenue cutter had approached the *Amistad* and, before the black man could become aware of what was happening, had taken it into custody. In his haste to return to his ship, Cinque lost a belt overboard containing 600 Spanish doubloons which neither he nor Captain Green, despite their best efforts, could recover.

What had happened was that Cinque and his fellow Africans were being transported along the Cuban Coast as slaves when they overwhelmed their captors, killed all but two of them, and seized their ship. With the help of the two survivors they managed to sail the ship north to Montauk where it was ultimately apprehended as Cinque and Captain Green were negotiating on the beach.

The ensuing trial of Cinque and his followers, which was held in Hartford, created a sensation, as abolitionists argued with the government lawyers that the slaves had the right to secure their freedom by whatever means. Cinque at first pretended that he spoke no English, a pretense that imputed perjury to Captain Green who had already testified to the negotiations at Fort Pond Bay. But when Green confronted Cinque on the witness stand the African eventually confessed to the truth, and the trial proceeded before a packed courtroom. Eventually the court denied salvage to all claimants, and turned the Africans and the ship over to the president of the United States. John Quincy Adams argued the case for Cinque and his followers before the Supreme Court which ruled that since the rebellion had occurred on the high seas even the president had no right to detain the Africans, who were then given passage home. The trial and its outcome were a victory as much for the abolitionists as for the Africans. Cinque returned to Africa where he entered the slave trade himself.

Between 1820 and 1850, 490 whaling vessels landed at Sag Harbor, bringing a total of 83,101 barrels of sperm oil, 821,595 barrels of whale oil, and 6,728,809 pounds of whalebone, worth some $15 million. In 1847 alone there were thirty-two arrivals worth $996,413. In these years several Sag Harbor vessels were chartered out for the slave trade, and when their crews, which were usually Portuguese, managed to elude the authorities and land their cargoes on the Cuban coast, the owners made even larger profits from "black ivory" than from whaling. Only two of these ships, the *Montauk* and the *Augusta,* were captured by the authorities. How many other ships were involved in the trade remains obscure.

As late as 1858, with the whaling industry in decline, seven Portuguese sailors arrived in Sag Harbor with their pockets full of gold. They turned out to be part of a crew that had brought a cargo of slaves to the Cuban coast, collected their profits, and scuttled their ship off Montauk. Perhaps on the theory that eastern Long Island was a safer place than most for men in their situation, they arrived that September in Sag Harbor, where one of them, Favieo Maiecola, died under mysterious circumstances. His tombstone in the Oakland Cemetery reads,

> *Though Boreas' winds and Neptune's waves*
> *Have tossed me to and fro,*
> *By God's decree, you plainly see*
> *I'm harbor'd here below.*

In 1845 a fire destroyed much of Sag Harbor, but the prosperous village soon rebuilt itself. By 1847, however, the Sag Harbor whaling industry had begun its long decline, the result of the gradual extinction of the whales, the greater cost of outfitting the ships for increasingly longer voyages, and the discovery of gold at Sutter's Mill which lured much of the Sag Harbor fleet and most of its personnel through the Strait of Magellan to the California gold fields. In the 1850s the price of whale oil rose sufficiently to justify a brief revival of the industry. But by 1870 petroleum had largely replaced whale oil, and Sag Harbor was left with only two barks and a single brig in its fleet. The once thriving port, according to a New York newspaper, had become "a deserted village." After a disastrous fire in 1887, the buildings along Bay Street were not replaced and the area became what it is today, open land facing the harbor. A map drawn after the arrival of the railroad in 1870 shows the central part of the village to be pretty much as it is now.

Yet the commercially defunct port revived briefly every

The "W.W.Coit" sailed from Sag Harbor to Greenport and then to New York.

summer. A new economic force had arisen; the rural vacation, especially the vacation by the sea, was fast becoming an annual rite for well-to-do Americans. But summer tourism was of no great benefit to Sag Harbor, for the town was only a stopover where travelers arriving by packet hired a stage to drive them on to where the Atlantic surf beat against the south shore, to the sleepy little village of East Hampton that would soon economically surpass its more cosmopolitan neighbor to the north.

THE RESORT

East Hampton's favorable reputation as an attractive resort was longstanding. Officers of the crown once came here for the "waters," presumably as guests of the Gardiners, and those who were not invited by the lords of the manor stayed at the tavern kept by Thomas Baker overlooking the village green or later at Samuel Huntting's inn.

Its agricultural prosperity made the town a study in picturesque rusticity. When Timothy Dwight visited it in the first decade of the nineteenth century, he found besides the windmills, the church, and Clinton Academy some eighty houses and two schoolhouses. The town was compactly arranged along its broad village green and, with its already old, unpainted houses, was, to Dwight's eye, remarkably unpretentious. He wrote that "the passion for appearance, so far at least as building is concerned, seems hitherto, to have fastened very little on the inhabitants of East Hampton. A general air of equality, simplicity and quiet is visible here in a degree perhaps singular."

Lyman Beecher, who came to East Hampton at the age of

twenty-four to serve from 1799 until 1810 as the Presbyterian minister, undoubtedly entertained Dwight and showed him his orchard, a novel experiment at the time, since East Hamptoners were convinced that the sea breezes, which contributed so much to their own good health (Dwight said that their chief complaint was hypochondria), were harmful to the fruit trees. For Beecher, who had spent his youth in bustling New Haven, the town was something of an outpost, and he described it as consisting of "the plainest farm-houses, standing directly on the street, with the wood-pile by the front door, and the barn close by, also standing on the street." The recently built windmills stood at either end of the green. "There was," wrote Beecher, "so little travelling that the road consisted of two ruts worn through the green turf for the wheels, and two narrow paths for the horses." Just such a scene as Beecher painted would serve as a magnet for the numerous artists who started arriving a generation later.

Though at first the townspeople were suspicious of the summer visitors, they soon saw them as a source of profit and rented out their best rooms to them. By the 1850s the rooms for boarders at seven dollars a week were fully booked, and the New Yorkers would stroll along Main Street, under the sycamores and willows that lined the old green and past the young elms which have grown to such venerable proportions today. The roadbed was still grassy; in spring freshets of water coursed through it, emptying into Town Pond. An elderly resident said of the village at this time:

> *There were resting places all along the Green, and here the neighbors met at twilight for friendly gossip. . . . Every morning and evening various herds of milch cows crossed the Green going to pasture on Mill Plain or Lily Pond, returning at nightfall to bathe in Town Pond. Almost everybody kept geese, and every morning after the cows passed the Green, flocks of geese and goslings marched to the Pond. They owned it by day but deserted it when the cattle came back at night, and fled honking to their respective barnyards.*

John Howard Payne once referred to the town of his "Home Sweet Home" as "Goose Heaven."

Though in 1863 the Mulford house welcomed as a boarder such a distinguished visitor as General George McClellan after he had lost command of the Army of the Potomac, the town remained relatively isolated until after the Civil War. The long journey from New York, the lack of hotels and other resort facilities in East Hampton, and the availability of resorts closer to the city guaranteed the preservation of East Hampton's rustic somnolence.

But by the 1870s summer visitors began to arrive in increasing numbers, either by Rackett and Fithian's horse-drawn omnibus from the railhead in Bridgehampton six miles away or, after an overnight trip from New York to Sag Harbor by packet boat, in Jerry Baker's three-passenger stage. The boarding houses had become famous for their hearty breakfasts. After breakfast the holiday-makers would ride the stage to the beach where they would sit under rustic arbors until it was time to return for dinner, the main meal of the day, which was served at noon. Afterward there were omnibuses for excursions to Three Mile Harbor and Fireplace. Afternoons were for picking berries and mushrooms in the woods. An evening supper, called tea, was served promptly at six.

In the summer of 1877 *Scribner's Magazine* commissioned a group of writers and artists to write and illustrate a series of articles on the villages of Long Island. They called themselves the Tile Club, as each member was expected to decorate a tile at the club's weekly meetings. These artists were so taken with East Hampton that they decided to make it their summer home. Boarding at various houses along Main Street, they remained throughout the Eighties and Nineties, and their presence soon attracted other visitors.

In their dark-brown velveteen suits, their knee breeches, their heavy ribbed, hand-knit stockings, and their berets, the artists soon became a fixture in East Hampton, and their easels and umbrellas were to be seen everywhere, in the cow pastures, along the beaches, and on the country roads. Among them only Winslow Homer, Childe Hassam, and Thomas Moran produced works of real distinction, but they added glamour to the town's inherent attractions and by the Eighties East Hampton had become a thriving resort for rich New Yorkers.

By the 1920s the first generation of East Hampton artists

The first Maidstone Clubhouse.

had largely disappeared, but the area continued to attract painters and writers. During the Second World War Gerald and Sara Murphy, who lived on the Wiborg estate, just west of the Maidstone Club at Pink Beach, brought a number of European artists to East Hampton including Max and Jimmy Ernst, Fernand Léger, Salvador Dali, André Breton, and Marcel Duchamp. Many of them stayed, and by the 1950s a more or less permanent artists' colony established itself.

The second Maidstone Clubhouse.

In 1869 the East Hampton Lawn Tennis Club—the precursor of the present Maidstone Club—was formed, and in 1891 the Maidstone Club itself was organized. It opened the following year with a dinner dance, the music supplied by Professor Van Houten's Sag Harbor orchestra. That summer a society writer for a New York newspaper said of East Hampton that it was "innate with good breeding and good family"; that it "excluded the vulgar parvenus that so often make life wretched at the conventional summer resort. Six miles to the nearest railroad (at Bridgehampton) keeps off the rabble." Another writer said that year that in East Hampton, "You wear fancy blazers, dress a good deal, play tennis and attend hops."

The summer residents who formed the Maidstone Club

and whose style came to dominate the summer colony were genteel, Episcopalian, and rich. They tended to be lawyers, businessmen, doctors, and clergymen. They were at least as much interested in good works and good behavior as in good times. Their games were golf and tennis. They swam in the ocean and rocked on the vast porch of the original clubhouse.

In their club they didn't drink and the only boisterousness they may have allowed themselves was at the fox hunt. They raised trotting horses and built a track on Pantigo Lane just west of Spring Close. There was another track in Sag Harbor, on the site of the present Mashashimuet Park, and a third where the East Hampton high school now stands. While the rest of America had begun to transport itself by automobile, the East Hampton summer residents clung to their surreys and dog-carts. Unlike the visitors to Newport and Southampton, they did not consider themselves members of "society" nor did they display their wealth. Though a few of them built mansions, most of the houses they built for themselves were in the shingled style of the local dwellings. On Sundays they filled the local churches and, until 1906, forbade themselves golf, and after 1906 permitted it only after 12:30. They shot snipe and plover at Georgica Pond, and the women were thought daring when they wore bloomers as they rode their bicycles along Main Street or to the beach. The artists they befriended painted moonlit scenes on clam shells and added such verses as "Where ocean kisses Apaquogue and then retires confused."

The local celebrity was the actor John Drew, who would drive along Main Street in his carriage with his niece Ethel Barrymore beside him or with the actress Mary Boland. Drew rode to hounds on his white Irish hunter Tornado and gave an annual hunt breakfast. He donated two swans to Town Pond, and these, together with eight others placed in Georgica Pond by Albert Hunter in 1914, were the progenitors of East Hampton's present flocks. When Drew died in San Francisco at the age of seventy-two after a performance of *Trelawney of the Wells,* Major John Vernon Bouvier, the grandfather of the present Mrs. Onassis, eulogized him at the Maidstone Club's Saturday night dance.

The first pink coats were seen in the town in 1890. In 1902 "Dickie" Newton, a summer resident, organized the Suffolk Hounds in a large house on the south side of Montauk Highway in Hayground, just west of Bridgehampton, now the tavern Another Time. In 1896 the town built a bicycle path along Main Street; in addition, there were bicycle paths to Bridgehampton and Sag Harbor.

The favorite artist of the summer colony and a founder of

the Maidstone Club was Thomas Moran, a protégé of John Ruskin, who brought back from Venice a gondola that had once belonged to Robert Browning. He kept it in Hook Pond and hired George Fowler, a Montauk Indian, as his gondolier. His fellow clubman, William King, kept a dog-cart, drawn by a bob-tailed horse, with a coachman in buckskin livery perched on a high seat behind the passengers. When Goelet Gallatin's two-hundred-pound coachman saw this costume, he demanded livery for himself. By 1902 there were enough liveried coachmen in East Hampton to hold a grand ball for seventy-five couples. Membership in the Maidstone was simple. The secretary-treasurer kept his account book with him wherever he went, and whoever wanted to join had only to approach him at the beach or on Main Street, pay his fee, and become a member. Among the local residents, however, only the Gardiners belonged.

The club itself was built on eighteen acres purchased for $14,000 from Henry Hedges, whose house was then moved several feet away to make room for the club's driveway. The original building burned down in 1901 and was replaced a year later with a two-story clubhouse in native shingle, 190 feet long by eighty feet wide, with a piazza sixteen feet deep

An East Hampton mansion.

on all four sides. Rocking chairs abounded. There were tennis courts and the beginnings of a golf course. This second clubhouse also burned, to be replaced in 1924 on a different site by the present building with its white stucco façade and its oak beams in imitation of an English country house.

By 1895 when the railroad reached East Hampton the town found itself with 800 summer visitors. To accommodate this new wave of holiday-makers that summer the directors of the Maidstone Club voted to build the Maidstone Inn, adjacent to the club. It opened the following year and operated until 1935 when it burned. The Huntting Inn, the oldest in the town, installed East Hampton's first bathtubs.

In 1873 C. P. B. Jeffery built "Sommariva," East Hampton's first summer home. In 1888 the Reverend Dr. E. Heber Newton built a summer home on the dunes on the East Hampton side of Georgica Pond. On the western banks of the pond

Prohibition Days in East Hampton

All, however, was not conservative repectability in East Hampton. During Prohibition eastern Long Island was "the wettest place in the country" and a "bootlegger's paradise," according to the Reverend George Brown of Patchogue's Methodist Episcopal Church. During Christmas week, 1923, the East Hampton *Star* affirmed that "everyone knows that nearly every night from one to five trucks pass through East Hampton loaded with liquor. . . . Last Saturday night over 500 cases passed through the town. . . . It is said that last week there were nearly 20 boatloads of liquor landed on the shores of eastern Long Island."

It is unclear to what extent the townspeople themselves were involved in this traffic, though legends abound that would, if they were true, implicate them heavily. During Prohibition three ships laden with liquor came ashore in storms and inspired among the baymen and others a vogue for bottle fishing. At the least, the town seemed to accept the illegal traffic calmly: "Last Sunday," according to a report in the East Hampton *Star*, "about twenty-five rum runners and gunmen visited East Hampton in search of two hijackers who, they claimed, had stolen twenty-five cases of liquor from their warehouse near Devon." As they assembled at the corner of Main Street and Newtown Lane, "several of them became quite noisy in their threats to get the highwaymen who had robbed them." Chief Morford, however, "told them to act orderly as they would be placed under arrest and this quieted them down." According to the *Star* they left town later in the evening. What happened to the hijackers is unknown. However, the *Star* estimated that some 3,000 cases of liquor were successfully landed and carried through town that week.

in the village of Wainscott William S. Wood bought the hundred or so acres that were to become the Georgica Association. Wood and his heirs parceled out their Georgica property on a lot by lot basis to congenial friends, and to ensure the continued upright character of their settlement they put strict covenants into their deeds of sale. Georgica Association residents were forbidden to "erect, maintain, or permit to be maintained . . . any hotel, club-house, liquor or beer saloon." Although of a puritanical bent, the association founders were more pliant in regard to the Sabbath than the trustees of the nearby Maidstone Club, for Maidstone members, who were forbidden to play on their own golf course on Sunday, sailed their boats across Georgica Pond and played on the course in Wainscott.

By the 1890s East Hampton real-estate promoters were offering farm land for residential development. A thirty-acre farm with buildings was available for $3,000. A "large, elegant Queen Anne country seat with barn, carriage house plus ice house on 10 acres" could be had for $24,000. With the establishment of the Maidstone Club the houses along Dunemere Lane were built, and houses along the southern end of Main Street were bought and expanded by summer residents who would often arrive for the season with ten or more servants. By the turn of the century East Hampton was no longer simply a picturesque village, inhabited in the summertime by artists and writers, but a sedate resort for rich and conservative New Yorkers. It was not until the end of Prohibition that the Maidstone Club opened its first bar.

FARMING AND FISHING

The coming of the railroad to East Hampton in 1895 not only precipitated the town's development as a resort but influenced other changes in its economy as well. The townspeople had enjoyed a fairly self-contained existence for 250 years, trading goods and services among themselves and, except for such items as rum, molasses, and timber imported by Sag Harbor traders, living off their own lands and the bounty of the sea and surrounding bays. The railroad and later the highway changed all this. Whereas in the era of water transport East Hampton had been linked with coastal New England and even the West Indies much more intimately than with New York, now the railroad tied the town to the growing metropolis. New York was beginning to consume vast tracts of its immediate Long Island hinterland. The farms of

69

Brooklyn and Queens were being paved over by new streets. As the potato fields of Nassau County were converted into estates and later into subdivisions, produce farming became an increasingly attractive occupation to old-time Suffolk County farmers, particularly those who were lucky enough to own or rent the extraordinarily fertile soil known as Bridgehampton loam, a soil formed by mineral-rich sediments left by the glacial outwash of the last ice age. This soil occurs throughout the southern half of Southampton and East Hampton (see p. 77) and is among the most fertile in the United States. In addition, the South Fork averages slightly more rainfall and considerably more fog than the rest of the island. Moreover, Bridgehampton loam is remarkably porous and spongy with the result that while Riverhead typically irrigates 90 percent of its farm land, East Hampton farmers irrigate only about 20 percent of theirs. Because of the moderating influence of East Hampton's bays and ocean on local temperatures the number of frostless days here is greater than anywhere else on Long Island. The growing season on the South Fork begins, on the average, on April 13 and ends with the first killing frost about November 14. In Roslyn, by contrast, the respective dates are April 23 and October 27. Thus, the mild weather,

rich soil, and abundant moisture combined with the advent of the railroad, then the highways, and finally the suburbanization of the farm land to the west created the conditions for a profitable monoculture in the Hamptons.

Farmland and a summer home on Further Lane at Two Mile Hollow Road.

By the 1920s the once diversified crops geared to livestock production and self-sustenance had given way to something approaching a single crop economy. The farmers still grew corn and some summer vegetables for the East Hampton resort colony, but the potato had become the major source of income for most East Hampton farmers. Reinforcing the change to potato culture was the settlement of several Polish families on eastern Long Island in the years following World War I; with them they brought a familiarity with this staple crop of middle Europe. By the 1930s the hedgerows that separated the old fields were torn down to make way for the new crop, much to the dismay of conservationists and hunters, who admired the beautiful old privets and complained that without them the birds would have no nesting places.

Although today only 5 percent of East Hampton's land, or some 2,300 acres, is under cultivation, nevertheless with Southampton it is among the leading agricultural areas of the state. Each spring as the ground becomes warm enough for planting, last year's cover crop of rye grass is plowed under and the farmers, whose machines have been dicing potatoes into seed, plant their new crop. The main variety is Katahdin which, though slightly watery and not as flavorful as the Russet or Idaho potato, has a heavier yield. East Hampton farmers do plant some fields of Russets and hope for a growing season with regular periods of rainfall; otherwise this potato will grow knobby and misshapen. They also plant the Superior, an early-maturing variety of the Katahdin. The Superior does not store well and is therefore not put into potato barns to be sold later in the year but is sold right out of the ground to the summer market.

In June and July the fields are white-flowered with the star-shaped potato blossoms. Throughout the summer months the farm machines lumber up and down the furrows, cultivating and spraying the potato plants with pesticides. By mid-August the fields in which the Superiors were planted lie brown and bare; the blossoms have vanished from the Katahdins and Russets, and their plants are now a matted mass of vines. Along the margins of the fields are summer wild flowers: blue chicory, clover, pink lady's thumb, yellow mustard, and the lovely trumpet vine called hedge bindweed, a relative of the morning glory.

In September and October, until the first frost, East Hampton farmers harvest their potatoes and store them in huge barns insulated by earth berms or in the warehouse barns beside the railroad tracks in Bridgehampton. Soon the green shoots of newly sown rye grass emerge from the fields. This is the cover crop, planted before the ground freezes to keep the winter winds from blowing the soil away in huge clouds of yellow dust. The appearance of the cover crop marks the end of the harvest.

In 1972 the two towns produced some two million hundredweight of potatoes on 7,500 acres, with a market value of $6,697,500. The net value to the growers from this highly mechanized crop was estimated to have been about $2 million. 1973 and 1974 were still more profitable for the local growers, though inflated costs together with all the usual agricultural risks by no means assure these farmers an uninterrupted prosperity.

Today as many potatoes go to market by truck as by rail, while all of East Hampton's fish goes by truck. Nevertheless, large-scale commercial fishing for the city market, like commercial farming, dates from the coming of the railroad. To be sure, Sag Harbor fishermen for years had been catching and salting quantities of cod for export, and the menhaden industry was at its height in the 1880s when oil from these fish was widely used in paint. By 1889 there were 232 sailing boats and twenty-four steam vessels operating purse seines for menhaden in Gardiners Bay, and the shoreline was studded with small factories, or "pot works," for rendering the oil and drying the scrap for fertilizer. Moreover, smoked eels were shipped by boat out of Sag Harbor, and fishermen could take fresh fish packed in ice cut out of Fort Pond in Montauk or Accabonac Harbor over to Orient or Greenport and load them onto the old *Shinnecock* bound for the Fulton Fish Market. However, the shipment of fresh fish from East Hampton to city markets did not become a major source of income until convenient fast transportation was at hand.

When sturgeon and roe were plentiful and profitable in the late 1890s many carloads were shipped into New York each spring. As bay scallops became a delicacy on the menus of New York restaurants, Accabonac baymen ("Bonackers") started scalloping in the winter. Clamming became another

Haul seiners on the beach at East Hampton.

profitable year-round enterprise; between the 1890s and the present tens of thousands of bushels of Cherrystones and Little Necks have been shipped to New York. Clams are also sold to the local cod fishermen to bait their trawl lines and to canneries for clam chowder. Though bay fishing is usually a secondary source of income, a bayman, working part time, can often clear $10,000 or more for a season's work.

The oyster beds of Accabonac Harbor in Gardiners Bay are unparalleled; because of the configuration of the current here these beds are bathed twice daily by nutrient-rich waters. Oystering was at its height in the early 1900s when commercial operators seeded the beds and harvested the superlative "Gardiners Bay salts" which they marketed out of Greenport. Though periodic infestations of starfish have damaged the oyster beds, a plant in Greenport continues to seed and harvest oysters in Gardiners Bay.

Fyke-fishing—fishing for fluke with funnel-shaped traps made from twine and hickory saplings—was once practiced extensively in the town's harbors. Haul-seining is still widely practiced; it is the method whereby coastal migrations of striped bass are netted in the spring and fall; three or four thousand feet of net are set in a half circle, and once the nets are full they are pulled ashore by winches operated simultaneously from two trucks on the beach. Bottom draggers work all year round, and the dragger fleet operating off Montauk accounts for the largest proportion of fish sold out of East Hampton.

Because of the proximity of the Gulf Stream whose warm waters carry tropical species such as swordfish, white marlin, tuna, bluefish, striped bass, and sharks into northern latitudes, Montauk has become an important sport fishing center; its charter fleet has been successfully operating since the 1930s.

Since the completion of the Long Island Expressway and the Sunrise Highway Extension, East Hampton's popularity as a resort has increased. Together with Southampton it attracts some 240,000 short-term visitors annually and as many as 42,300 full-time summer residents. These vacationers are estimated to spend some $200 million per year in the towns of East Hampton and Southampton and are by far their largest source of income and employment.

A
Natural
History of
East
Hampton

A Landscape Left by Ice

Gardeners on eastern Long Island often find smooth, rounded pebbles studded in their soil. Of quartz or some other durable mineral, these stones resemble the water-worn rocks one finds on the beach. Local sand quarries have enormous piles of them of various sizes which have been sorted out to be crushed into gravel or sold as aggregate. Farmers plowing their fields will pile up the larger ones by the roadside, where at a casual glance they look like potatoes. Why should the Bridgehampton loam, as the fertile eastern Long Island farm land is known to agricultural scientists, thus resemble a fruit cake? This question intrigued Timothy Dwight, the president of Yale, who visited East Hampton in the first decade of the nineteenth century:

When we commenced our journey on this Island, I proposed to companions to examine with a continual and minute attention the stones of every size. . . . The result of this examination was that all stones, which we saw were without an exception destitute of angles, appearing as if worn by the long-continued attrition of water; and in all respects exactly like those which in a multitude of places we found on the beach of the ocean.

From these "aquatic" stones Dwight deduced that Long Island had been swept by the Deluge of Biblical times. He also reasoned that the residual waters of the Flood had created Long Island Sound.

Dwight's contemporary, the scientist Samuel Latham Mitchell, remarked the similarity between the loose rocks that littered the Long Island landscape and the bedrock of Connecticut and mainland New York. He concluded that during the Deluge the rivers in those places had overflowed their banks and that the velocity of their currents had detached rocks from the surrounding hills and propelled them southward.

Mitchell had correctly figured out the dynamics of Long Island's creation; what he did not guess was that the transporting agent was not water but ice. For contemporary geologists the explanation of Long Island's soil structure lies not in a Biblical flood but in the no less astonishing fact that a massive glacial shield a few millennia ago plowed southward, incorporating into itself as it moved sand and water-washed pebbles from the primordial beach of Long Island Sound. In addition, the glacier, like a giant bulldozer, shoved boulders across the Sound and left them randomly poised here and there on Long Island. Called erratics, they make convenient monuments;

Jackson Pollock's grave in the Green River Cemetery in the Springs is marked by such a boulder.

The ridge of hills that forms Long Island's central spine and the two "flukes" which give it the appearance of a whale, one fluke tapering into Orient Point on the north, the other into Montauk Point on the south, are a physiographic expression of the so-called terminal moraine, a heavy load of sedimentary accumulation that was dumped by the leading edge of the glacier as it melted. East Hampton on the south fluke is part of what geologists call the Ronkonkoma moraine. This same moraine crops up again beyond Montauk Point on Block Island, Martha's Vineyard, and Nantucket. On the north fluke, the Harbor Hills moraine, created by a later phase of glacial unburdening, also has its offshore extensions: Plum Island, Fishers Island, and Cape Cod.

Glacial meltwaters flowed out of this morainal mass in braided rivulets carrying a large quantity of sediments: clay and fine-grained sand intermixed with smooth water-worn pebbles. Shelving toward the sea, these sediments formed what geologists call an outwash plain. It was this rich sedimentary mantle of Bridgehampton loam that attracted East Hampton's early settlers and which makes Suffolk County New York State's number one agricultural-producing county today.

One of the great virtues of East Hampton's soil is its porousness and thus its permeability by rain water. Relatively little water runs off, and the water table is readily replenished in areas that have not been built up or heavily paved over, an important factor since the town depends entirely on its own ground water.

Some streams that cross the coastal plain simply sink out of sight. Others drain into the bays and ponds that rim the south shore. Originally these latter streams emptied into the ocean; however, as a berm, or ridge, of sand was created by westward-migrating ocean currents, their waters became impounded behind it. In this way Mecox Bay, Sagaponack Pond, Fairfield Pond, Wainscott Pond, Georgica Pond, Lily Pond, and Hook Pond were formed.

An "erratic" boulder left by the glacier.

Besides the "collect" ponds next to the south shore, there are numerous kettlehole ponds, most of which are found in depressions of the moraine ridge or in the adjacent outwash. Kettlehole ponds were formed as large chunks of ice left behind by the retreating glacier became trapped here and there in the moraine. As these melted the surrounding earth caved in and in many instances the depressions thus formed filled with water. The double kettle of Poxabogue and Little

Poxabogue ponds is part of a kettle plain around Bridge-hampton. Round Pond, Long Pond, and Crooked Pond are part of a kettle chain near Sag Harbor.

As one drives east on the Montauk Highway across the flat agricultural plain formed by the glacial outwash one notices in the distance on the left—that is, to the north—the gentle hills of the moraine. But beyond Amagansett there is an abrupt change in the appearance of the landscape. Napeague, a name which has been translated as "land overflowed by water," is a narrow bar of heavy sand. It is in effect a causeway linking Amagansett and Montauk. Originally this area was open sea, and Montauk and Hither Hills were separate islands formed by glacial debris. Promised Land, where an abandoned fish factory stands today, was another small island lying in what is now Napeague Bay. Westward-trending currents kept transporting the sands that are constantly being eroded from Montauk Point. Eventually a long sleeve of sand extended westward from Hither Hills pointing in the direction of Promised Land. Promised Land itself grew a tail trending toward Amagansett. Finally these sandspits linked with each other and with the mainland at Amagansett. When they first joined they formed a gentle arc, leaving a shallow bay between Amagansett and Hither Hills. Gradually this bay filled in with more eroded sand from the east as the projecting headlands on Montauk were torn away by wave action. Geologists call this type of built-up, filled-in, straightened shoreline a "pro-graded" beach.

Successive stages of Napeague's accretion are marked by the parallel lines of dune ridges which once fronted on the ocean, but which became "stranded" as new dune ridges were formed in front of them. A particularly noticeable one is found between Cranberry Hole Road and the Long Island Railroad tracks beside the primitive roadbed of the old Montauk Highway. Some years ago a weathered whale skeleton was found in the Napeague dunes nearly a mile inland from the present beach, giving additional support to the geologists' theory that accreted sands have built up this area and in the process converted Montauk from an island into a peninsula.

Montauk with its steep promontories and roller coaster terrain is called knob and kettle country in the language of the geologists. Timothy Dwight noticed that "on Montauk Point, the stones have a different aspect, being angular." The rocks which Dwight observed are part of a much thicker, much more violently contorted ice contact deposit known as Montauk till. If one examines the high bluffs near Montauk Point one can see an exposed section of Montauk till. It is partially cemented be-

cause of the great pressure exerted on it when it lay buried under hundreds of feet of ice.

The chief difference between the Montauk till and the Ronkonkoma moraine which was laid down several thousand years later is one of stratification. The Ronkonkoma moraine is an evenly bedded stratum of fine-grained clay, sand, gravel, and smooth, rounded pebbles, whereas the Montauk till is a wildly undifferentiated mass of unsorted, unstratified clay, sand, angular stones, and rough boulders.

In the fifteen or so millennia since the last glacier reteated from Long Island, East Hampton's vegetation has changed drastically. At first there were only the hardy lichens like those that grow in the Canadian tundra today. Eventually as the climate warmed up a forest similar to the present northern New England forest of birches, sugar maples, white pines, and hemlocks grew up. But this forest disappeared as the hardy pitch pines, oaks, and hickories—trees of a yet more temperate climate—assumed a dominance which they still hold. Beneath the oaks, flowering dogwood, mountain laurel, huckleberry, and blueberry grew. These are the trees and shrubs one sees in the woods around Sag Harbor. In the predominantly oak woods around Amagansett gray birch and American beech developed along with a shrub layer of dogwood, maple-leaved viburnum, and hackberry. Damp depressions such as the Sagg Swamp, a remnant of a glacial outwash stream and now the largest surviving fresh-water marsh on the South Fork, became a habitat for red maples and an understory of highbush blueberries mixed with swamp azalea, shadbush,

A typical collect pond at Wainscott.

79

viburnum, chokeberry, summer sweet, and, in the wetter spots, a groundcover of lily of the valley.

While East Hampton does not have intermingling in its present oak-hickory-pine forest such warmer-climate species as the sweet gum which one finds on western Long Island, it does have a fine stand of white pines on Barcelona Neck near Northwest Harbor, a relict feature surviving from a colder era. And, of course, many southern and northern native trees not strictly indigenous to the area exist in East Hampton gardens along with numerous imported specimens.

As the great shield of ice that had once imprisoned the waters of Peconic Bay and Gardiners Bay retreated, the necks and islands around Sag Harbor, Northwest Harbor, Three Mile Harbor, Accabonac Creek, Napeague Harbor, and Montauk Harbor were built up by glacial drift. Sandspits elongated, and some 4,000 years ago in the protected coves *Spartina* grass, a vegetation particularly adapted to the semi-salinity of estuarine areas, gained a foothold. As this grass died back each winter it formed organic sediments to feed the crustaceans and other small organisms that were reestablishing themselves as East Hampton's climate grew warmer. In addition, these

sediments formed new soil which helped extend the developing marsh a bit farther offshore each year. We live in an age of continuing glacial retreat, which means that sea level is constantly rising as the polar cap melts. Because of this Long Island is submerging, and East Hampton's marginal salt marshes are not only extending seaward but landward as well, a fact which has been confirmed by various instances where old tree stumps and logs have been discovered several feet below the low-tide level.

It is not surprising then that over the last four millennia the town's various harbors became thickly fringed with marsh vegetation: *Spartina alterniflora,* a tall cord grass, grew along the shore and the tidal creeks meandering through the marshes; *Spartina patens,* the short cord grass which the colonists prized as hay for their cattle, was found in the higher, drier places. In the Springs, Kaplan Meadow and Merrill Lake Sanctuary, under the stewardship of the Nature Conservancy, are part of the Accabonac salt marsh. Although it is no longer mown for salt hay, this marsh still plays a vital role in the economic life of East Hampton; its protected location and sediment-laden waters make it an excellent nursery for marine

Looking west at Napeague from the overlook at Hither Hills.

81

life. Studded through the marsh are small knolls topped by oak or red cedar and rimmed with marsh elder. Other protrusions in the marsh mark the tops of glacial boulders, or erratics, which have been nearly blanketed over by vegetation. In the salt-saturated depressions, which are called pannes, one finds the fleshy, segmented-stemmed glasswort, pale green in the summer but translucent scarlet in autumn. In late summer there are wild flowers: marsh pinks, mallow roses, and, here and there, the delicate feathery sea lavender.

On the south shore, where the gradually lengthening sand berms impounded the once open waters to form such ponds as Hook, Georgica, and Sagaponack, salt marshes also came into being. An especially extensive one around Mecox Bay was known as Hayground; here the townsmen of Southampton had their salt meadow allotments. In East Hampton Village, Hook Pond has now been stabilized, and, as its waters are no longer saline, its salt marsh vegetation has given way to cattail and rushes. Still, it attracts a variety of waterfowl: coots and mallard ducks, American widgeon and Canada geese. The fern-fringed nature trail at the head of Hook Pond is a favorite place to bring children to see the mallard ducks that invariably parade there.

At Napeague, during the post-glacial eon, the sands that eroded away from Montauk Point continued to accrete until an extensive series of dune ridges, some twenty to thirty feet high, were formed. Typically, these dune ridges are crescent-shaped with their "horns" pointing northwest, the direction of the strongest winds. In the basins between the arcing dune ridges are fresh marsh areas known as "slacks." The "slacks" are actually exposed sections of the water table. They are created when rain water soaks into the highly permeable dunes and then seeps out at their bases as the pressure of fresh water above equalizes with the pressure of the sea water without and below. In the past boats were often floated in the open water of the "slacks," but today they have become mostly filled with fresh-water bog vegetation. Wild cranberries grow in their bottoms as well as the sticky little insect-trapping sundews. Fresh-water rushes, black willows, cattails, and sphagnum moss can sometimes be found (one can squeeze a handful of this spongy material several times before it will be wrung dry). Along the margins of the "slacks" are highbush blueberries. In some, black and mallard ducks breed, and muskrats live in the banks. Frogs and red-wing blackbirds also are at home here. Rabbits, pheasants, and quail sequester themselves in the brush.

Where the ground rises a few feet a change of vegetation

Pitch pine

The nature trail on David's Lane.

occurs. There are pitch pines, often so wind-stunted that they simply prostrate themselves, their branches creeping along the ground. There are red cedar and bayberry too. Where the sand becomes drier and the water table less accessible to plant roots on the dune slopes one finds an extensive heath-type vegetation: bearberry, a low, lustrous green, creeping mat with beautiful, tiny pink, urn-shaped flowers in the spring; hudsonia; and the pale-gray reindeer moss which is not actually a moss but a lichen. Stabilizing the dune crests are the tall beach grasses which shimmer and undulate like waves when the wind blows.

The older, more developed dunes lie to the east of Napeague Harbor north of the Long Island Railroad tracks in Hither Hills State Park. Some are fifty feet tall, the highest dunes on Long Island. Their wind-blown northwestern slopes are practically bare; they descend precipitously on their leeward southeastern sides to boggy basins of small scrub-oak forest mixed with· pitch pine and carpeted with spongy emerald moss and gray-green lichen. It is obvious why these dunes are sometimes referred to as the "walking dunes" when one sees how the shifting sands have buried some trees until only their tops show. Farther west and nearer the ocean, the Nature Conservancy has rescued Sheppard's Dunes and the Atlantic Double Dunes from the threat of real estate development.

Besides the *Spartina* grass of the salt marshes which provided hay for their cattle in winter, the first settlers found another exceptional natural resource in the grasslands on Montauk. The rolling Montauk downs once spread out for several square miles and must have reminded the town's founders of the Kentish downs near their native Maidstone, just as the Accabonac and Napeague salt marshes were similar in appearance to the tide-washed marshes of the Medway as it emptied into the North Sea.

Now it is hard to visualize the once luxuriant tall grasses waving in a great unbroken expanse across the Montauk peninsula, for what was described in a botanical survey of Montauk made by Norman Taylor of the Brooklyn Botanic Garden in 1923 as "little islands of thicket in an ocean of grassland" have since become a fairly dense shrubbery, and the meadows exist only as irregular patches today. At Indian Field County Park one finds an interesting mixture of grassland and scrub: there is sand reed and several different grasses—purple love-grass, tall cord grass, little prairie bluestem, big prairie bluestem, and Indian grass—interspersed with such shrubs and wild flowers as woolly false heather, sweet pepperbush, maleberry, Virginia winterberry, dwarf sumac, sickle-leaved golden aster, seaside goldenrod, quobsque weed, yellow thistle, southern swamp shadbush, beach plum, wild indigo, partridge pea, and bayberry. This thick mat of vegetation is here and there flattened in rough circles where deer have bedded down.

Cranberry.

To imagine the great stands of trees that greeted the first settlers one must be invited to Gardiners Island, the site of the town's only intact remnant of virgin forest. Taylor in his 1923 survey remarked, "On Gardiners Island there is perhaps the finest growth of timber to be found within hundreds of miles of New York. On a given acre there are sixteen trees nine feet or more—usually much more—in circumference; and many times that number between six and nine feet in circumference." Although many of these venerable trees were destroyed by the devastating hurricane of 1938, the hoary oaks of Bostwick Wood are yet an extremely impressive sight. With their rude implements the early townsmen must have laboriously cleared their lands of similar trees. But East Hampton's forests were much less of an obstacle than an asset as they provided wood for fuel and building materials and were filled with game for food.

By the time Lyman Beecher became minister of East Hampton in 1799, the village itself was practically treeless. He said, "The only trees in the place were a line of poplars between two of the principal residences, and a large elm, standing at an enormous height, which had been trimmed up to a head, and was a conspicuous waymark for miles around."

John Lyon Gardiner, a contemporary of Beecher's, complained that the countryside surrounding the town was becoming deforested; he remarked that "thousands of cords are annually cut down in this county for sale." Timothy Dwight, who was also a contemporary, was more sanguine. He found that, in spite of extensive clearing, "Still, a great proportion of [Suffolk] County is a mere wood: so great a proportion, that the City of New York, and many other places, are to a considerable extent furnished with fuel from this source."

As wood became an increasingly valuable commodity during the eighteenth and early nineteenth centuries, double-bladed axes rang out in the forests   Fireplace, Northwest, and Barcelona Neck. Friction developed with the Indians who complained that they were not being allowed to cut their own firewood in the Hither Hills forest; in 1764 they petitioned the lieutenant governor of New York for relief from the oppression of "their English neighbors at East Hampton who deny them necessary fuel." Their petition was largely ignored, and woodchopping remained an important industry in East Hampton until after the Civil War. Besides the thousands of cords of wood shipped to New York City for firewood, thousands more cords were sent to the brick kilns at Greenport, Sag Harbor, and Noyac.

Lacking wire and the large stones New Englanders used to build their pasture walls, the people of East Hampton developed the lopped fence—a natural barrier to straying cattle and sheep. It was made by partially cutting trees in the spring when their sap was flowing, bending them over in a straight line, and letting their sprouts grow into a hedgerow. George Washington did not think much of lopped fences when he toured Long Island in 1790, since, as he remarked, they were "no defense against Hogs." Some of these curiosities can still be seen beside old fields in the Springs.

The black locust was not a native Long Island tree, but, because of its durability, it was in great demand for fence posts, and practically every farmer planted plots of locusts to serve as an inheritance for a son or dowry for a daughter, until eventually this tree became a ubiquitous feature of the landscape.

People began to plant ornamental as well as utilitarian

One of East Hampton's elms.

trees, especially after cuttings from foreign plants became available during the heyday of whaling. Two giant Japanese Pagoda trees brought back from the Orient by a whaling captain at the beginning of the nineteenth century stand in the back yard of Mrs. D. F. Mulvihill on Main Street, Sag Harbor; the trunk of the larger of these two venerable specimens measures eighteen and one half feet in circumference. The Parrish Museum in Southampton has a notable collection of exotic trees including one of the only two Chinese Cedrella trees on Long Island. Some exotic plants including the famous ship's rose that is found in many East Hampton gardens were purely accidental imports, arriving on the beach as cargo from shipwrecked vessels.

It is the American elm more than any other tree that gives East Hampton its unique character. Originally rare on Long Island, it was widely planted by the first settlers as a shade tree around their homes. It became a favorite street tree as well, and in 1841 S. B. Gardiner and the Reverend L. Lord planted fourteen on Newtown Lane. The Dutch elm disease has, alas, decimated the American elm within the last generation, and George Peters notes in *The Trees of Long Island* that in the village of East Hampton this tree is "making its last significant stand on Long Island." It is in large measure due to the tree care program sponsored by the Ladies Village Improvement Society that East Hampton's extremely fine elms continue to throw a great filigreed vault of green over Main Street and Newtown Lane.

Man's activities will continue to alter the face of East Hampton in the future; one hopes that a growing awareness of the principles of sound land use will prevent further destruction of valuable tidal marshes, the protective dune barrier, and the open lands that soak up rain to recharge the water table. Forces that have been set in motion by nature's own inexorable dynamic will also continue to change the appearance of the town. The Montauk lighthouse, which, when it was built in 1795, stood several hundred feet from the Point, is drawing close to collapse as the waves below relentlessly eat the cliff upon which it stands. If the present glacial retreat and warming trend continue, the town's vegetation will become more invaded by southern species like that of western Long Island today. And if sea level goes on rising several inches each century, the shoreline will move further inland. Moreover, there is nothing to prevent us from imagining that eventually these present trends will be reversed and that East Hampton will some few thousand years hence be once again a frozen waste, or in some few million years be entirely

eroded into the sea. Indeed, the only certainty is that the earth's crust is constantly in flux, and particularly transient and mobile are its continental fringes.

THE RESTLESS SAND

Two jetties to the east of Georgica Pond; they trap the westward-migrating littoral sand, causing serious erosion of the Wainscott beach.

Summer visitors returning to East Hampton for a winter weekend may notice that the broad beach that was crowded with sun bathers on Labor Day has considerably narrowed. Ocean-front homeowners are dismayed that the encroaching surf will sooner or later tear away their dune foundations.

Beach erosion and beach replenishment are, in fact, seasonal phenomena, the two sides of a coin which shore geologists have labled the progradation-recession cycle. In summer the beach progrades, or builds up. This is because wave action is generally mild and the sand grains that are transported with every oncoming wave are deposited as a thin new layer on the berm, or beach face. The gentle backwash does not have the energy to suck all of the grains back offshore.

However, the normal coastal storms of late fall and early spring scrape away the terrace of sand that was created in summer. The turbulent waves keep the waterborne sand in suspension; little accumulates on the beach face. Much that was already there washes away—but not too far away, for it accumulates in an offshore bar. This underwater bar will be important in replenishing the beach later. Tens of thousands of cubic feet of sand can be ripped away from the beach dunes and the high morainal bluffs at Montauk during a single bad storm; it is not unknown for a hundred or more feet of beach to disappear in this fashion. But with calmer weather, the waves trip over the now bulky offshore bar, scouring sand and pushing it once again landward.

Summer calm, winter storm: this is the oscillating rhythm that keeps the beach expanding and contracting.

There is another factor at work which complicates these relatively simple mechanics. It is the littoral current. Sea bathers are familiar with the "set" or current which more often than not deposits them after a swim some yards distant on the beach from the point where they left their towels on the sand. This is because waves rarely travel in a perpendicular line to the shore. The general movement of the waves is in a slightly westerly direction. Therefore the sands that are pulled offshore to form a post-storm underwater bar are not in the succeeding calm weather redeposited on the same portion of the beach where they lay before. Rather, the sands of East Hampton will have traveled a bit farther toward New York.

Old maps of Long Island graphically illustrate this. When we compare them with contemporary maps we see that the barrier beaches of Fire Island, Atlantic Beach, and the Rockaway Peninsula have grown considerably in a westerly direction over the years. An estimated 600,000 cubic yards of sand is moved westward each year by the littoral current; one source of this great load is Montauk Point. Indeed, the same old maps that, when compared to modern versions, show the accreting barrier beaches also show the whittling down of Montauk Point. The lighthouse on the Point which was commissioned by George Washington in 1790 was said to have been built "to last two hundred years." It may—just. The old maps and photographs show that the lighthouse, which now stands so precariously close to the Point, was once several hundred feet inland.

Jetties or groins interfere with the normal drift of beach sand. Their efficacy in stopping beach erosion is a keenly debated local political issue. Only recently are engineers beginning to realize what shore geologists had discovered earlier: when sand is impounded behind jetties it cannot nourish the down drift beaches.

The early settlers certainly had no compulsion to live in the same proximity to the sea as some modern vacationers, although many of them depended upon it for their livelihood.

Their attitude toward the Atlantic was respectful rather than romantic, and, as we shall see, the village Main Streets of Amagansett, East Hampton, and Wainscott were prudently laid out some half mile inland from the restless sand.

The East End of Long Island is an especially favored spot for bird watching. Situated on the Atlantic flyway, the area attracts migratory shore birds, waterfowl, and upland species like the hosts of warblers that appear in the woods each spring. Jutting into the Atlantic, Montauk Point, particularly after a storm, is a fine vantage point for glimpsing such sea birds as gannets, shearwaters, and oceanic gulls who normally don't make an appearance on shore.

The relatively mild winters of the area make it attractive to year-round residents: cardinals, blue jays, nuthatches, chickadees and other freeloaders at back yard bird feeders. Although decimated by sportsmen during the last century, various shore birds still breed on the extensive marshes at Accabonac and Napeague; and the quiet waters of the town's harbors, bays, and ponds shelter many kinds of waterfowl. The mixture of salt and fresh water in such ponds as Georgica and Sagg produces an amazingly rich eco-system and an attractive breeding ground for large numbers of aquatic birds. The fields of winter rye draw an occasional snowy owl in years when lemmings are scarce in the north and these impressive predatory creatures must extend their range as far south as Long Island in search of field mice.

The serious bird watcher will find rewards in any of the state or county parks, Nature Conservancy areas, or the Morton Wildlife Refuge in Noyac (see pages 217-219). Following are some well-known birds that are closely identified with the East Hampton locale.

The Birds of East Hampton

CANADA GOOSE (*Branta canadensis*)

One of the great sights signaling the arrival of fall is the V-shaped flight pattern of a flock of honking Canada geese streaming overhead. These birds, whose leader is probably an experienced old gander, can fly at a steady pace of 55 miles per hour. Because of inbreeding, they vary in size, but usually they are large birds, the males weighing up to twelve pounds and attaining a wingspread of six feet. They settle down beside ponds or in open fields. Mainly they are vegetarians. Their long necks permit them to forage like swans for pond weeds. They also graze on the new shoots of rye grass which farmers sow as a cover crop to keep the dirt of their bare winter fields from being whipped into clouds of dust by the wind.

Canada geese are considered to be very cunning; they are extremely wary birds. Their salient identification mark is a black head and neck interrupted by a broad white cheek patch.

Though some remain in the area year round, most return north in the spring to breed on cold marshes or the lakes of the tundra. They do not breed until the age of three, and then they mate for life. If it is not killed, a Canada goose will live for many years.

MALLARD DUCK (*Anas platyrhynchos*)

Because of its familiarity bird watchers are somewhat blasé about the sight of the ubiquitous mallard, the most abundant wild duck species. Many people, however, delight in these gregarious waterfowl, and children never tire of watching them parade at the Nature Trail on Dunemere Lane. The Nature Trail forms an arm of Hook Pond. Hook Pond was once, like Georgica Pond, a brackish tide-washed embayment. Some years ago engineers stabilized it by sealing it off from the ocean with a man-made dune and then running a pipe through the dune. Now its waters are entirely fresh. Ferns, cattail, rushes, and other fresh-water vegetation fringe it, and muskrats dig tunnels in its banks. It is an ideal habitat for mallards, and these dabblers are seen there, tails upended, as they extend their necks to forage for seeds and plants on the shallow pond bottom. Snails and aquatic insects also form part of their diet.

Mallards breed in the sheltering reeds around Hook Pond; their nests are made of grass mixed with down. Soon after birth the buff and blackish baby ducks can be seen swimming behind their drably colored mother, while the beautifully plumaged drakes, with their bright, irridescent green heads, white collars, and velvet black feathers curling above their tails, congregate together. The female does share with the male one touch of vivid color: the white-framed irridescent blue patch on each wing known as the speculum (window). In midsummer the birds molt, and for a few weeks the eclipsed plumage of the male makes him nearly as dull as the female.

BLACK DUCK (*Anas rubripes tristis*)

The black duck is the common duck of the East Hampton salt marshes where it nests in small colonies. In the fall it warily tries to avoid the hunters' guns; then large rafts of these birds may float offshore or in the middle of a pond, returning only at night to the shallows where they feed on pond weeds and other aquatic vegetation. In the winter black ducks survive by adding to their diet small shellfish, crustaceans, and insects.

MUTE SWAN (*Cygnus olor*)

Unlike the whistling swan and the rare trumpeter swan, the mute swan is not a native American bird but an Old World import. Long before the founding of East Hampton, or any other American town for that matter, the mute swan enjoyed great status in England. Edward IV decreed it a royal bird in 1482, and private ownership of swans was forbidden except as a privilege granted by the king. Eventually mute swans were brought to this country to decorate ornamental ponds and park lakes. Even today private ownership of swans is not common, and a pair sells for several hundred dollars. Wild mute swans are, however, quite common in East Hampton, one of the few areas in the United States frequented by them. The actor John Drew is credited with introducing a pair on Town Pond; subsequent generations of their offspring became wild and multiplied on other ponds in the area.

The swan's long neck, which we interpret as the very image of gracefulness, is actually a utilitarian feature that permits it to forage for aquatic vegetation growing in the muddy depths of ponds. When necessary, the swan is a fast swimmer—another contradiction to the impression of calm serenity conveyed by its usual gliding progress through the water.

Like Canada geese, swans mate for life. They prefer to build their nests—large piles of sticks which look like small islands—on fresh-water ponds. In cold weather they keep a small area of water from freezing by swimming around. Should ice form nevertheless, they will move offshore to open sea temporarily. A large flock is usually seen on Georgica Pond, a mixed salt- and fresh-water pond.

Mute swans can migrate hundreds of miles, although the ones that are sometimes seen here flying in a line overhead, their long necks outstretched, are usually just changing their grazing grounds temporarily from one pond to another. They are fast fliers and the largest of all flying birds. Unlike Canada geese, they do not vocalize in flight; their passage through the air is signaled rather by the musical throbbing sound made by their great beating wings. Their only sounds consist of a hiss when angry (they are rather aggressive toward other waterfowl) or a feeble bark when summoning their young.

OSPREY (*Pandion haliaëtus*)

Except for a few pairs on Shelter Island and a still thriving colony on Gardiners Island, these impressive, once numerous fish hawks are a rare sight on eastern Long Island. With its five-and-one-half-foot wingspread the osprey is a superb glider. A lucky watcher might see one of these dark-brown-and-white birds hovering over Gardiners Bay before plunging with lightning speed and sinking its long curved talons into a fish. These talons operate like double-pronged pincers; each foot has two pairs of opposing toes and a rough surface which helps the bird to grip its slippery prey. Because they run in large schools that swim near the surface of the water the menhaden that have played such an important role in the East Hampton fishery also form a significant portion of the osprey's diet.

Like some other birds of prey, ospreys mate for life, and a pair continues to inhabit the same nest, adding sticks and seaweed year after year, until it becomes a huge unwieldy pile. These nests are usually built in treetops or other elevated perches so that these keen-sighted birds can gain the necessary altitude to scan the nearby waters for fish. Some old osprey nests can be seen in the trusses of the radio towers at Napeague.

GULLS AND TERNS (Family Laridae)

The ubiquitous gulls gliding effortlessly over the town's bays and beaches are a familiar sight as they float from air current to air current with only an occasional series of slow, measured wing beats. Unlike the osprey, gulls do not dive for their food, nor do they live in isolated pairs. Rather, these noisy communal birds congregate in large colonies, scavenging greedily along beaches, mud flats, and even in the town dump for mollusks, dead fish, and morsels of man's garbage. Within their colonies gulls are fiercely territorial. Their seaweed nests are usually found in protected dune areas. The male helps incubate the speckled greenish eggs until they hatch after about a month; then for five or six weeks he feeds the chicks until they are ready to fly and find their own food.

The herring gull (*Larus argentatus*), which is distinguished by its white-and-pearl-gray plumage and the red dot on its yellow beak—a spot which its young tap when they want food—is by far the commonest species. While the largest gull species, the great black-backed gull (*L. marinus*), is usually found farther north, large numbers have nested in recent years on Long Island. Here they congregate in the midst of flocks of herring gulls. They are quarrelsome birds, intent on showing dominance, preying on the eggs of other water birds and usurping the most elevated nesting positions. Their colonies are much smaller than those of the herring gulls. Immature gulls of both species are brownish and do not acquire their adult plumage until they are around three years old.

Terns are sometimes called sea swallows, and with their forked tails and swooping, arcing flight they do bear a superficial resemblance to the land swallows which nest in nearby barns each summer. They lay their mottled eggs directly on the sand, usually in the vicinity of similarly colored stones which help to camouflage them. If one walks too near a tern's nest, the bird does a series of bombing dives which only narrowly miss the intruder's head. Terns dive for their dinner as well; their long pointed beaks can quickly snap up a swimming fish. Sometimes instead of diving they skim along the water's surface in search of prey. However, they rarely alight and bob about on the water for periods of time like the gulls whose strong webbed feet make them better swimmers.

The two tern species most frequently seen on East Hampton beaches are the common tern (*Sterna hirundo*) and the least tern (*S. albifrons*). The larger bird, the common tern, is distinguished by its red beak. The least tern's beak is yellow. At the end of the nineteenth century the graceful least tern became a highly coveted fashion item; dead birds were stuffed and mounted on ladies' hats, and the market price for them was sufficient to ensure their slaughter in vast numbers. No longer persecuted, this prolific bird is now so firmly re-established that it is a frequent sight on all the beaches of eastern Long Island.

SANDPIPERS (Family Scolopacidae)

Visitors to the beach enjoy watching the lines of sandpipers rushing back and forth with each oncoming and retreating wave as they search for their meal of tiny crabs or insects in the wet sand. There are seventy-seven species of this familiar shore bird, and even avid bird watchers have a hard time getting them straight. The semipalmated sandpiper (*Ereunetes pusillus*) is the most abundant species. When it is not busily working the intertidal zone for food it may be seen on the upland beach or in marshy inlets, balanced on one foot, its bill tucked beneath its feathers. It migrates to the arctic usually in May to nest, but returns as early as mid-July when its hatchlings are a scant two weeks old.

PLOVERS (Family Charadriidae)

Closely related to the sandpiper, the plover appears to be a somewhat stockier bird. This is due in part to its powerful wing muscles which have developed as an evolutionary adaptation to migration. For many East Coast plovers the long migratory journey begins in the arctic where they breed and does not end until the birds have settled down on the pampas of South America. Its name derives from the Latin *pluvia*, meaning rain, because of its habit of scolding before rain.

The ring plover (*Charadrius hiaticula*), distinguished by a black neck band, is the most common plover to be seen on Long Island. It feeds on sandy flats such as those surrounding Georgica Pond in Wainscott.

AMERICAN OYSTER CATCHER
(*Haematopus palliatus*)

The oyster catcher is a striking black-and-white bird which can sometimes be seen probing its long coral-colored beak into the shells of the oysters and clams that proliferate in the waters of Gardiners Bay. The colony nesting on the rocky shore at Goff Point represents something of a local rarity for this once common bird.

A Bibliography for Bird Watchers

Bull, John. *Birds of the New York Area*. New York: Harper & Row, 1964.

———. *Birds of New York State*. New York: Doubleday, 1974.

Matthiessen, Peter. *Shorebirds of North America*. New York: Viking Press, 1967.

Peterson, Roger Tory. *A Field Guide to the Birds: Eastern Land and Water Birds*. Boston: Houghton Mifflin, 1947.

Pough, Richard H. *Audubon Bird Guides*, 2 volumes: *Land Birds*; *Water Birds*. New York: Doubleday, 1951.

Robbins, Chandler S.; Bruun, Bertel; Zin, Herbert S. *Birds of North America: A Guide to Field Identification*. Racine, Wisconsin: Western Publishing Co., 1966.

Touring the Town

Sag Harbor
East Hampton
The Springs
Wainscott
Amagansett
A Nature Walk
at Napeague
Montauk
Three Bike Tours

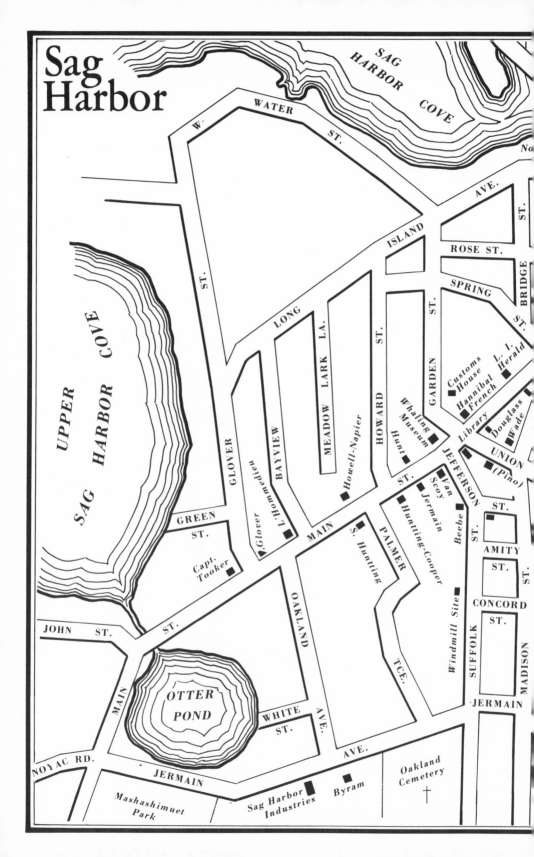

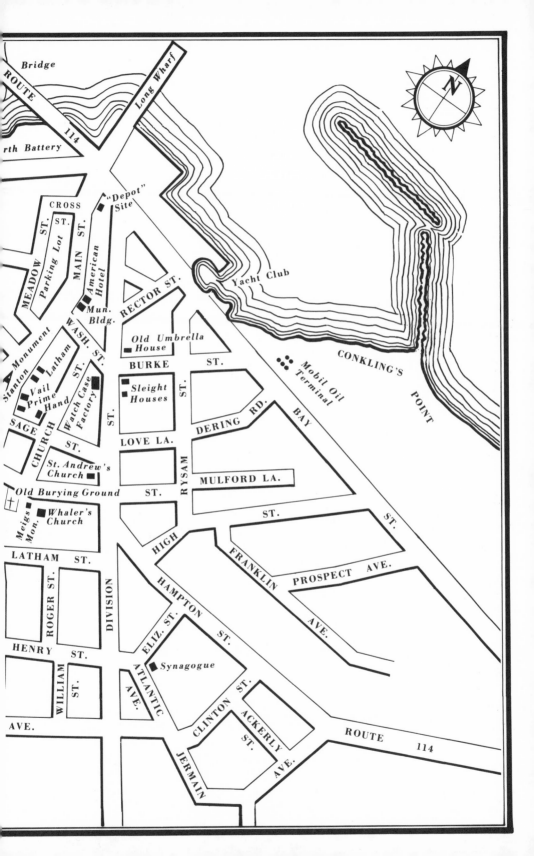

Sag Harbor Tour

Visitors to Sag Harbor should park their cars in the lot behind the stores on the west side of Main Street and proceed on foot. A stay of two or three hours will provide an adequate first impression of the village and its handsome old houses, and allow time for visits to the Whaling Museum, the old Customs House, a tour of the antique shops, and even a half hour for lunch. Though the more interesting part of Sag Harbor lies west of Division Street and is therefore in the town of Southampton, the visitor might as well ignore this distinction as the village itself has traditionally done.

For visitors with a special interest in early American architecture Sag Harbor will repay repeated visits and careful study. Because of its peculiar economic history (see pages 48-62) Sag Harbor is a kind of living museum of pre-industrial Americana, a nineteenth-century manufacturing city that never advanced beyond its infancy and so has been spared the pattern of rapid industrial development and subsequent decay characteristic of more "successful" places such as New Bedford or New London. For those who want to study the architecture of Sag Harbor in some detail, *Sag Harbor: Past, Present and Future,* published by the Sag Harbor Historic Preservation Commission, is a useful reference. A shorter guide is supplied free of charge by MASH, The Merchants Association of Sag Harbor.

Sag Harbor reached the height of its prosperity as a whaling center in the 1840s. Thereafter it declined, and repeated attempts in the years after the Civil War to create new industries failed. Only the watchcase factory, the large brick building on lower Division Street, flourished, and its original sections remain today virtually in the same condition as when they were opened in 1881. It is now a part of the Bulova Company and employs about 200 people.

The reasons for Sag Harbor's interrupted economic development are not entirely clear. Certainly there was no shortage of capital. The whaling industry is estimated to have provided the tiny settlement with revenues of some $15 million between 1820 and 1850 alone, and a total of perhaps $25 million between 1785 when the whale fishery commenced and 1870 when the last whaling ship left port. Sag Harbor, with its bulging oil cellars, was the Kuwait of its time, and the handful of whaling families, in their great houses along Main Street, were its sheiks. In addition the whale fishery spawned a variety of subsidiary industries, such as shipbuilding, rope and sail making, and metal working; activities that attracted a variety of skilled craftsmen and merchants to the village. Moreover there was an active trade between Sag Harbor and the cities of New England and the South as well as the West Indies, with ships carrying grain, hides, and salt fish for export and returning with cargoes of rum, mahogany, and timber. Sag Harbor ships were frequently chartered and fitted out for the illegal slave trade, and local investors are said to have shared in the proceeds of these ventures. A successful whaler might return with forty or fifty thousand dollars worth of oil and bone after a voyage of two to three years. A slaver might earn much more for a shorter and less hazardous voyage.

As the whales became scarce and whaling less profitable, local entrepreneurs invested repeatedly in new ventures, but neither the flour mill (which burned in the great fire of 1877), the cotton mill (built in 1850 and burned in 1879), the pottery works, the stocking factory, the hat factory, the brass foundry, nor the clockworks succeeded. Though the ever hopeful owners of the Long Island Railroad built a connection from Bridgehampton to Sag Harbor in 1870, the village's distance from major inland markets undoubtedly hurt its chances, despite its well-established water routes to ports both in America and abroad.

But a more important reason for its decline may have been the deadly nature of the whale fishery itself. In the Oakland Cemetery on Jermain Avenue there stands a handsome monument, a shaft of marble carved in the shape of a broken mast, a coil of rope around its base and beneath it a carving in bas-relief that shows a smashed whaleboat, the skipper dead, the crew clinging to the wreckage, and in the background two

The American Hotel

spouting whales. In the distance are two whaling ships.

This monument was erected in 1840, the year the cemetery opened, by the three grandsons of Stephen Howell, who, some fifty-five years earlier, had founded the Sag Harbor whale fishery with his partner Colonel Benjamin Huntting. The monument commemorates their brother John E. Howell who at the age of twenty-eight died in the Pacific in an encounter with a sperm whale. The same monument honors five other captains with such good Hamptons names as Topping, Glover, Payne, and Pierson who lost their lives as well. Of these the oldest was thirty, the youngest twenty-seven. Most of these captains had first gone to sea at the age of twelve or thirteen, and those who survived the rigors of their early voyages came of age as boat steerers or harpooners. Often they found themselves in hand-to-hand combat with their enraged prey. The attrition among these young men must have been terrible, and though the Oakland Cemetery also includes the graves of captains who lived into their forties, fifties, and beyond, perhaps a thousand American whaling men lost their lives each year when the fishery was at its height.

To achieve manhood in Sag Harbor in the 1840s must have been a perilous affair. To survive beyond that must have required the greatest skill and good fortune, and not only for those so fortunate as to return alive from their long voyages. The psychological consequences for those young men who fell behind in the competition for places in the fragile whaleboats must have been debilitating in other ways.

No wonder then that when word of the California gold fields reached the village in 1849 a general exodus to the tented shores of San Francisco ensued, even though the American whale fishery was at its height in the years 1846-1851 when total revenues rose from $5,553,817 to $10,042,536. One ship, the *Sabina,* commanded by Captain Henry Green, sailed for California in 1849 with eighteen former whaling captains among its passengers. Few of these men returned, and the vital population thus lost was never replaced. The whales had, so to speak, taken their revenge on the village that had profited so greatly from their destruction.

New Bedford with a more densely populated hinterland from which to replace its losses maintained its whale fishery into the Seventies and Eighties. But Sag Harbor had only the decimated Hamptons to draw upon. By the 1850s its population had begun an irreversible decline, and by the end of the Civil War the more adventurous young men routinely headed west. "The girls stay home and grow into old maids," a resident complained. "A glance on Sunday at the congregation reveals only a male head here and there in a forest of bonnets." By the 1870s, Sag Harbor had become a typical frontier town, left behind in the rush for new opportunities. Though the old whaling entrepreneurs invested their fortunes in new industries, there simply were not enough able young men left to staff them. Only the watchcase factory took root, probably because when its owner, Joseph Fahys, moved his business here in 1881 from Carlstadt, New Jersey, he brought his crew of German workers with him. Later he brought some forty Jewish families directly from Ellis Island to work in his factory. In 1900 they built the first synagogue on Long Island. It still stands on Atlantic Avenue. The watchcase factory remains today as Sag Harbor's largest employer.

The village's loss, however, is the antiquarian's gain. Sag Harbor survives as an invaluable historical asset. Many of its old houses have been carefully restored by their present owners, and the interested visitor will soon find himself in touch with a rare and living example of the American past.

The visitor should walk first to the foot of Main Street and from there proceed past the flagpole, where originally a liberty pole and whipping post stood, to the end of Long Wharf. The liberty pole was destroyed by lightning in 1903. The wharf is 1,000 feet long and was completed between 1770 and 1820. For years it was the center of Sag Harbor's commercial activity, crowded on either side with warehouses and oil cellars, cooperages and smithies, and dense with workers and seamen attending to the ships tied up alongside. At the height of the industry there were some eighty businesses at the foot of the wharf.

To the northeast is Cedar Point, the entrance to the harbor, where a stone lighthouse, built in 1868, can be seen. The headland directly to the east is Barcelona Neck, named for its resemblance to the entrance to the Spanish port and now a part of the county park system. To the north is Shelter Island and to the west is the eastern shore of North Haven, originally called Hog Neck or Hoggonock. Drunken sailors were held in hulks in an anchorage there that was then called Indian Jail. The boundary between East Hampton and Southampton bisects this wharf. Route 114, which crosses the North Haven bridge, joins the ferry to Shelter Island. Until 1834 a ferry connected Sag Harbor and North Haven. Then a drawbridge was built which provided access to the shipyards in the Cove. In 1891 this was replaced by a new wooden bridge which collapsed nine years later. The present bridge, much restored, was built in 1938.

**Cedar Point
Lighthouse**

According to tradition the village of Sag Harbor was settled in 1730, though the area was apparently inhabited by scattered settlers as early as 1707. An account of the early history of the village, the origins of its name, its division between the two towns, and its importance in the early history of whaling will be found on pages 48-62.

The Indians who had for many years maintained a settlement here called the place Wegwaganock or "land at the foot of the hill." Where Main Street now stands there was originally a wetland or tidal meadow called the Great Meadow which nestled beneath a ridge of high ground that ran from the Old Burying Ground on Union Street along Garden Street to the bay. This ridge formed the southern boundary of the original settlement. Another ridge known as Turkey Hill ran along the east side of Main Street, and it was here that the original inhabitants built their first dwellings, which were hardly more than cellars dug into the side of the hill. Later Turkey Hill was leveled and used to fill the meadow, though some of it was carried away as ballast by outgoing ships.

When President Timothy Dwight of Yale visited the harbor in 1804 he found the place "to be situated on a mere mass of sand." He counted 120 dwellings on streets that wound through the partly filled marsh. Apparently he was in error. The census of 1810 shows only eighty dwellings. Dwight found the village "unpleasant, not from want of prospect, but because it furnished unpleasant streets and walks·and is unfriendly to every kind of vegetation."

But within twenty years the flourishing whaling trade had transformed the village completely. In 1875 an old resident, recalling the past glories of Sag Harbor, wrote that "the years from 1828 to 1848 were the flush times of whaling. The village was prosperous. Everyone lived well and laid up money. Business failures, vagrants, tramps, and extreme forms of poverty were unknown. Most of the ships were owned by companies and these companies embraced everybody. Not a family in the village or the surrounding country but owned stock in some blubber hunter. Thirty and thirty-three percent dividends were not uncommon.

"There was work too on every kind of ship's rigging. [There were 200 shipwrights in the village at the time.] Every sailor who came in after a two or three months voyage had from a hundred to four hundred dollars to spend. [At the height of its prosperity the village employed about 1,000 seamen.] In those days they did not go to New York to get rid of their money. New York was a long way off. Under the arches of the old Suffolk House and into the stable yard there used to roll every other day the old-fashioned stage coach, bringing mails, news and passengers three days from the city. Only the richer merchants and shippers—the Hunttings, Derings, Sleights and Mulfords—went to New York." (In 1810 the population was 850. By 1845 it was 3,621. In 1855 it had declined to 3,067. Today it is 2,346.)

But by the 1870s, according to these recollections,

a generation has grown up who know little or nothing of their birthplace. Since 1847 disaster and decay have attached themselves to the whalers. . . . The houses all have a comfortable cozy look. [Sag Harbor] is a finished village. It stopped growing a quarter of a century ago. The old-time merchants and shippers are nearly all in their graves. Sag Harbor is merely a place where a few farmers do a little trading.

The little shed termed a depot stands on a waste of empty cellars, vacant lots, tumble-down cooper shops and deserted buildings. This was once the most stirring spot in the village. Twenty ships refitting at the wharf; two large hotels facing each other; a dozen cooper shops turning out casks, half a score of blacksmith shops, and for the rest stores, sailors, farmers, wagons, fast horses and fancy buggies were some of the features of this spot thirty odd years ago. Now there is only heard the ripple of waves washing over piles, black and rotting, marking the site of former wharves.

Two years later the devastating fire of 1877 was to destroy even these last relics of Sag Harbor's vigorous past.

Where "the little shed termed a depot" once stood there now stands a bank on the east side of Main Street, opposite the foot of Long Wharf. The area on the other side of Main Street where an abandoned gasoline station now stands was once known as the North Battery and had been the site of gun emplacements during the War of 1812. It was here that Nathan Fordham, Jr., one of Sag Harbor's earliest settlers, was given leave by the town of Southampton to build a wharf and try-works in 1761, and where his son, Peletiah Fordham, built his tavern, later known as Duke Fordham's or the Suffolk House. It was Sag Harbor's leading hostelry, and here James Fenimore Cooper lived at various times between 1819 and 1823, and commenced his career as a novelist (see page 59). This building was destroyed by the fire of 1845 which also destroyed dozens of other thickly clustered frame buildings that occupied the northern end of Main Street at the time.

The brick building on the east side of Main Street which now houses Carruthers's flower shop survived this disaster. It was built in 1824 by Nathaniel Tinker, a well-known cabinet-maker, and in the year following the fire Tinker added an extension to the south of his original building. This extension now houses the American Hotel. It stands on the site of James Howell's house and tavern, built in 1730 and burned in 1845, and one of the first three houses in the village. Howell himself was a Tory during the Revolution and his house was occupied at the time by British officers. Here in 1777 Meigs (see page 43) captured the commander of the British garrison. James Howell's tavern later became a coffee house known as Eldridge's.

Tinker and his son leased their buildings as offices and warehouses to various tradesmen. After the fire of 1877 Addison Youngs and his father-in-law, Captain William Freeman of Bridgehampton, exchanged their farm for these buildings and opened the American Hotel. They added the porch at

The house of
Cornelius and Hannah
Sleight.

that time. The columns in the Gothic revival style along the
ground floor façade are an especially graceful detail. The
hotel has been carefully restored by its present owner and is
Sag Harbor's most popular bar and restaurant.

To the south of the American Hotel stands the Municipal
Building. Contemporary with the American Hotel, it originally
housed the Mansion House Hotel owned briefly by Ezekiel
Mulford, a member of one of the village's prominent whaling
families. It did not prosper and became the Union School
Building in 1873. When Pierson High School was opened
in 1907 the building was given to the village as a municipal
center. Its handsome cupola is a Sag Harbor landmark. The
building is now sadly in need of repair.

Beyond the Municipal Building to the left is Washington
Street, opened in 1787. Proceed along Washington Street past
the watchcase factory and you will come to Division Street,
which marks the boundary between East Hampton and Southampton. On the east side of Division Street to the north is the
little hip-roofed building known as the Old Umbrella House.
It is the oldest brick building in the village and may be the
village's oldest building of any kind. The bricks on the north
wall are Dutch, probably brought here as ship's ballast. Its date
is in dispute, but in 1790 it housed the Denison brothers' hat
factory. Today it is a craftsman's shop.

To the south stand the two imposing Sleight houses, the
larger one built in the Georgian style, the smaller in the
later, federal style, both five bays wide with handsome, centered doorways. These houses stand on what had once been

the Conkling farm, owned by original settlers of Sag Harbor. The Conklings suffered severe losses during the Revolution and in 1799 sold their land, which extended eastward to the bay, to William Rysam, a retired sea captain.

Rysam, a widower with five daughters, had settled in East Hampton during the Revolution. There he married an East Hampton widow and at her urging abandoned an option to buy the Stuyvesant farm in Manhattan, which she felt was too far away from home. Rysam bought the Conkling property instead, leaving the Astors to pick up his abandoned Manhattan option. Since Sag Harbor handled more foreign shipping than New York at the time, Rysam's decision must have seemed reasonable and prudent. Though Rysam's descendants had reason to regret the choice, Rysam himself prospered, building the large house for himself and his family and incorporating into it parts of the old Conkling farmhouse. To the north, along Burke Street between Division and Rysam streets, he built a ropewalk or factory, and his other enterprises included a shipyard at Conkling's Point where the Mobil Oil terminal now stands, a factory that made candles from sperm oil, and a salt works. He traded extensively with the West Indies and owned a large mahogany plantation in Honduras.

His daughter Hannah attended Clinton Academy in East Hampton (see page 44) where she met Cornelius Sleight, a fellow student descended from a distinguished Hudson River Dutch family. They eventually married and established themselves with Captain Rysam in his large house. They then built the smaller house to the south between 1820 and 1830. Both houses contained furniture made of Captain Rysam's Honduran mahogany. Note especially the handsomely framed doorways with sidelights and transoms, and the rows of boxwood.

Sleight himself prospered as his father-in-law's partner, and for a time was involved with General Washington in the manufacture of cypress shingles taken from the Great Dismal Swamp in Virginia. One of his ships, the *Cadmus*, brought Lafayette to America in 1824. His son, William Rysam Sleight, married the daughter of Henry Packer Dering, the first collector of customs in Sag Harbor, and with his brother-in-law William Mulford, his neighbor to the south (Mulford's house no longer stands), formed the whaling firm of Mulford and Sleight with offices at the wharf. Sleight's widow died in Sag Harbor in 1905 at the age of ninety-four. Her son, Brindley Dering Sleight, who edited the Sag Harbor *Corrector*, the predecessor of the present Sag Harbor *Express*, died in 1913

106

The house of
Captain David
Hand, the original
of James Fenimore
Cooper's Natty
Bumppo.

at the age of seventy-eight. Today no members of the family live in the village.

Proceed south on Division Street, past St. Andrew's Catholic Church (1872) to the corner of Union Street, which originally marked the southern limit of the village. Turn right and proceed along Union Street. At the northeast corner of Union and Church, where there are now a playground and parking lot, is the original site of the house of Henry Packer Dering, the first collector of customs at the port and William Rysam Sleight's father-in-law. This house has now been moved to the corner of Main and Garden streets, where it has been painstakingly restored and is open to visitors during the summer months. From the hill on which the Customs House once stood it was possible for the collector to observe the ships as they entered and left the harbor.

Turn north on Church Street, cross Sage Street, and you will find, just beyond the Montauk Hose firehouse, the one-and-a-half story "half house" of Captain David Hand, a descendant of one of the original East Hampton settlers. He served bravely as a privateer during the Revolution and later became one of Sag Harbor's leading citizens and most colorful characters. James Fenimore Cooper based Natty Bumppo, the hero of his *Leatherstocking Tales*, on Hand (see page 59). The house was built originally in Southampton, probably around 1690. It was then moved to Sagaponack, and later to the corner of Main and Madison streets on the site of the present Admiral Stanton house (see below) just behind the

107

Civil War monument. This area was once known as Hand's Corner. In keeping with the observation that "when they have nothing else to do in Sag Harbor they move a house," Hand's house was then transported to its present location in 1832.

Return to Union Street and opposite the parking lot you will see the Whaler's (Presbyterian) Church, Sag Harbor's most interesting building. Designed by Minard Lafever, a New York architect of great reputation, it was dedicated on May 16, 1844, at the height of Sag Harbor's prosperity. Its cost was $17,000, an enormous sum at a time when the carpenters who built it were paid $1.50 for a twelve-hour day. It is in the style of an Egyptian temple, a reflection of the romantic preoccupation with Napoleon's archæological investigations of Egypt. Though the style was more commonly adapted to furniture design it was occasionally used for tombs and prisons, and supplied the motif for the original New York City prison, known thereafter as the Tombs. Except for a poor copy in Essex, Connecticut, the Whaler's Church is the only ecclesiastical example of the style known to exist. At its dedication the Reverend J. A. Copp compared the church to the temple of Solomon.

The center of the façade is a truncated, pyramidal tower some 100 feet high and 40 feet square at the base, flanked by two smaller towers. The cornices are ornamented with stylized blubber spades.

A spectacular steeple 135 feet high was destroyed in the hurricane of 1938. The spot where it landed can be seen between the church and the Old Burying Ground where a new section of concrete walk has begun to buckle. Though a local critic once deplored this spire as a fantastic cross between a Turkish minaret and a Chinese pagoda, it was in fact a handsome ornament built by whalers who wanted to see it as their ships rounded Montauk Point. It was constructed in three sections, each smaller than the one beneath it, rather like an extended telescope. The lowest section was an octagonal shaft in the style of Christopher Wren, surrounded by eight Corinthian columns. Four clocks were built into its pediment. The second section was a truncated paneled cone, decorated with Phoenician swastikas, a symbol of good luck. At the top was a towering pagoda with fluttering eaves. A bell that once hung in the steeple now stands in the entrance to the church.

The interior of the church, 130 feet long, 65 feet wide, and three stories high, with room for 1,000 worshipers, is uncommonly beautiful, its dazzling white woodwork interspersed with panels of sea green, its balconies and choir loft ornamented with a blubber-spade freize. The rostrum is flanked by two

The most imposing building in Sag Harbor. The carpenters who built it in 1846 were paid $1.50 for a twelve-hour day. Even so, the church cost $17,000 to construct. The steeple fell in the hurricane of 1938.

delicate Corinthian columns like those that once supported the Wren tower, and two identical columns flank the entrance to the auditorium. The pews of Cuban mahogany are marked with the silver nameplates of their original occupants—Hunttings, Coopers, Howells, and so on. The effect of this towering room with its vaulted ceiling is not at all austere but calmly luxurious, as if to suggest the serenity that its sponsors must have longed for after their long and dangerous voyages. On a bright day, with the light filtering through the softly tinted windows, you can almost feel the room rocking on a gentle sea.

To the west of the church is a monument commemorating the raid of Colonel Meigs on a British fort which once stood there. On this site there later stood the Old Arsenal. Built in 1810 and destroyed, after it had been abandoned, in 1886, it was a stone building fifty feet long, twenty feet wide, and two stories high. It housed the guns and other equipment used to defend the village during the War of 1812, and later served as the customs house and post office as well as a courthouse.

The Old Burying Ground to the west of the Meigs monument was opened in 1767. The infant son of James Howell, the Tory innkeeper, was the first village resident to be buried there, and later his sister recalled how her mother had wept bitterly because her child was buried "way out in those lonesome woods," an odd complaint since the Burying Ground is hardly a five-minute walk from the site of Howell's tavern. Among the stones to be found in the Old Burying Ground is one in memory of William Havens, captain of the privateers *Beaver, Jay,* and *Retaliation* during the Revolution. Another reads simply Robin, Negro. Still another commemorates the death of two young men who were killed at the age of twenty-two when a cannon exploded during a celebration to mark the end of the War of 1812.

On the northwest corner of Union and Madison streets is the federal house of Jared Wade built about 1797. Wade was a whaling captain and a member of a prominent Sag Harbor shipping family who in 1849 sailed the forty-eight-ton schooner *San Diego* through the Strait of Magellan to San Francisco, setting record for a ship of that size. Later he became a boat builder with a shop at Long Wharf. Note especially the handsome doorway with its well-proportioned transom and sidelights and the elliptical fanlight above it. The ornamental brackets under the eaves are of hand-carved mahogany. The twelve-over-twelve window design suggests that the Wade house is an early example of the federal style. Later federal houses generally had a six-over-six arrangement.

Jared Wade's house.

On the opposite side of Union Street the handsome Italianate house now occupied by the Pino funeral home was built originally in 1796 for Lester Beebe, a shipbuilder. It was remodeled in 1870 for Stephen B. French. Stephen and his brother Hannibal, relative latecomers to the village, were involved in a number of Sag Harbor enterprises from the 1850s through the 1880s. They were merchants, they built and outfitted ships, and invested in whaling ventures. They owned the first Sag Harbor steamships and the *Myra,* the last of Sag Harbor's whalers. At one time they also owned the Maidstone flour mill which burned in 1877. As a young man Stephen made a voyage in a Sag Harbor whaler and in 1849 sailed to San Francisco, possibly as a passenger aboard Jared Wade's schooner. He later became a prominent Republican politician, served as Suffolk County treasurer from 1868 to 1872, and became appraiser of the Port of New York and chairman of the Board of Police Commissioners. He belonged to Roscoe Conkling's New York City Republican machine and was a lifelong and intimate friend of Chester A. Arthur, who is said to have visited the French house during his presidency. Whether or not Arthur actually visited Sag Harbor, French frequently visited the White House and became Arthur's confidant. He committed suicide in Boston in 1905. Stephen's older brother, Hannibal, became village postmaster under Arthur and later under Grover Cleveland and William Henry Harrison. Upon his death his daughter carried on his duties.

At the northeast corner of Union and Main streets stands

the John Jermain Memorial Library. It was built in 1910 as a gift to the village from Mrs. Russell Sage, wife of the millionaire philanthropist, in honor of her grandfather, an early Sag Harbor merchant.

In 1907 Mrs. Sage bought and restored the Benjamin Huntting mansion, now the Suffolk County Whaling Museum, the large Greek revival building on the southwest corner of Main and Garden streets, opposite the library. She used the house as a residence. Later it was sold to the local Masonic lodge which deeded it in turn to the museum. Note the lance-and-blubber-spade ornaments along the cornice. The museum is the most imposing building in the village. It was probably designed by Minard Lafever, the architect of the Whaler's Church, and built in 1846.

Benjamin Huntting, for whom the mansion was built, was one of three sons of the original Colonel Benjamin Huntting (1754-1807), who was himself a grandson of East Hampton's second Presbyterian minister. With Stephen Howell he fitted out the brig *Lucy* for a whaling cruise to the Brazil banks in 1785. The voyage was a success and the origins of the Sag Harbor whaling industry can be dated from that time. Colonel Huntting became the leading citizen of the village, and later formed a partnership with David Gelston, a Sag Harbor native who became collector of the Port of New York. Their ship *Abigail* came to be known as the school for Sag Harbor whalers. It made seventeen successful voyages to the coasts of Brazil and Patagonia as well as to the African coast, and was finally retired in 1822. Colonel Huntting served in the state senate from 1800 to 1804. Upon his death, his affairs were taken over by his widow and his three sons, who were able to lend substantial sums to the United States government after the War of 1812.

The Whaling Museum is Sag Harbor's most popular attraction, with some 60,000 visitors each summer. In the parlor stands the highboy made by the Dominys of East Hampton in 1796. The skylight over the staircase is especially impressive.

In the harpoon room there is the bomb lance or exploding harpoon invented by Captain Thomas Royce of Sag Harbor in the 1850s. In 1848 Royce in the bark *Superior* passed through the Bering Strait and became the first whaler to enter the Arctic Ocean. He found the water crowded with whales. A year later 154 ships followed Royce's example and left for the Arctic. They returned with cargoes worth $3,500,000. Nantucket and New Bedford were the main beneficiaries, most of the Sag Harbor fleet having gone to San Francisco by this time. An ingenious as well as an intrepid man, Royce invented

112

The house of
Hannibal French, the
scene of many
grand parties in the
1880s.

his bomb lance soon thereafter. Later he journeyed to London where he designed a gun from which to fire his lance. The device exploded and Royce lost his left hand. On the same voyage he met and married a French woman. They returned to Long Island where she gave piano lessons. While Royce was away on one of his whaling ventures, she abandoned him for a husband closer to home. Royce's fortunes declined thereafter. His whaling voyages proved unsuccessful, and he died penniless and alone in Mazatlán, Mexico.

Across from the Whaling Museum, on the northwest corner of Main and Garden streets, is the home of Hannibal French, Stephen's brother. It was rebuilt for French in the 1860s from an earlier house, and its interior as well as certain exterior details were done by Lafever. It is the ultimate expression of Sag Harbor's prosperity, a prosperity which had begun to erode even as the house was being built. It is in the so-called Italianate style, with twisted baroque columns and an elaborate bird house, in the style of an Italian villa, under the southern gable. The fleurs-de-lis above the upper windows are probably in recognition of the owner's surname.

Behind the Hannibal French house stands the old Customs House, which was moved to this site from its original location on Union and Church streets to make room for the St. Andrew's parking lot. It has been faithfully restored under the auspices of the Society for the Preservation of Long Island Antiquities and is open to the public. The Customs House was built by Henry Packer Dering as his residence shortly after the Revolution. It became the Customs House in 1790, when Sag Harbor was declared a port of entry, and Dering became its collector. Later Dering became village postmaster and his house served as the post office as well, until both the customs and post offices were moved across Union Street to the Arsenal after 1810. Upon his death Dering left an inventory of his possessions. Many of these have been found and restored to their original places in the house.

When you visit the Customs House be sure that the two congenial and knowledgeable guides—one on each floor—are on hand. They know the house and its details intimately. In the parlor note especially the handsome captain's chair made by the Dominys of East Hampton. In the kitchen there is a pie safe which looks like a big bird cage. A similar kitchen and identical implements are to be found in the historical museum at Maidstone, Kent, from which many of the early settlers of East Hampton and Sag Harbor originally came. The doors are hung with "Heaven & Hell" hinges, an H on the upper joining, an L on the lower. On the second floor notice the tapering upright beams. These beams were cut from oak trees, and were set with the wider end up to support the second-story floorboards. Note too the way in which two houses must have been joined to form the present building. From the daughter's room—the room presumably of the future Mrs. William Rysam Sleight—one could have seen the ships entering and leaving the harbor when the house was in its original location. The original stenciling along the wall borders in this room is especially interesting.

On the east side of Main Street on the corner of Jefferson Street opposite the Whaling Museum is the house of Arnold Van Scoy, a Dutch daguerreotypist. The house was built about 1810 by Benjamin Glover, Sag Harbor's master builder. Its gambrel roof and gable end windows are typical of Glover's work. The small bricks in the foundation are Dutch.

The fifth house to the south on the same side of Main Street was the home of John Jermain and the birthplace of Mrs. Sage's mother. It was built before 1798. At one time it belonged to Luther D. Cook who married the only daughter of Colonel Benjamin Huntting. It dates from the colonial or early federal period and has the twelve-over-twelve window arrangement typical of the period. Cook was a whaling agent who bought the house when Jermain died in 1820. Mrs. Sage bought and restored the house in 1901. It has since been extensively restored by its present owners.

Directly opposite, on the west side of Main Street, is the John Hunt house of the same period. The Hunts were the original owners of the Sag Harbor *Corrector*, founded in

The Howell-Napier house, one of the last mansions built in Sag Harbor.

1822. When Hunt's father sold the paper to Brindley Dering Sleight in 1859, John Hunt started the *Express,* Sag Harbor's present newspaper.

Beyond the Jermain house on the northeast corner of Palmer Terrace is the federal-style house of Huntting Cooper, captain of the whaling ship *Thames* owned by Mulford and Sleight, and later the owner of the ships *Gem, Franklin,* and *Konohasset.* This last vessel was wrecked on an uncharted reef off Pell's Island in the Pacific on May 24, 1846. Its crew built a sloop from the wreckage and after a voyage of forty-six days arrived safely at Honolulu. The Coopers were another of Sag Harbor's important whaling families. The brothers William and Gilbert Cooper have been described, dressed in tall white stovepipe hats, gray trousers, and Prince Alberts, and with gold-headed canes, rowing out to meet their ship *Nimrod,* home from the Indian Ocean. In 1845 Mercator Cooper was one of the first Americans to bring his ship, the *Manhattan,* into a Japanese port.* He was forbidden to land but the charts he brought back were used by Commodore Perry eight years later (see page 56). In 1848 Ronald McDonald of the Sag Harbor whaler *Plymouth* went ashore in Japan with a supply of books and provisions and was immediately captured. He was kept in a bamboo cage, released a year later, and sent home. While in captivity he learned the Japanese

---

* The first American ships to land in Japan were the *Lady Washington* of Boston and the *Grace* of New York in 1791. From 1798 to 1802 the Dutch chartered one American ship each year to carry cargo from Batavia to Nagasaki. No further American ships reached Japan until Cooper's voyage in 1845.

language. The Huntting Cooper house was built around 1800. The main cornice, with its egg-and-dart molding, is original and a typical federal detail. The porch was added later.

On the southeast corner of Main Street and Palmer Terrace stands the house of Samuel Huntting, one of the three sons of Colonel Benjamin Huntting and a brother of Mrs. Luther Cook. The house, which is in the Greek revival style with its columned porch, its row of wreathed eyebrow windows, and its gables at either end, had been built originally by Dr. Nathaniel Gardiner in 1797 and was embellished in the 1830s by its new owner. Gardiner was the son of Colonel Abraham Gardiner of East Hampton and Gardiners Island (see page 41). He married the only sister of Henry Packer Dering, was said to have failed in the whaling trade because his crews and captains were not sufficiently experienced, and eventually left Sag Harbor. The new owner, Samuel Huntting, inherited the famous whaling ship *Abigail* upon his father's death, and during the War of 1812 sailed it past the British blockade into New York where he sold its cargo of oil for one dollar a gallon, an extraordinary price at the time. Later he joined Captain David Hand and other villagers to help beat off a British attack on the village in 1813.

The house directly to the south on the same side of Main Street was occupied by Samuel's brother, Gilbert. Earlier the house had belonged to John Hulbert, who raised the first company of Minute Men from the Hamptons and the Harbor. He designed a flag of thirteen stripes and thirteen stars which his company carried with them to Ticonderoga. In 1775 they presented their flag to the Continental Congress in Philadelphia. This may have been the flag that a member of Congress commissioned Betsy Ross to "copy" and which was officially adopted in 1777. The Hulbert flag is now in the Suffolk County historical museum in Riverhead. After the Revolution Hulbert made saddles for export to the West Indies. He also built houses, among them the one later occupied by Stephen French.

Directly opposite the Samuel Huntting house on the west side of Main Street is an imposing Victorian mansion in the Italianate style, known locally as the Napier house. It was built in the 1860s by Nathan P. Howell, grandson of Stephen Howell who, with Colonel Huntting, sponsored Sag Harbor's first successful whaling venture. Later it was bought by Dr. Charles Napier, the great-grandson of Isaac Hand, David Hand's brother. The house, which had fallen into disrepair, has been meticulously restored by its present owners. Like the Hannibal French house, it was built after the village had en-

Samuel L'Hommedieu
built this house
in the 1840s
when it appeared
that Sag Harbor
might become a
proper city.

tered upon its decline and was among the last buildings of consequence to be built in Sag Harbor.

Beyond the Howell-Napier house on the southwest corner of Main Street and Bayview Avenue stands the Greek revival town house built by Samuel L'Hommedieu in the 1840s at the height of Sag Harbor's prosperity. This brick house with brownstone details was typical of the sort that was being built in New York City at the time and suggests that its owner was among those who expected Sag Harbor to become an urban center. The two-and-a-half story house with its handsome columned doorway could as easily have been built in New York's Washington Square. The L'Hommedieus were French Huguenots who settled in Southold on the North Fork of Long Island in 1690. They were said to have been "romantic, sentimental and to have possessed 'temperament.'" The house in Sag Harbor was built by the great-grandson of this original settler and the son of Samuel, Sr., who fought in the Revolution first as a soldier, then as a privateer. He helped choose the site for the Montauk lighthouse. He also made and supplied rope to the whaling trade, later traded with the West Indies, and bought the whaling ship *Alknomack* from Colonel Huntting. The name was pronounced locally as Lum-a-doo. Though Samuel, Jr., and his wife had eight children the family declined with the decline of the village and there are no members left today. The house was bought eventually by Oliver Wade, who fitted out the first Sag Harbor ship for San Francisco in 1849 and whose shipyard also built the schooner *San Diego* in which Jared Wade made his record voyage to San Francisco later that year.

117

On the northwest corner of Glover and Main streets is the house of Benjamin Glover, the builder. Note the gable end windows and the gambrel roof, typical of his work. The house is of the federal period, built around 1810. Glover was a real-estate developer as well as a builder, and many of the houses along Glover Street were built and sold by him. On the opposite corner is the house of Captain George Tooker with its characteristic Greek revival front end gable. Tooker navigated the bark *Martha II* which carried America's first consul to Japan in 1865. Later he became keeper of the Cedar Island lighthouse.

From here proceed around Otter Pond, whose inlet to the Cove was cut in 1783. Mashashimuet Park was a gift to the village from Mrs. Sage, as was Otter Pond itself. The park, whose name is said to derive from the Indian word for great spring, which was the Indian name for Otter Pond, includes six tennis courts, baseball diamonds, and other recreational facilities. In the latter half of the last century it was the site of a trotting track and fairgrounds. In the 1840s Sag Harbor's red-light district was on the opposite side of Main Street from the park entrance.

Proceed past the park along Jermain Avenue. The small factory occupied by Sag Harbor Industries originally housed the Engravers and Printers Machinery Company. In the 1920s this company made engraving machinery for the United States Mint. The plant now manufactures electronic coils. Beyond it is the oddly shaped house with its wooden campanile, built by Ephraim Byram, whose father Eliab was one of the builders of the old arsenal. Byram was an astronomer and inventor who was said to have been a mechanical genius. A globe built by him is displayed in the Whaling Museum. He made clocks in a factory next to his house, one of which he sold to New York's City Hall. He is said to have built his campanile in order to test his pendulums. He was also a builder of orreries or mechanical models of the planets in their orbits. His business failed and was replaced by a hosiery mill which, after three years, also failed. Thereafter a barrel stave factory, a morocco leather business, and a hat company were all attempted in Byram's former factory and they too failed. In 1882 the building burned. Its site was bought by Joseph Fahys and Stephen French, and donated to the cemetery.

To enter the Oakland Cemetery after having learned something of the Sleights, the Hunttings, the Howells, the Wades, the Coopers, the Mulfords, the Frenches, the Byrams, and the Fahys is to undergo something of a shock, for here they all

The broken mast
monument in
Oakland Cemetery.

are, together with their wives and husbands, their brothers
and sisters, and their various children. With a slight effort one
can almost see the men in their plug hats and their swallow-
tailed coats, the women in their shawls and bonnets standing
about as mourners as yet another of their number is laid to
rest. The eastern section of the cemetery contains the graves
of more recent Sag Harbor families.

Note especially the broken mast monument in the western
section of the cemetery with its touching bas-relief of the stove
boat and the names of the young mariners lost at sea in "actual
encounter with the monsters of the deep." Just to the north of
it are the graves of Captain David Hand and his five wives.
In their original location in the Old Burying Ground the
wives' graves were arranged in a semicircle around that of their
husband. When they were moved here after the Oakland
Cemetery opened in 1840, the graves were arranged in a straight
line. The epitaph, composed by Captain Hand and now in-
decipherable, once read:

> *Behold ye living mortals passing by*
> *How thick the partners of one husband lie;*
> *Vast and unsearchable are the ways of God,*
> *Just but severe his chastening rod.*

From the main entrance take the first carriage road to the
left and in the third aisle you will find a boulder in memory
of Prentice Mulford, marked with the word Philosopher and
the legend "Thoughts are Things." Mulford was born in

119

1834 and grew up in the Mansion House Hotel (now the Municipal Building) of which his father Ezekiel was proprietor. After a few years in New York he went to San Francisco where he became a writer for a newspaper called *The Golden Era*. He lived on a converted whale boat anchored in San Francisco Bay, dressed in a one-piece knitted garment, like an old-fashioned bathing suit, which had once been blue but later turned a rusty brown with age. He insisted that this was all the clothing a man needed. He lived on fish, vegetables, fruit, and bread, and once a day he landed his boat to buy his provisions and the newspapers. He was something of a mystic and had the idea that one's thoughts, if sufficiently intense, assumed physical shapes. He is said to have predicted the invention of the radio and to have experimented with the idea of a flying machine. He had no use for money and composed, in addition to his journalism which was said to have been extremely witty, thirty-six volumes of spiritualist writings. A cult eventually formed around these writings and his memorial was erected, some thirty years after his death in 1891, by a group of his San Francisco followers.

He returned to Sag Harbor late in his life and though he had not himself been a whaleman, he was considered, by the old whalers who exchanged tales in French's store, Sag Harbor's foremost teller of whaling tales. One of these had to do with a whaleboat painted green. This boat was fastened to a whale which, instead of sounding, started off across the ocean at a tremendous speed. As Mulford told the story the line smoked as it ran around the loggerhead, through the chock from the coil tub, so that water had to be poured on it to keep the boat from catching fire. The friction caused the boat's seams to melt and the men had to bail with their hats. Soon the hair had blown off three whalemen and another lost his eyelashes. Finally the captain looked over his shoulder and saw another green boat just behind. He then looked over the gunwale and saw that his own boat had no paint at all. "Boys," he said, "it's time to cut clear when that a're critter tows us so fast he pulls the boat right out'en its paint."

Mulford was not the first of Sag Harbor's eccentrics. Before him there had been Byram, the clockmaker, and Byram's contemporary, John Sage. The son of the village doctor, Sage also had a medical degree but did not practice. Instead he pursued astronomy and mathematics, and in the cellar of the old arsenal built a flying machine. It didn't work, but a balloon he built, with Thomas Dering, son of the customs collector, was apparently a success. His chief contribution to the village, however, was his mathematical skill which enabled him to

Admiral Stanton's house. He sailed with Commodore Perry to Japan and later fought in the Civil War.

settle disputes as they arose among the holders of shares in whaling ventures. He mistrusted doctors and took only what today would be called organic medicines. He lived to be ninety-four and lies not far from Prentice Mulford in the Oakland Cemetery.

Leaving the Oakland Cemetery, walk east past Oakland Avenue and Palmer Terrace to Suffolk Street. Originally known as the Road to the Mill, it was the site of Jason Beebe's windmill, built in 1820. From the top of this mill the returning ships could be seen as they entered Gardiners Bay (see page 58). The mill was sold in 1837 and moved to Bridgehampton. Suffolk Street was also known once as Academy Street after a school that had been built here in 1845. It was burned in 1864 by its prankish students. At the southeast corner of Suffolk and Jefferson streets stands a fine house of the federal period, with a Greek revival portico added. Notice the Chinese smokebush in the yard, and the elegant transom and sidelights framing the ten-panel door. Directly across, on the southwest corner, is the Beebe homestead, built at about the same time as the mill and subsequently enlarged. The large boxwoods behind its fence are well over a century old. The English walnut tree in the front yard is probably one of those that came ashore in 1835 from the wreck of the *Louis-Philippe,* a French ship with a cargo of shrubs and trees.

Returning to Main Street and walking north toward the business district you will notice on the west side of Main Street, beyond the Hannibal French house, the Long Island *Herald* house, one of the oldest houses in the village, built

121

around 1735. The porch and the dormer window are recent additions. The house itself is in the typical Cape Cod style. In 1791 David Frothingham established Long Island's first newspaper in this house (see page 54). Opposite the Long Island *Herald* house, on the east side of the street, is the Sybil Douglass house, a Georgian building with interesting gable end windows but with a Greek revival porch framing its doorway. Beyond the Sybil Douglass house on the east side of Main Street, directly south of the monument, is the Greek revival house of Admiral Oscar Stanton, who sailed with Commodore Perry to Japan and later fought in the Civil War. The house was probably built in 1834 by David Hand for his son Forrest, after he had moved his own house to Church Street in 1832. Lead eagles ornament the triangular windows at the front and rear of the house. The porch was added later, probably between 1860 and 1870. Further north on the east side of Main Street is a gingerbread Gothic house built in the 1850s. Though Shelter Island has several houses in this style, this is Sag Harbor's only example. Beyond it is the house of Peleg Latham, in the federal style. Like many merchants of the period he built his house over his shop. The Latham house was built originally on Turkey Hill. As the hill was leveled to fill in the Great Meadow, the basement and foundation of the house were exposed above ground, as they are today.

If you will turn south again and walk a few steps along Madison Street, you will see on the east side of Madison the federal house of Abraham Vail with its double doorway and the molding at the cornice in the shape of a twisted rope. Vail was a carpenter who built this house in 1820. It is said to stand on the site of an Indian burying ground.

Next to Vail's house is the original Presbyterian manse, once occupied by Nathaniel Prime, Sag Harbor's fourth Presbyterian minister (1806-9) and better known as the historian of Long Island. His wife, Julie Jermain, started one of the first Sunday schools in America in this house. The minister himself seems to have been a convivial fellow. He recalled that when he lived in Sag Harbor, "I have had a half gallon of different liquors consumed by the callers of a single evening." The house, which was built around 1797, is an excellent example of the federal style with its three bays and its doorway to one side. Its foundation of brown sandstone is not local. It may have been brought here as ballast in ships built in New England and sent here for fitting out. Just east on Sage Street is Meeting House Hill, the site of Sag Harbor's first Presbyterian Church (1767), known locally as God's Old Barn.

By the turn of the century the population of Sag Harbor

The Latham house
on the remains of
Turkey Hill.

included few descendants of these early residents. Instead the
various attempts to industrialize the village had encouraged
the settlement here of the families of European immigrants.
In 1900 there lived in the part of Sag Harbor that lies within
the town of East Hampton forty-one Irish immigrants, thirty-
three Germans, fifteen Russians, fifteen Hungarians, thirteen
Swiss, three Italians, three Bohemians, and three Rumanians,
as well as 100 blacks. Though the old East Hampton families
were by now very much in the minority, among the five village trustees in 1927 there was a Hand, a Wade, and a Byram.

By 1929 the village supported six barbers, five cobblers,
two pool parlors, three hotels, seven clergymen, two dentists,
three lawyers, and three doctors, and served chiefly as a trading
center for East Hampton farmers. The economy of Sag Harbor
hovered between stability and stagnation. In 1929, a troubled
YMCA secretary observed that in addition to two single
ladies who entertained gentlemen callers and had no apparent
means of support, Sag Harbor abounded in "loafers." On Main
Street from March 16 to 22, between the hours of 7:00 and
10:00 P.M., he counted an average of twenty-four "loafers"
under the age of twenty-one, and forty-two above that age.

Sag Harbor's industrial activity continues to decline, but
the village has steadily drawn new residents attracted by its
handsome old houses, its informality, and its curious history.
Sag Harbor now attracts thousands of visitors each summer
and an increasing number year round. During the Christmas
weekend in 1974 some 600 visitors came to Sag Harbor for
a tour of its historic houses.

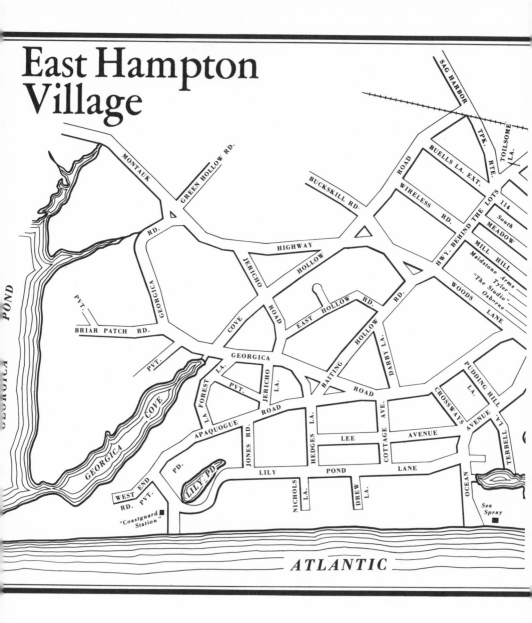

East Hampton Village

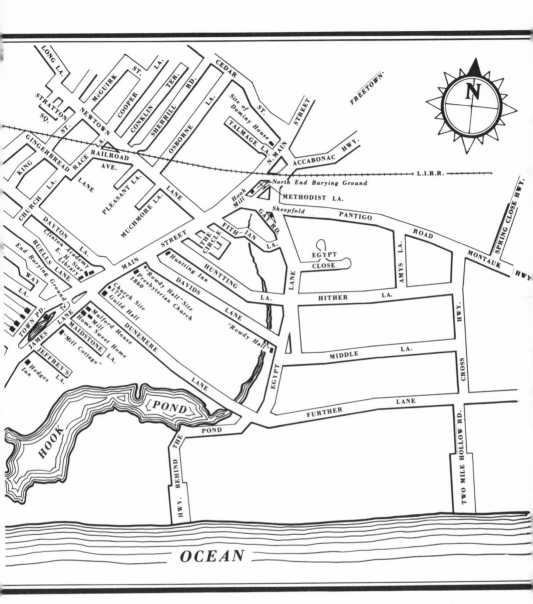

East Hampton Village Tour

Few visitors are indifferent to the charms of East Hampton Village. Though throngs of summer vacationers and automobiles have replaced the geese and cows on Main Street, this wide thoroughfare is still overarched by venerable elms and lined with equally venerable houses, and East Hampton remains a rare specimen of a well-regulated, well-to-do, but unostentatious American colonial town. To be sure, much of the current air of sedate prosperity comes not from the colonial past but from the affluent resort community that increasingly over the last hundred years has come to dominate East Hampton's economy and physical appearance. Because that influence has been conservative in character and was slow in coming, the underlying nature of the village is still fairly tranquil and rural. Blessed by geography, natural resources, and the circumstances of its development, East Hampton has retained a hold on its native population to an extent that is unusual in American history; the names of the town's founders are in the local telephone directory as well as on successive generations of headstones in the cemetery.

The portion of the Montauk Highway entering East Hampton from the west is called Woods Lane, presumably named because this part of the road from Bridgehampton once ran through the forest that was the town's main fuel source for many years. At the blinker light turn right on Ocean Avenue, once Calf Pasture Lane. For 200 years the single religious denomination of East Hampton was Presbyterian, and the town's minister received among other benefices the Calf Pasture for grazing his cattle. To pass south of Town Pond to the ocean, one had to take down the bars that kept the minister's cows from straying.

According to early records the town herd was sometimes driven that way to the fine grazing lands beside Lily Pond. Lily Pond Lane, which runs west off Ocean Avenue, is today lined with mansions, many built by the summer residents around the turn of the century. They are huge rambling Victorian shingled houses designed to accommodate and be maintained by the large staffs that once accompanied well-to-do people to their summer establishments each year.

Before you come to Lily Pond Lane, you pass Pudding Hill Lane, also a street of fashionable large old summer homes. Between this street and Woods Lane there is a slight elevation (once somewhat more pronounced than today). According to legend, the Osborn mistress who lived there during the revolutionary war was cooking a suet pudding when she was beset by a band of hungry redcoats. The rest of the story, which was immortalized in verse, is as follows:

"Hurrah boys!" said the leader bold,
"We're just in time! Come on—"
"Oh, no you're not," she made reply,
Then seized the boiling pot,
Ran with it through another door,
And threw it blazing hot
Pudding and all, adown the hill
And left it in the sand,
Amid the curses loud and deep
Of all that hungry band.

Hence Pudding Hill and Pudding Hill Lane. In another version of the story the British soldiers saw an Indian pudding steaming in a bag over the open hearth and, considering the dish unfit to eat, shoved a stick through it and rolled it down the hill.

If you turn on to Lily Pond Lane you will eventually pass Lily Pond on your right and will notice the Coast Guard public beach on your left. Continuing straight, Lily Pond Lane makes a T-intersection with Apaquogue Road. Apaquogue, incidentally, is the Indian word for "the place where the flags grow," in this case the cattail flags of Lily Pond. Turn right and you will observe some fairly old, unpretentious houses that look as if they might have been boarding houses back in the mid-nineteenth century. Apaquogue was in those days a farming hamlet which catered to those vacationers who did not want to board on Main Street and ride the stage to the beach, but preferred instead to be in easy walking distance of the ocean.

A popular establishment there during the 1840s and 1850s was Abraham Candy's boarding house. Candy was an Englishman who taught school at Clinton Academy. In 1863 he inherited a house on Main Street from his brother-in-law, Captain Josiah Mulford, and converted it into another boarding house. He hired William Gardner, a one-armed Civil War veteran and ex-keeper of the Montauk Light, to run it for him. Enlivened under the genial Mr. Gardner's administration by oyster suppers and dances in the parlor, it soon became a popular vacation spot and was patronized by the artists Thomas and Mary Nimmo Moran when they "discovered" East Hampton in 1878. Ten years later this house underwent new management and was named Sea Spray. In 1902 it was sold and moved to its present location. If you return to Ocean Avenue and turn right, you will see this same Sea Spray Inn, with some alterations, in front of the parking lot beside the beach.

Return to Town Pond from the beach. The pond was originally just a marshy depression which the early settlers excavated in order to make a drinking place for their cattle. Below the pond's east side, opposite the blinker light, is the Hedges Inn, named after the Hedges family which owned the property from 1652 until 1923. The inn has been much altered and added to; the oldest part dates from 1774. A small outbuilding in back is over 100 years older; it was a cordwainer's, or shoemaker's, shop when the Hedges engaged in that trade. The inn became a famous restaurant between 1954 and 1964 when it was owned by the late Henri Soulé.

The first house on the west side of the pond at the intersection of Main Street and Woods Lane once belonged to Dr. Osborne, a beloved family physician of the second half of the nineteenth century. The second house from the corner is "The Studio," the home of Thomas and Mary Nimmo Moran, now a registered national historic landmark. In 1884, six years after the Morans began coming to East Hampton to spend their summers etching and painting, they built their large pleasant house, now the home and real-estate office of Mr. and Mrs. Condie Lamb. Today Moran's extraordinarily fresh water colors are prized by museums and collectors of nineteenth-century American art; he first rose to national prominence when his large canvases depicting Yosemite and Yellowstone were unrolled in the halls of Congress, thus influencing the legislature to establish our national park system.

The house at 217 Main Street, two doors down from "The Studio," was the summer White House when President John Tyler came there in September, 1845, with his wife, the fair and worldly Julia Gardiner Tyler. Julia, daughter of State Senator David Gardiner, was known as the Rose of Long Island. A contemporary East Hampton diarist and sidewalk philosopher, commenting on the attractive pair who created a sensation every time they walked down Main Street, wrote: "Mrs. Tyler for beauty and nobleness in appearance is said by many not surpassed by any of her Sex in the United States. (But Beauty Fades.)"

Beyond what was for many years known as "the old Tyler place" is the Maidstone Arms. This inn is the site of the old Osborn tannery, begun by Thomas Osborn when he came to East Hampton from New Haven in 1660 and continued by subsequent generations of his descendants.

In front of the Maidstone Arms on the village green is a flat-topped knoll, an artificial mound, with a large maple tree growing on top. This elevation was created so that the mill which was built there in 1771 could better catch the breezes to turn its sail-covered arms. It was moved to Pantigo Lane in 1850 and then moved again in 1915 to the lawn behind

The studio of
Thomas Moran
where he lived with
his wife, Mary
Nimmo.

"Home Sweet Home" where it can be visited today. Unlike the old Hook Mill at the north end of Main Street, it no longer has millstones or gears.

Walk east across the green, imagining the clamor of honking geese in a more bucolic age waddling each day down Main Street to and from Town Pond. On your right you will see a stile which you can climb over to enter the cemetery or South End Burying Ground as it is called to differentiate it from the North End Burying Ground behind Hook Mill at the opposite end of Main Street. The cemetery was not always fenced, and the early residents of the town apparently didn't mind that their cows wandered among the graves of their relatives and forebears.

The most notable monument in the South End Burying Ground, that commemorating Lion Gardiner (1599-1663), was erected some two centuries after his death. A stone effigy of an armored soldier, hands folded in prayer, rests under a Gothic revival arch designed by the well-known nineteenth-century architect James Renwick. Sarah Diodati Gardiner, who commissioned the monument, also had the bones of the founder exhumed. According to Robert David Lion Gardiner, the skeleton was that of a six-foot man—an uncommonly tall height in the seventeenth century—with broad shoulders and narrow hips. By his account, his ancestor's bones were encased in a steel vest and helmet, and the red fragments of a British officer's uniform. People who saw the remains commented on the old gentleman's fine set of teeth. Before he was reburied, the grizzled reddish hair was clipped and distributed to family members in various rings designed by Tiffany.

Other members of the Gardiner clan are buried nearby. A tall obelisk marks the grave of State Senator David Gardiner (1784-1844) who was killed along with several others in an accident aboard the steam frigate *Princeton* when the ship's gun burst. His daughter Julia (1820-1889), the wife of President John Tyler, lies nearby. A broken column marks the resting place of their son, John Alexander Tyler (1848-1883), a Confederate soldier, veteran of the Franco-Prussian War of 1870 and surveyor of Indian lands in the American West.

Not far from the congregated Gardiners is the simple red sandstone marker of Lion Gardiner's friend and protégé, Thomas James, the first minister of East Hampton. James's headstone is the earliest found in the East Hampton cemetery. It is probable that in their desire to abandon all "popish" trappings, the puritanical town founders memorialized their dead with mere wooden markers that vanished in time.

In their day James and Gardiner were frequently seen walking up Main Street together as they discussed the town's business; they must have have made an odd-looking pair, for if Gardiner was unusually tall for his time, James was diminutive. Besides attending the spiritual needs of his flock, James proselytized among the Indians with a catechism he had written in their language. In fact, his proficiency with the Indian tongue was such, he said, he could have been an interpreter from one end of Long Island to the other during the busy period of Indian land purchases in the 1660s. Upon his death his estate was valued at £500, a considerable sum in that period, most of which represented real-estate holdings gained from the Indians. He also operated a whaling company with boats manned by Indians. His wealth was further increased by an extraordinary allotment of oil from beached whales resulting from a special agreement with the Indians and his fellow townsmen. One notices something unusual about Minister James's headstone. It does not face west toward Town Pond as do almost all the other markers, but rather east because of instructions in James's will. It is said that he wished to be buried in a position so that at the Resurrection he would be facing the congregation he had served so long.

James Lane, named for the minister, is a short street bordering the eastern edge of the cemetery. It is East Hampton's most historical thoroughfare. It was here that the Montauk Indians during their calamitous warfare with the Rhode

James Lane at the
cemetery.

Island Indians in the 1650s sought protection and set up an encampment between Lion Gardiner's house and that of Reverend James (see page 34). James's house is gone. After his death his property was sold, according to the terms of his will, to John Gardiner, the grandson of Lion Gardiner, and Gardiners have owned it ever since. Winthrop Gardiner's "Mill Cottage" at 36 James Lane is a very old house, a south-facing salt box, much altered and moved from its original location somewhere else on the property. The mill itself, which was built in 1771, was in operation until the hurricane of 1938 tore off its arms. The Gardiners, being wealthier than their neighbors, could afford their own mill, which obviated having to wait in line to have grain ground at one of the town mills.

"Home Sweet Home," a shrine to the songwriter, actor, and playwright John Howard Payne, is at 14 James Lane. Payne was the son of William Payne, who came to East Hampton to teach at Clinton Academy when it opened in 1784, and Sarah Isaacs Payne, the daughter of Aaron Isaacs, Jr., son of a Jew from Hamburg who immigrated to East Hampton, became a successful man of property, and married a girl from the town. Young Isaacs married Esther Mulford, the daughter of Matthew Mulford, and went to live in her girlhood home, the house that was to become Home Sweet Home. Built in 1650, it had been embellished by Matthew Mulford who installed in the parlor handsome pine paneling and a corner cabinet which he carved himself. (Matthew Mulford was a prosperous whaling captain and the son of Samuel "Fishhook" Mulford, see page 37.)

After Sarah Isaacs married William Payne they lived with her parents until 1791, when he took another teaching position in New York City. By that time she was expecting John Howard, and it remains a point of debate to this day whether or not he was born in Home Sweet Home or in New York. In any case, Sarah frequently brought him to stay with his grandparents, and the old Mulford-Isaacs house remained the only real home the peripatetic Payne ever had. The song which brought him lasting fame was written when he was homesick and broke in Paris. Its sentimental lyrics became an immediate sensation; Jenny Lind is reputed to have brought tears to Daniel Webster's eyes when she sang it.

In 1908 the old house was sold to Gustav H. Buek, a Brooklyn businessman, for a summer home. He and Mrs. Buek made it into a Payne shrine with memorabilia they collected. Now open to the public, it has, in addition to numerous Payne relics, an extensive collection of lusterware china, glass, and pewter. The Bueks were also responsible for bringing the old 1771 windmill to its present location behind Home Sweet Home.

East Hampton's other ancient homestead, the Mulford house, is next door to Home Sweet Home at 12 James Lane. Also dating from the 1650s, it is one of the oldest houses on Long Island. In 1698 it became the property of Samuel Mulford, who deeded it to his son Matthew, who later came into possession of Home Sweet Home. Generations of Mulfords lived in it until 1944 when it was put up for sale. Funds were raised to buy it for a town museum, and in 1948 it was presented to the East Hampton Historical Society. The society restored it and maintains it now as a period piece furnished exclusively with local furniture and artifacts showing a bygone way of life.

James Lane rejoins Main Street at Guild Hall, home of the John Drew Theater and the Woodhouse and Thomas Moran galleries. It was designed by the architect and summer colony resident Aymar Embury II in 1931. Twenty years earlier Embury had designed the East Hampton Free Library across the street in the style of an Elizabethan half-timbered house, a conscious reference to the town's Kentish origins. In 1946 he added the Gardiner Memorial Room to house the valuable Morton Pennypacker collection of Long Island history. The library is on property that once belonged to Samuel Buell, who was installed as East Hampton's third minister in 1746 in a ceremony presided over by the famous divine Jonathan Edwards. More convivial than the puritanical Edwards, Buell was a sportsman and raconteur. According to the East Hampton historian David Gardiner, "He was always active and sometimes impetuous. The style of his sermons had the fault of being rather diffuse; but they are neither lukewarm nor undecided." Over his long life he had three wives, the last of whom was nearly fifty years younger than he. Dr. Buell is credited with being a great educator; in 1753 he founded a library and in 1784 Clinton Academy.

Clinton Academy at 151 Main Street was begun as a college preparatory school (see page 44). Before it was established young men who wanted to go to college were tutored by the town's ministers. (According to the East Hampton historian Jeannette Edwards Rattray, the town's first college graduate was Recompense Osborn, who finished Harvard in 1661.) Although only young men went on to college, Clinton Academy was from its inception co-educational. After the school was discontinued in 1881, the building was remodeled as a community center and called Clinton Hall. For a period it also housed the East Hampton *Star* and the East Hampton Free Library. In 1921 it was restored to more or less its original appearance and turned into a museum of local history under the auspices of the East Hampton Historical Society. The wealth of artifacts it houses reveals much about the occupations and pleasures of the town over ten generations.

The church in which Samuel Buell preached stood across Main Street from Clinton Academy; a historical marker a few yards north of Guild Hall locates the site of this once famous landmark. Built in 1717 with massive oak beams

The Mulford House where "Fishhook" Mulford lived. It was built in the 1650s and remained in the Mulford family until 1944.

brought over from Gardiners Island, it had a clear-toned bell donated by Queen Anne, and was for many years considered to be one of the finest and most costly churches on Long Island, a symbol of the town's prosperity. The predecessor of this church was a very modest thatched-roof structure built in 1650 in the middle of the Old South Burying Ground. The present white church, a short distance north on Main Street, was built in 1860, and a few years later the church of Buell and Lyman Beecher (see page 35) was torn down.

Just north of the present Presbyterian Church on the corner of Main Street and David Lane was a house that has since been moved to the corner of Egypt and David lanes. In the 1890s it was known as "Rowdy Hall" and was the center of the summer art colony. Every morning the artists, who had since the 1870s been coming to East Hampton in increasing numbers, would fan out into the nearby fields and set up their easels and umbrellas. Then at the end of the day they would gather at Clinton Academy where John Ward Stimson criticized their work. After this they would return to their boarding house where their cheerful noise over beer and cards earned the place its name.

After "Rowdy Hall" was moved to its present location it was renovated and, following their marriage in 1928, rented by Janet and Jack Bouvier, the parents of Jacqueline Onassis. A society columnist once reported that "little Jackie Bouvier made a charming hostess at her second birthday party given at the home of her parents, Rowdy Hall, on Egypt Lane."

The Huntting Inn on the corner of Main Street and Huntting Lane encloses a house of 1699 built for the Reverend Nathaniel Huntting, East Hampton's second minister. Nine generations of Hunttings lived in the house, making various additions to it until the original structure was completely invisible from the outside. It was an inn during the revolutionary war and a boarding house after 1875.

The town's windmills were ever popular subjects for East Hampton's first wave of artists. Hook Mill at the north end of Main Street, built in 1806 by Nathaniel Dominy, is the third successive mill to be operated on that spot. It is called Hook Mill because it is located slightly north of "the Hook" or low-lying drainage basin that curves around to become Hook Pond. According to an account book kept by John Lyon Gardiner, Nathaniel Dominy took three Indians and a Negro, Shem, to the island to chop down the huge oak timbers that were needed for the mill shaft and cog wheels. In 1893 the windmill was almost sold for an exhibit at the Chicago World's Fair, but the transaction fell through. Reconditioned in 1931,

"Rowdy Hall" where East Hampton's artists gathered in the 1870s. Later it was rented by Mr. and Mrs. Jack Bouvier. Their daughter Jacqueline celebrated her second birthday here.

the gears are in good working order, and the mill, which is open to the public, can still grind grain.

Nathaniel Dominy (1737-1812), who built the mill, was a highly skilled clockmaker and cabinetmaker. The clocks and furniture that he and subsequently his son and grandson made are now valuable family heirlooms or museum pieces. The old Dominy house a few yards beyond Hook Mill on North Main Street was built in 1715 and torn down in 1946. The Winterthur Museum near Wilmington, Delaware, has reconstructed the Dominy clock shop, complete with original account books, tools, furniture patterns, clocks, and finished cabinetwork.

Continuing on North Main Street you pass through Freetown, once an enclave of freed slaves. From its earliest days East Hampton had a small black population; the Gardiners worked their island plantation with slave labor. At the beginning of the nineteenth century the rate of manumissions increased, and the freed slaves, followed at a later date by the Montauk Indians, took up residence in Freetown.

If you return to Hook Mill and follow the Montauk Highway toward Amagansett you will be "going down Pantigo." Pantigo, like Jericho or Apaquogue, was an outlying farming district. It was part of the area referred to in the early records as the "eastern plain." Imagine if you will the herds of cattle and sheep jostling as they bleated and bellowed down Pantigo on their way to the grassy downs of Montauk. East Hampton has changed much since those days, but a good deal of its history can still be deduced by what remains along its Main Street and side lanes.

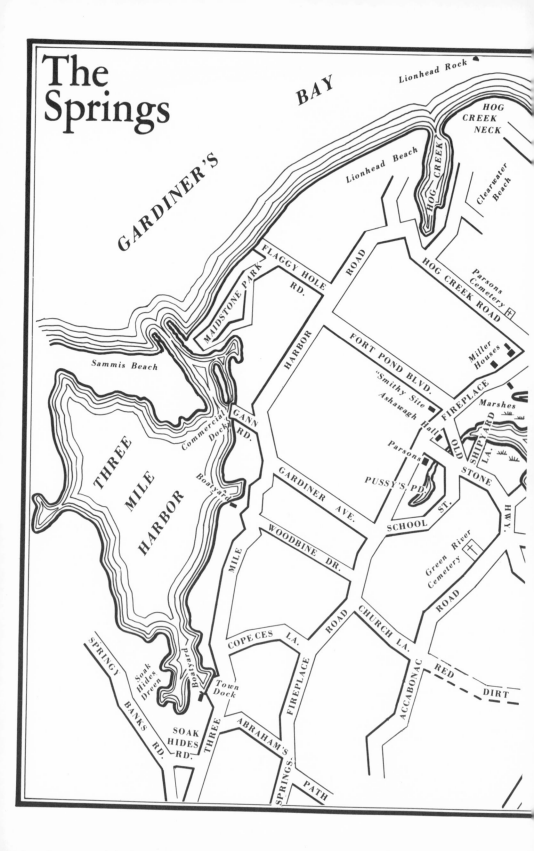

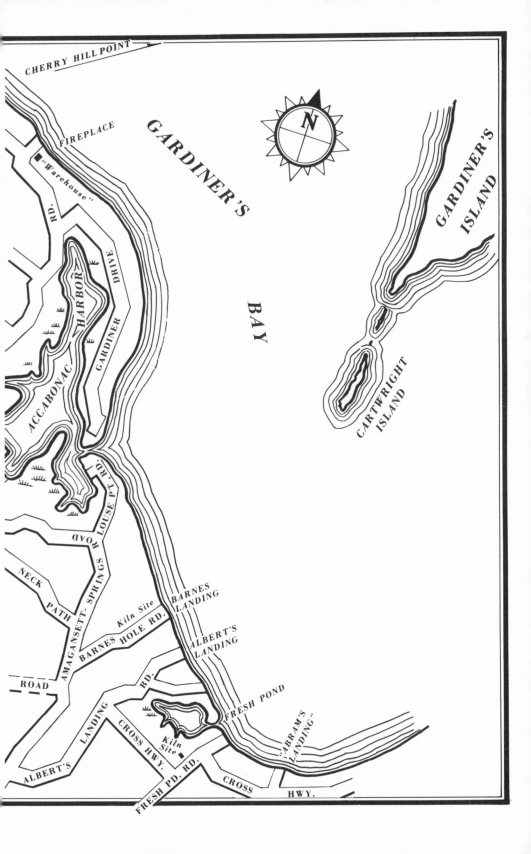

The Springs Tour

The first-time visitor to the Springs, like the first-time visitor to Wainscott, does not immediately know when he is "there." Amagansett, Montauk, Sag Harbor—all have their commercial centers; the closest thing the Springs has to a visible heart is Ashawagh Hall at the corner of Fireplace Road and Old Stone Highway. Once the village school, Ashawagh Hall is now a community center and the site of an annual fair and artists' exhibition. But to think of the Springs as merely an outlying suburb of East Hampton is to be mistaken, for the Springs is perhaps richer in local folklore and local sentiment than any other part of the town. In addition, it has in the last twenty years acquired considerable cachet as a summer colony of well-known New York artists.

To the east of Ashawagh Hall are the Accabonac marshes. "Accabonac" and "Sagaponack" are differently anglicized versions of the same Indian word meaning "the place where the ground nuts grow." Like the Indians, the first settlers prized ground nuts both as a vegetable for themselves and as feed for their livestock.

"Bonacker," the term often used to describe any East Hampton native, originally meant a person who lived on Accabonac Harbor, particularly the baymen who made their living from the fish and shellfish in the harbor. When it first gained currency "Bonacker" was a derisive epithet akin to "hick," "hayseed," or, more appropriately, "lazy clamdigger." Subsequently it has become a chauvinistic badge, and today there is even a thriving business in "Bonacker" bumper stickers.

The "Springs" refers to the fresh-water springs at the head of Accabonac Creek. From colonial days until recent times salt hay from the Accabonac marsh was an important crop for the people of East Hampton and the Springs. On July 5, 1653, the "great meadows" at Accabonac were parceled out among the founders of East Hampton into allotments of approximately one and a half acres. According to the terms of the 1686 Dongan Patent the East Hampton trustees are still vested with ownership of this and other town wetlands. The settlers cut the *Spartina* grass growing in these luxuriant meadows with scythes every summer and dried it for hay which they used for livestock feed and bedding during the winter. Eventually salt hay acquired a commercial value, and the Springs farmers sold what they didn't need for garden mulch on the estates of the East Hampton summer colony.

For many people in the Springs the waters of Accabonac Harbor and Gardiners Bay provide their entire livelihood. The baymen dig for soft and hard clams, and from 1890 to the

Ashawagh Hall was
once the village
school.

present Accabonac clams by the thousands of bushels have
been shipped to New York and Connecticut or sold to the
Amagansett cod fishermen to bait their trawl lines. According
to one estimate, some twenty to twenty-five families support
themselves by the Accabonac clam flats. Scallop dredging is a
major winter industry; in fact, the first bay scallops ever
shipped to the Fulton Fish Market reputedly came from the
Springs.

In addition the baymen carried eels, butter fish, porgies,
bluefish, and weakfish to the East Hampton train depot to be
shipped to New York. Since these fish had to be packed in ice,
ice cutting in the days before refrigeration was another important Accabonac industry. Men with hand saws cut large
blocks from the frozen harbor in the winter; these were
then packed between layers of salt hay in ice houses dug into
the ground. Today the fish harvested in Accabonac waters
are carried to market by refrigerated trucks.

In the latter part of the nineteenth century when wild
duck was standard fare on the menu at Delmonico's, many
Accabonac men made a living shooting shore birds and waterfowl, principally coots, old squaw, and broadbills. The birds
were first shipped out of Sag Harbor and later went by railroad from East Hampton.

In recent years some portions of the Accabonac wetland
have been filled in and built upon, much to the dismay of
those who realized its value as an incubator of marine and
bird life. Now the Nature Conservancy has acquired various
sections of this marsh, the most notable of which are Kaplan

Meadow and Merrill Lake Sanctuary. These preserves are accessible from Fireplace Road to those who wish to examine the intriguing flora of the marsh floor. Rubber-soled shoes are recommended.

Continuing east on Fireplace Road one passes various houses of the Millers, a family of successful Springs farmers for several generations. Their family chronicle comprises the history of the Springs agriculture.

The soil that the Millers farmed in the Springs is generally poor and acid. For fertilizer and lime they spread bay scallops on the ground before this seafood became a select item on restaurant menus in New York. Early generations of Millers raised pigs and sheep. Their chief crops were wheat, oats, and rye which they used mainly as animal feed. They grew flax which they wove with wool to make linsey-woolsey, the common cloth of colonial people here as elsewhere. They grew hops for making beer, and grapes for wine. Unlike the farmers in East Hampton Village who grew no fruit trees for fear of the sea wind, the Millers had orchards of apples, pears, and quinces.

With the almost simultaneous arrival of the railroad and the summer colony in East Hampton in the 1890s, new kinds of farming and new opportunities to practice mechanical skills

were opened to the Springs residents. Poultry raising became a major element in the local economy. The Millers provided thousands of broilers and thousands of dozens of eggs every summer to feed the well-staffed households of the resort folk. With the departure of the seasonal residents in the fall, instead of carting their eggs in horse-drawn wagons and selling them from door to door, they would take them to the train platform in East Hampton for shipment to New York. Other farmers grew produce, and vegetable wagons from the Springs plied a busy trade in East Hampton.

Accabonac Harbor. Louse Point is to the left, Gerard Point to the right. A New Haven sharpie is on a reach as it enters the channel into Gardiners Bay.

When refrigerated trucks and supermarkets became commonplace the poultry and produce businesses in the Springs perished, and the Millers turned to dairying. Now dairying too has disappeared since milk processors buy bulk shipments of milk and no longer rely on local producers. The land that used to grow feed for the dairy herds has been sold for house lots. Old fields awaiting development have become overgrown with cedars and wild cherry saplings. Asa Miller still raises a few calves, but sells them when they are two years old and ready to produce milk. He and his brother George Sid Miller board horses on the remaining acres of their ancestral farm.

Fireplace Road leads to Fireplace, just east of Hog Creek

141

Point and directly opposite Cherry Point Hill on Gardiners Island. It is so named because of the signal fires which were lit there to communicate with Gardiners Island. (Today communication between the island and the mainland is by radio.) During the long period when Gardiners Island was a thriving manor plantation with large herds of sheep and cattle, a boat was kept at Home Pond ready to "come off" the island for various provisions. When the Springs people had supplies ready a fire was kindled and seaweed piled on top of it to create a cloud of smoke. Wool was a major export item from Gardiners Island, and in June many Springs men would assist in washing and shearing the sheep and parceling the fleece for shipment out of Sag Harbor.

Near the corner of Fireplace Road and Hog Creek is a small family cemetery in which every stone bears the name Parsons. Generations of Parsons living at Fireplace Landing were agents and mechanics for the Gardiners. In fact, the Parsons had such a flourishing trading post that John Lyon Gardiner relocated the signal position from old Fireplace, which was somewhat south, to the Parsons property in order to avail himself more conveniently of their services. In 1791 he bought a few acres from David Miller for a warehouse at the water's edge. That warehouse—now converted into a summer cottage—still stands at the end of Fireplace Road.

An eighteenth-century ledger indicates the scope of the Parsons' activities. They sent the hides of horses, goats, and cattle to a place at the head of Three Mile Harbor called Soak Hides Dreen where they were softened, cleaned, and then returned to their tannery on Hog Creek Road. The leather thus produced was fashioned into boots and shoes which the Parsons turned out in almost factory proportions. Joseph Osborn, himself a tanner, bought hides and tanbark from the Parsons, three wagonloads at a time, and carted them back to his tannery in East Hampton where the Maidstone Arms now stands. Between 1795 and 1801 Nathaniel Dominy, the East Hampton clock and furniture maker, had shoes made at the Parsons' for Phoebe, Clara, Temperance, John, Asa, Nancy, and Nathaniel. He was also charged for cider, meat, tallow, wool, weaving, wheat, timber, pigs, vinegar, and tanning a dog's skin.

The Gardiners were dependent upon the Parsons for overland transportation and many entries in the ledger charge them for horses ridden to East Hampton or Sag Harbor. The rental of a horse to East Hampton was one shilling if ridden single; one shilling, sixpence if ridden double. The single fare to Sag Harbor was two shillings, ninepence. In 1788 John Gardiner

Pussy Pond.

was charged for "riding Seth's mare to town," as well as for a hog and for carting wheat.

Before the Revolution when there was free trade with the West Indies, some coastal trading sloops may have landed directly at Fireplace rather than at Northwest or Sag Harbor. The Parsons sold prodigious quantities of rum and molasses to their neighbors. Cash was scarce, and they were often paid in goods and services. The Indian Samson Cuffee is on record in 1791 as having borrowed money and bought groceries, shoes, tobacco, cheese, and hay; he then paid for these things by coopering, working on the grindstone, ditching, shingling, fencing, mowing, and woodcutting. Isaac Plato, another Indian, paid for his shoes, boots, and rum by hoeing, spinning, and weaving thirty-seven yards of cloth.

The versatility of the Parsons persisted down through the generations. Charlie Parsons, who was known as "the Edison of the Springs," lived in this century and was famous as a blacksmith and mechanic. His smithy near the old Parsons homestead at the end of Fireplace Road is gone now. When it was in operation it turned out, among other things, clam rakes and bailing irons for the Accabonac baymen. In 1904 Charlie Parsons built a five-horsepower automobile wagon for Peter Koppelman, a well-known Springs vegetable man.

In the old days huge quantities of seaweed washed ashore on Accabonac beaches. Springs people used it as insulation in their houses, as bedding for livestock, and as fertilizer for their crops. Like salt hay and wood, it was also sold commercially and at one time was considered ideal by New York manufacturers as fireproof packing.

Some of the many loads of seaweed and firewood carried away from the Springs were shipped by Captain "Sinnie"—Sineus M. Edwards—the owner and operator of the coastal sloop *Florian* between 1837 and 1873. He transported such items as paving stones, shingles, coal, grain, flour, molasses, and fish to towns along the New England coast, the north shore of Long Island, and up the Hudson as far as Albany. The paving stones, incidentally, were rounded, water-washed rocks gathered on the Gardiners Bay beach. Many of these stones were used to pave New York City's streets.

Much of the forest on Hog Creek Neck has become house lots. But in the days when wood was the primary fuel these woods were of critical importance in the economy of the Springs. In wintertime some 200 men would cut thousands of cords of wood which were sent to the brick kilns at Greenport and Amagansett. Some cords were also shipped to New York and New England for household firewood. The Amagansett kilns were located at Barnes, Albert's, and Abraham's (now Devon) landings. Bricks made from gray Gardiners Island clay and the red dirt of Amagansett were used in local chimneys or transported by barge and sold elsewhere.

Returning to Ashawagh Hall and continuing south on Old Stone Highway one crosses a little bridge skirting one end of Pussy's Pond. Ducks are usually found dabbling in this pond which allegedly got its name because the cries of the mistress of the adjacent Parsons house calling for her cat often rang out across its waters.

A few yards beyond this pond is Shipyard Lane, so named because of the boatyard there in the nineteenth century.

Clamming with a bullrake in Accabonac Harbor.

The construction of the large "cottages" of the East Hampton summer colony around the turn of the century promoted various trades, and the Springs men became plumbers, carpenters, and electricians. Independent by nature, the legendary Bonacker prefers self-employment, although this means that in the winter when service jobs are scarce many Springs families are on the welfare rolls. But life is seldom grim, for Accabonac Harbor is an immense source of fish and game, and an unemployed Bonacker carpenter will often dig clams, fish, or bag a wild goose for dinner. This self-sufficiency has led to some proud Springs culinary traditions such as "smooched clams" and "smooched fish." The clam pie is a Springs specialty; in fact, the Springs cooks boast of being able to serve clams twenty different ways.

Bear right on Accabonac Highway where it intersects Old

Stone Highway to visit the Green River Cemetery. Jackson Pollock, whose resting spot is marked by an impressive boulder imbedded with a small bronze plate bearing a facsimile of the artist's signature, was the first artist to be buried here after his tragic death in an automobile accident in 1956. Soon so many fellow artists had purchased plots that one of them was heard to quip, "Everyone's dying to get into Green River Cemetery." The poet Frank O'Hara, the writer A. J. Liebling, and the painters Stuart Davis, Ad Reinhardt, and Wilfrid Zogbaum are among the other artists buried here.

Pollock was the first member of the New York School to take up year-round residence in the Springs. He was soon joined by Willem de Kooning, James Brooks, Charlotte Park, Ibram Lassaw, John Little, and Constantino Nivola. A host of other well-known painters and sculptors have established the Springs as their summer headquarters.

The Springs is, in summary, the wide expanses of Accabonac Creek, the woods of Hog Creek Neck, and the waters of Gardiners Bay with the wide-arcing curve of Gardiners Island on the horizon. It is a community of independent artists working in a variety of mediums and styles, and of other equally independent people with roots as deep as the seventeenth-century origins of East Hampton, people with various trade skills as well as the immemorial skills of working with and living off the land and sea.

The grave of Jackson Pollock in the Springs.

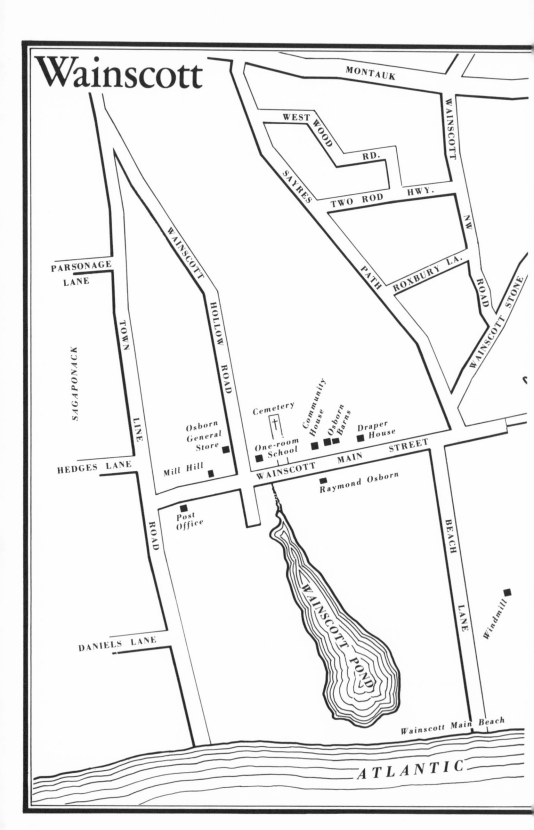

Wainscott

MONTAUK

WEST WOOD RD.

TWO ROD HWY.

WAINSCOTT

SAYRES PATH

NW

ROXBURY LA.

ROAD

WAINSCOTT STONE

PARSONAGE LANE

WAINSCOTT HOLLOW ROAD

TOWN LINE

SAGAPONACK

HEDGES LANE

Cemetery

Community House

Osborn Barns

Draper House

Osborn General Store

One-room School

Mill Hill

WAINSCOTT MAIN STREET

Raymond Osborn

ROAD

Post Office

BEACH LANE

Windmill

DANIELS LANE

WAINSCOTT POND

Wainscott Main Beach

ATLANTIC

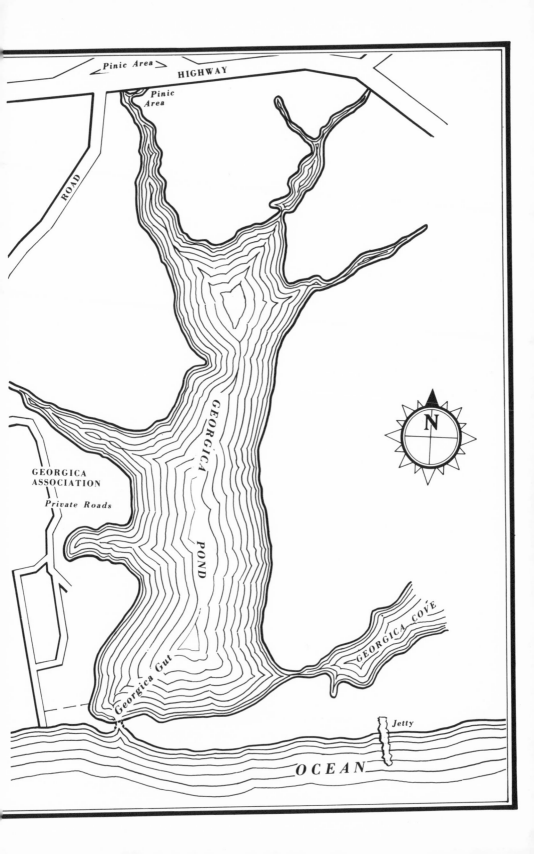

Wainscott Tour

Just as the men of East Hampton christened their settlement Maidstone after their Kentish birthplace, so they named Wainscott after a village a few miles north of Maidstone at the mouth of the Medway River, opposite Whitstable's extensive North Sea oyster beds. Charles Dickens, who died at Gad's Hill, a mile from Wainscott, used its foggy marshes as the scene of the first encounter between Pip and Abel Magwitch in *Great Expectations.*

The new Wainscott was hardly as forlorn and desolate as Dickens's version of the original. Instead of bleak marshes there was the fertile land of the Wainscott Plain. Georgica and Wainscott ponds abounded in fish and eels. There were more fish and whales in the ocean, and a variety of game in the surrounding oak forest. With such abundance, there were probably also periodic encampments of Montauk Indians in the environs. Georgica Pond is believed to be named for an Indian, Jeorgkee, who lived beside it; his name appears in a document of 1679 which states that one Jeorgkee "goes to sea to kill whales for Jacob Schellinger of East Hampton and partners."

Of all the East Hampton villages Wainscott, because of its fertile agricultural lands, has remained the most rural. A community house, a one-room school, and a little gray-shingled post office are the only public buildings in this hamlet of less than 200 houses hidden in the woods around Georgica Pond or dotted along the margins of the flat potato fields whose furrows meet the ocean dunes. The Wainscott school and the one in the contiguous village of Sagaponack are the last surviving one-room schoolhouses on Long Island. The two villages are separated by Town Line Road, the boundary between East Hampton and Southampton.

The post office stands a few yards east of Town Line Road on Wainscott Main Street. Continuing east on Main Street one passes what was once the site of the village windmill on the left. Mill Hill is now covered with cedars and other scrub growth, but it was a favorite sledding slope for Wainscotters in bygone years. Like many of the mills of eastern Long Island, the Wainscott mill has stood in different places during its long life. Built in Southampton in 1813, it was moved to Wainscott in 1852; then in 1922 it was transferred to Montauk where it was used as the sitting room of a summer residence. When Montauk became a defense outpost during World War II and the property upon which it was then located was appropriated by the US military, the members of the Georgica Association, a private group with summer homes on or near the western shore of Georgica Pond, ac-

Osborn's General
Store.

quired the old Wainscott landmark and resurrected it on the
south side of the association's tennis courts.

Wainscott Hollow Road used to be the major north-south
axis of communication for the village. Wainscott fishermen
and farmers drove their wagons over it to the railroad station
on the other side of the Montauk Highway until the station
was closed down in 1921.

Just north of the intersection of Wainscott Hollow Road
and Main Street is the relic of the Osborn General Store, its
Coca-Cola sign almost rusted into oblivion. Tradition recalls
a cracker barrel and Chauncey Osborn's anecdotes relieving the
tedium of the farmers' long winters. Crutchley's General Store
in what is now the Draper house on Main Street was the
original village emporium.

Running through Wainscott Hollow is a small feeder
stream of Wainscott Pond. This stream was dammed with
sand when Wainscott Main Street was built. Main Street was
originally called Sandy Bridge Road, and the remnant of the
dammed stream formed Sandy Bridge Pond. Today reduced to
a tiny trickle, it was ample enough for ice skating and a game
called bendigo until the early years of this century.

Today twenty or so pupils attend the school, the fourth
one-room schoolhouse to occupy approximately the same site.
In the early days of the village the school was the nucleus of
all community life. It was a church; men and boys sat in rows
on the west side, women and girls on the east.

Behind the schoolhouse is the cemetery. The markers of
the first settlers, if they were buried in Wainscott, have never

been unearthed; the earliest headstone is dated 1709. While not as venerable as some other local cemeteries, still the Wainscott cemetery impresses the visitor with the continuity of life in one community. Osborns, Hedges, Hands, Conklins, Hoppings, Strongs—names one sees on signs in front of nearby houses—are grouped in family congregations with markers ranging from red sandstone with letters all but erased by erosion to recently chiseled gray granite.

The white Community House beyond the cemetery started its life as the Bridgehampton school on Ocean Avenue and was moved to Wainscott around 1910 with funds raised by the Village Improvement Society. For many years its bell called the village farmers and their families to evening hymn singing services, and visiting ministers regularly came to preach. Now the Community House is used as a voting precinct and for covered dish suppers sponsored by the Wainscott Sewing Society.

The fields surrounding the Community House and those on the opposite side of Main Street belong to the Osborn family. While ownership of the fields has passed in and out of the family at various times, Osborns have been farming Wainscott land for ten generations. The first mention of Wainscott in the East Hampton town records occurs in 1652 when it was ordered "that a cart way shall be laid out to Wainscott where it may be most convenient." The following year Goodman Osborn was ordered to drive the cows without calves to Wainscott every morning. The "Goodman Osborn" of this entry in the records must have been Thomas Osborn or perhaps one of his sons. Thomas Osborn, like his fellow townsmen, was originally from Maidstone, England; unlike them, he immigrated not by way of Lynn, Massachusetts, but rather from New Haven. He was a tanner, a trade his Wainscott descendants would follow as witnessed by the discovery of an old tanning vat when the basement of Raymond Osborn's house was dug in 1904. In 1668 John Osborn, the son of Thomas Osborn, exchanged his allotment of lands in East Hampton for lands in Wainscott owned by the minister Thomas James. The Hoppings and Hands were also pioneer families who, along with the Osborns, took up residence in Wainscott at this time.

Looking south through one of the Osborn fields, you can see Wainscott Pond. Judge Henry P. Hedges, the chronicler of East Hampton's history, was born in Wainscott, and in his *Memories of A Long Life* he reminisced: "Before I was eight years old I knew Wainscott Pond from shore to shore, from shoal to deep. There I gathered the fragrant and beautiful

Originally the Bridgehampton school, Wainscott's Community House was moved from Ocean Road to its present location around 1910.

lilies. There caught minnows on a pin hook. There paddled the old canoe." According to the Division of Fish and Game of the New York State Conservation Department, "on an acre for acre basis, this pond might well have the highest winter waterfowl use of any area on Long Island." The Fish and Game Division has also concluded that "if ruddy ducks can be found any-where in New York State it will be at Wainscott," and indeed they have been observed there in substantial numbers together with American widgeon and a multitude of Canada geese.

For several generations Wainscott remained a self-con-tained hamlet of fifteen families. All the men were farmers. Their main commodity was cattle, and they also raised horses which they shipped to the West Indies. They grew wheat, barley, rye, corn, oats, flax, and grass for hay. For fertilizer they followed the Indian method and used the menhaden their seine nets scooped out of the sea; however, by later standards, their crop yields were meager. Isolated from town and trade, they also became craftsmen: James Hand was a weaver, Bethuel Edwards was a shoemaker, James Edwards, his brother, a carpenter, and Jacob Hopping a cooper.

Captain Jonathan Osborn is thought to be the first native of the town of East Hampton to go on a distant voyage on a whaling ship. His log book of 1797 is in the East Hampton Free Library. Of course, in the days before men shipped out of Sag Harbor on long cruises that sometimes lasted several years, boats manned by Indians and commanded by whites went on two-week expeditions looking for whales along the coast. Beached whales were rendered for blubber as long as

151

they were extant in Long Island waters; as late as 1907 there was a tryworks on the Wainscott beach.

Raymond Osborn remembers his father, Oliver Osborn, rowing out in an old dory to capture his last whale in 1907. Whereas in earlier times a whale watch had been set up in a wigwam shelter on the beach, in the days after the Long Island Railroad made the Fulton Fish Market accessible, Wainscott fishermen were constantly patrolling the shore as they set out or hauled in their seine nets. Whenever they sighted a whale they raised a "weft"—a rag tied to a pole—which sent the men working in the nearby fields rushing to help them (or watch them) row out and harpoon the great beast.

Fishing was for a period a major Wainscott industry, and haul seiners can often still be seen on the dawn beach, although the fish houses that once occupied the dune ridge have been replaced by vacation houses. (One old fish house now stands in the Osborn barnyard and is used as a machine shop.)

Today the potato fields of the Osborns and their neighbors the Strongs, Hands, and Toppings are the dominant feature of the Wainscott landscape. Besides their potatoes the Osborns have a small sideline business in strawberries. For about ten days in late June and early July their strawberry fields are open to the public. The ripe berries dangle under their little canopies of three leaves invisible to the casual passer-by. Their pleasant fragrance, however, is noticeable as one bikes on Main Street or Beach Lane. In the fields berry pickers are bent double or creep about on their knees selecting the reddest fruit. Smiling, perspiring, their fingers stained fuchsia, they emerge from the field and present their boxes to Raymond Osborn or his twin brother Leroy to be tallied.

Beach Lane makes a T-intersection with Main Street. It was built in the 1890s to give the Wainscotters another access to the ocean after their old road to the beach—Georgica Road—was appropriated and partially obliterated by the founders of the Georgica Association. The coming of the Association to Wainscott meant other road changes as well. Once Main Street extended all the way to Georgica Pond, and from there a causeway carried travelers across the pond to East Hampton. Now Main Street ends at the gate to the Association, and public access is forbidden beyond that point.

Much larger than Wainscott Pond, Georgica Pond is a catchment basin for five creeks. Originally it emptied into the sea; however, the old tidal gut where the Association bath house and parking lot now stand was blocked with sand during

One of the last two one-room school-houses on Long Island.

the hurricane of 1938, and the once-deep southwestern corner of the pond where the Association had its boat dock became covered with dunes. Today town officials periodically open a gut to let the pond's brackish water flush out to sea; then fishermen come to catch the blues and other fish that swim into the artificial channel. In season blue crabs are also caught in the pond. It is a haven for shore birds and swans. Members of the Georgica Association use it for canoeing and sailing.

East Hampton residents with beach parking permits can reach Georgica Pond by walking east from Wainscott Main Beach at the end of Beach Lane. This walk presents a graphic demonstration of the dynamics of beach erosion (see page 89). One large, white-brick, ocean-front house once preserved its privacy from the public beach with a fifty-foot-wide screen of pitch pines. But this barrier was torn away by successive winter storms until finally in 1974 the house itself was de-molished in a storm. A late Victorian house built by one of the early Georgica Association members is similarly threatened. Beyond the pond to the east one notices a jetty, one of three jetties between Wainscott and East Hampton Village. These jetties are the villains in Wainscott's losing battle with the sea, for they are impounding the sands being borne westward from Montauk by the littoral current and thus preventing them from naturally accreting on the Wainscott shore.

From the beach the placid view of swan-dotted Georgica Pond with a few huge old summer homes nestled on its wooded shores has a Gatsby-like quality of romance. This quiet pond and the flat, white-flowered potato fields from which as yet only a few lots have been subtracted by development give Wainscott its atmosphere of seclusion from the rest of East Hampton.

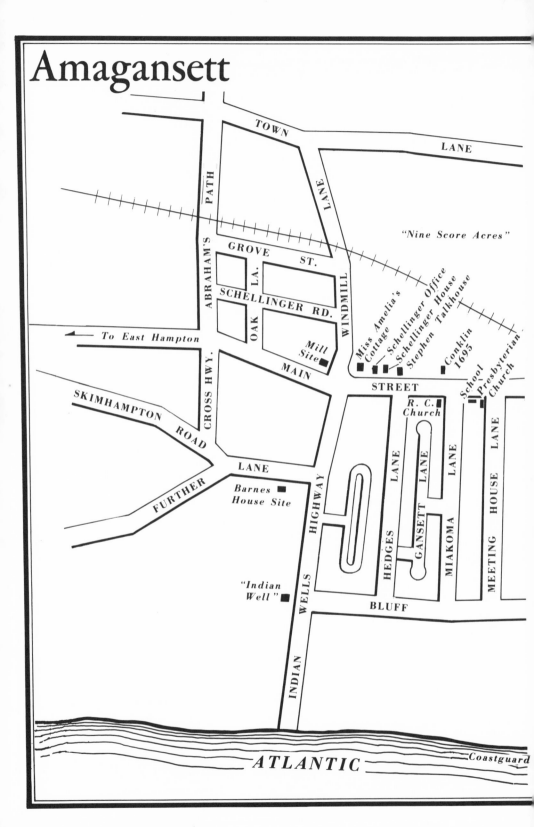

Amagansett

TOWN LANE

ABRAHAM'S PATH

"Nine Score Acres"

GROVE ST.

OAK LA.

WINDMILL LANE

SCHELLINGER RD.

To East Hampton

Mill Site

MAIN STREET

Miss Amelia's Cottage

Schellinger Office

Schellinger House

Stephen Talkhouse

Conklin 1695

School

Presbyterian Church

CROSS HWY.

SKIMHAMPTON ROAD

LANE

FURTHER

Barnes House Site

R. C. Church

HEDGES LANE

GANSETT LANE

MIAKOMA LANE

MEETING HOUSE LANE

HIGHWAY

"Indian Well"

INDIAN WELLS

BLUFF

ATLANTIC

Coastguard

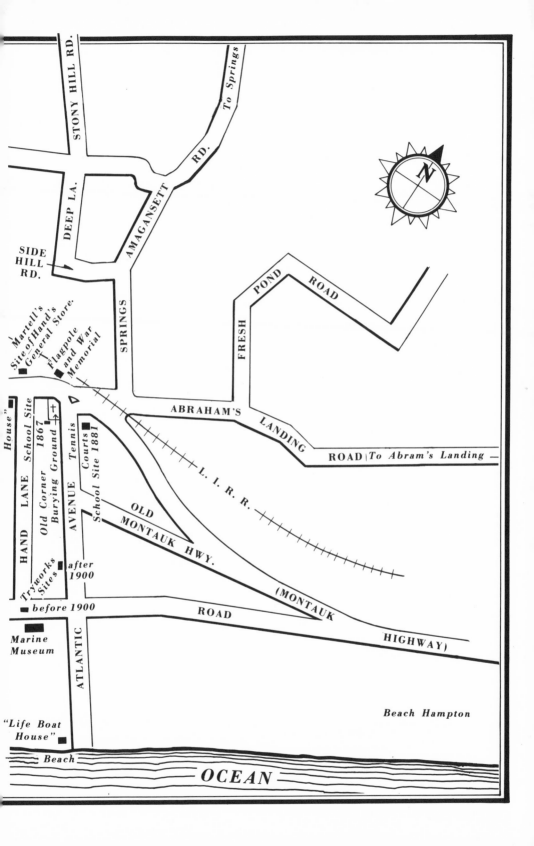

Amagansett Tour

The crowds overflowing Amagansett's restaurants and bars on a summer Saturday night are carrying on an old tradition. Centuries ago Indians traveling between Montauk and East Hampton would pause at Amagansett to drink from the wells for which it was then known. The Indian name Amagansett, in fact, means "place of good water," and in the early town records the Algonquian and English terms were used interchangeably.

Historical Amagansett is divided into two parts: a parcel of once open land near the ocean, which was used as a town commons for pasturing cattle by the founders of East Hampton; and a woods that has long since been converted to farm land and house lots. The open section, which contained the Indian wells, is bounded by Main Street (Montauk Highway), the ocean, Indian Wells Highway, and Atlantic Avenue. The Amagansett woods, or "Nine Score Acres," refers to 180 acres north of Main Street.

The visitor should begin his tour of the town by following Indian Wells Highway almost to the ocean. Opposite Bluff Road, part of the old Indian trail to Montauk, there is a boulder bearing a bronze plaque commemorating the wellspring of the Montauks. The legendary well near the site of the present marker was said to be a fresh spring flowing out of the hollow of an old pepperidge tree stump.

Returning to the village center, one faces Miss Amelia's cottage on the corner of Windmill Lane and Main Street. Built in 1725, it is now a historical museum, notable for its period furniture, especially the clock and other pieces made by the famous Dominy craftsmen of East Hampton (see page 24).

Miss Amelia's cottage stands on the property settled by the Schellinger brothers, Abraham and Jacob, in 1690. They were sons of Jacobus Schellinger (1625-1693), a New Amsterdam merchant who immigrated to East Hampton after the English took over the Dutch colony in 1664 and renamed it New York. Working with his stepson James Loper, Jacobus became a successful coastal whaler (see page 50). His own sons were also active in the family whaling enterprise, but, like other second and third generation sons, they needed land of their own to farm, and so they left East Hampton to found Amagansett. With them came their sister Catherine and her husband Nathaniel Baker. Today Schellingers still live in Amagansett, and the present generation is in the well-drilling business, redeveloping the function for which the town was named. Their office stands a few yards east of Miss Amelia's cottage next door to a handsome old shingled house which remains in the family.

A boulder on Indian Wells Road marks the site of an old Indian well. Amagansett means "the place of good water."

Miss Amelia's
cottage.

The land settled by the Schellingers is on the north side of Main Street within the Nine Score Acres. Abraham Schellinger purchased this land from the East Hampton minister Thomas James, who, besides being the town's spiritual leader, was also an enterprising capitalist (see page 130). In 1670 James and two fellow townsmen, Jeremiah Conklin and John Mulford, bought from the Indians a large tract of land on Montauk and traded it to the proprietors of Montauk—e.g., the East Hampton shareholders of the Montauk commonage—for 180, or nine score, acres "either at Accabonac Neck if they like it upon their view thereof or at the woodland lying against the Indian well in good land." The three associates chose the Amagansett woods. (Lion Gardiner was recently dead or he surely would have been a party to this transaction.)

The westernmost sixty-four of the Nine Score Acres were assigned to Thomas James who promptly sold them to Schellinger. A road had previously been laid out along present Town Lane, and Abraham Schellinger started to erect a house there; however, he found it difficult to obtain well water in that location, and a new road—Main Street—was built. It was here that he, his brother Jacob, and their brother-in-law Nathaniel Baker established homesteads along with Jeremiah Conklin and his wife Mary, the eldest daughter of Lion Gardiner. Isaac Barnes, another founder, built his house on Further Lane which, like Bluff Road, is part of the old Indian trail from Montauk to East Hampton.

Windmill Lane takes its name from the windmill that once stood on the rise a few hundred feet north of the Main

Street intersection. This mill was built in Setauket and was bought by a syndicate of Amagansett men, moved by boat to Abraham's Landing, and first erected slightly east of the present flagpole and war memorial before being moved once again to Windmill Lane at the western edge of the village. It was in operation until 1895 and remained a landmark until 1924 when it burned.

Continuing east on Main Street, one notices on the right first a Roman Catholic Church and, beyond the school, the squat double-towered church built by the Presbyterians, for many years the only denomination in the village. This church was built in 1860; earlier generations of Amagansett families journeyed every Sunday to East Hampton for worship.

In front of the present school in the roadbed of Amagansett's wide Main Street is the site of the first schoolhouse, built in 1808, a small wooden building with white-pine floorboards and hand-hewn rafters. Boys coming to school in the morning brought live coals from neighboring houses to light the stove in the center of the one room. In 1867 the schoolhouse was moved to the southeast corner of the Old Corner Burying Ground on Atlantic Avenue. As time passed there were approximately sixty scholars crammed into this building, and in 1883 funds were raised to build a new larger school across the street where the tennis courts now stand. That school still stands, although it was superseded by the present large brick Georgian-style school in 1936.

Returning a few yards west on the north side of Main Street, one notices directly opposite the Catholic church a house with the date 1695 inscribed over the door. This was the home of the village founder Jeremiah Conklin. Unlike the Schellinger brothers who settled in Amagansett as young men in their twenties, Conklin was in his fifties. He and Mary Gardiner had been married some thirty-odd years, and they had been living since their marriage in either the present Winthrop Gardiner house on James Lane, East Hampton (see page 131), which was built for them by Lion Gardiner, or in one very similar to it, which once stood next door. The Amagansett house which the couple built for themselves was, like the early houses of East Hampton, in the salt-box style, but has since been altered and raised off the ground by a new foundation.

Continuing east once again on Main Street one comes to the parking lot of Martell's, the currently popular restaurant, and the old site of Hand's General Store. Amagansett was, after Sag Harbor, a major home base for Long Island whaling captains, and many ships were provisioned from Nathaniel

The tower and weather vane of Amagansett's Presbyterian Church.

The Conklin house, built in 1695 by the founder of Amagansett Village. This is how the house appeared in 1900.

Hand's store in the 1840s when whaling was at its zenith. An old ledger lists 114 pounds of butter for the ship *Washington,* 229 hams taken aboard the *Noble,* and the provisioning of other ships such as the *Fanny* and the *Hamilton.* Besides conventional groceries Hand's varied emporium was stocked with snuff, chewing tobacco, laudanum, tallow, wagon springs, indigo, ochre, gunpowder, gunshot and caps, leather, vitriol, silk, calico, buttons, harness, lamps, hogsheads, wick yarn, suspenders, and pearlash and bunkers for fertilizer (these last sold ten for a penny).

Thirteen Amagansett men fought in the Revolution. Among them was 2d Lt. Nathaniel Hand, the father of the storekeeper, whose home on the corner of Main Street and Hand Lane was a public house during the war years. Here cadets who were part of the regiment raised for the protection of the livestock from British marauders on Montauk could be convivial; here also relays of horses were kept for messengers. Nathaniel Hand, incidentally, kept five slaves, a large number for a single owner in this area.

In the War of 1812 young Charles Hand distinguished himself by a Paul Revere-type ride to Sag Harbor, alerting the people along the way to British gunboats stealing up Gardiners Bay. A defense was mustered in the fort at Sag Harbor, and one boat and a large store of arms were captured.

The flagpole and war memorial stand just east of the boundary of the original Nine Score Acres. Running south from this point is Atlantic Avenue, the road to the ocean, and running east to Gardiners Bay is Abraham's Landing Road.

Both bay and ocean have been important in the life of the village from its earliest days. Abraham Schellinger was master of the sloop *Endeavor,* carrying cattle, horses, sheep, and whale oil to Boston and returning with lumber and products of the West Indies. Abraham's Landing (now Devon Landing) and Abraham's Path were named after him.

Among the legendary "salts" of Amagansett no one figures more prominently than "Cap'n Josh" Edwards, a deep sea whaleman of the last century. After he ceased going on long whaling voyages he became a menhaden fishing captain with his brother "Cap'n Gabe" Edwards, working fishing steamers out of Gardiners Bay.

Menhaden, or bunker, fishing was until recently an important occupation for Amagansett men. In the town's earliest days, as soon as the value of menhaden for fertilizer was realized, farmers began to "rally" for bunkers. A dune watch was kept around corn planting time; when a school of menhaden was spotted the weft went up, and everyone hurried to the beach to haul in the seine nets. Later huge purse seines dropped from boats in Gardiners Bay replaced shore seines. A mid-nineteenth-century customs house report shows 232 sailing boats and twenty-four steam vessels in the East Hampton menhaden industry. The menhaden are now less plentiful in Long Island waters in contrast to the days of the two "Cap'n" Edwards when ten to twelve million fish were netted during the five-month season; however they are still being taken, although modern processing plants are no longer located at Napeague but in New Jersey.

The great right whales that once roamed the East Hampton coastline have all but disappeared (very occasionally, as in the summer of 1974, a whale's appearance will be celebrated in the local papers). "Cap'n Josh" and "Cap'n Gabe" both participated in the capture of the last whale taken off Amagansett on February 22, 1907, the same day that Oliver Osborn harpooned another "last" whale in Wainscott. The Amagansett whale, a cow fifty-seven feet long, yielded 2,000 gallons of oil and netted $3,500. Dr. Roy Chapman Andrews of the American Museum of Natural History came to Amagansett to collect the whale's skeleton for preservation in the museum's Hall of Ocean Life.

Amagansett has its own marine museum. Situated on Bluff Road, it is a showcase of the various local fishing techniques past and present. Among the many artifacts it contains are "Cap'n Josh" Edwards's whaleboat, the wefts of coastal whaling days, harpoons used in the great bygone whale chases, and an ingenious contraption for skinning eels.

Cottages along
Bluff Road, once
the old Indian
trail to Montauk.

At the foot of Atlantic Avenue is Coast Guard Beach, on summer weekends a popular meeting place for singles. Before present-day helicopter Coast Guard patrols made the old Coast Guard Station, or Life Boat House as it was called, obsolete, Amagansett farmer-fishermen were active in manning it first as volunteers, later as paid trained officials. These experienced surfmen were kept busy since the stretch of coast between Amagansett and Montauk Point has some treacherous shoals which have been the cause of several shipwrecks. In 1851 the *Catherine* of Liverpool, bound from Dublin for New York, went aground with 300 passengers, all of whom were fortunately saved. An early spring snowstorm forced the schooner *Idabella* to founder in 1876. The mast from the *Bessie C. Beach* which was lost in 1912 was the flagpole on the Amagansett village green until it was replaced by a steel pole in 1950.

Salvage from wrecked vessels has played no small part in East Hampton's economy and natural history. Trees and shrubs, ostrich eggs, maltese cats, fence timbers, and Spanish gold pieces are among the items that have been washed ashore. Between 1787 and 1890 a wreck master, or vendue master, an official appointed by New York State for each shore-front locality, saw that these windfall goods were disposed of fairly at auction.

The Amagansett Coast Guard Station was discontinued in 1937 and only revived briefly during World War II. Stranger than a shipwreck was the appearance on June 13, 1942, of four men on the foggy midnight beach. A coastguardman hailed them, and they hesitated but then replied in fluent English that they were fishermen from Southampton who had run aground. When he invited them to come back with him to the Coast Guard Station and wait until daybreak to return to their boat,

161

they offered him a $300 bribe. He took the money to the little station house and sounded the alarm as the four men disappeared into the fog and the diesel engines of a submarine were heard rumbling offshore.

Coastguardmen from Napeague and an army detail from Montauk rushed to the scene and found an amazing array of clues to the identities of the blundering intruders. A dune search revealed stubs of a German brand of cigarettes, two German dungaree outfits, a reversible civilian overcoat, overshoes, and an overseas cap with a swastika. In addition, the searchers discovered buried in the sand four wood-covered waterproof tin cases containing small incendiary bombs disguised as fountain pens and pencils, various fuses, timing devices, and electric cable. The Nazi saboteurs were tracked down in an intensive fifteen-day manhunt, tried and, after a rejected appeal to the Supreme Court, executed. It turned out that they had made their getaway by purchasing four tickets from the Amagansett stationmaster for the 7:10 train to New York.

Because of its proximity to nearby Montauk, which has figured as a defense outpost in every American war since the Revolution, the military presence has always been strong in Amagansett. Relatives and friends of soldiers stationed at Montauk during World War I and II boarded with Amagansett families, and the village streets were thronged with soldiers and sailors. The families of army and navy officers who came to Amagansett in 1898 during the Spanish American War continued to return as summer boarders. Teddy Roosevelt and members of his staff were entertained at Mel Terry's newly opened Sea View Hotel. Early visitors arrived by Jeremiah Baker's stage from Sag Harbor; the visitors lodged up and down Main Street, and as many as thirty of them took their meals at Mrs. Phoebe Hand's. A journalist's description of this period extols Amagansett as "a reproduction of the Acadian village of Evangeline and Gabriel."

Soon large gray-shingled "cottages" lined Bluff Road, the old Indian trail to Montauk. The tryworks also stood on Bluff Road, but the objection of the new summer residents to the smell of boiling blubber soon necessitated its transfer around the corner to Atlantic Avenue. In the mid-1930s the bungalow development known as Beach Hampton began to grow in the dunes below Bluff Road. Today other subdivisions of vacation houses are sprinkled among the dunes, and the old Main Street has become lined with shops and restaurants catering to the resort clientele that packs it throughout the summer and on fall and spring weekends.

To reach the salt marsh and the "walking" dunes at the east end of Napeague beach, turn off the Montauk Highway on to Napeague Harbor Road. Continue to the end of the road where you may park your car or bicycle, but make sure you do not block access for four-wheel-drive vehicles that sometimes use this stretch of beach. You are now in Hither Hills State Park on the eastern rim of Napeague Harbor on Gardiners Bay. Across the harbor is Lazy Point, and to the west beyond Lazy Point is the area known as Promised Land.

Both the east and west shores bordering Napeague Harbor from the middle of the nineteenth century until the 1930s were studded with small factories where open brick furnaces processed the smelly menhaden fish into oil and fertilizer. The Smith Meal Company at Promised Land was the largest and most long-lived of these enterprises. It is now out of business, and part of its once extensive holdings is being acquired by the state for a public park.

To explore the salt marsh on the eastern side of Napeague Harbor climb a large dune ridge and then head north. This particular wetland is relatively unimpaired by man's activities and is therefore an especially good place to study marsh ecology. *Spartina patens*, the grass which is mown for salt hay, blankets the spongy ground with a rich green. On the outer edges of the marsh and in the hummocks which protrude above the tide-washed *S. patens* are beach grass, bearberry, hudsonia, and seaside goldenrod. In the depressed, salt-saturated areas known as pannes, there is glasswort, its fleshy, segmented stems turning a beautiful clear red in autumn. Where tidal brooks invade the marsh *S. alterniflora*, a coarser, taller grass than *S. patens*, grows. To watch the traffic in one of these estuarine streams is to be impressed with the fecundity of the marsh as an incubator of marine life. Miniature eels no bigger than one's little finger slither past and hundreds of newly hatched fish ply their way seaward. The marsh is a place for wild flowers, too; there are clumps of mallow roses and marsh pinks in late summer as well as an occasional touch of sea lavender.

As you walk through this salt meadow you may stumble upon a granite marker. It denotes the western boundary of the Proprietors' land at Montauk. When cattle were pastured on Montauk a fence ran from this marker into Napeague Bay. It was called Water Fence and was installed to prevent livestock from wandering west.

As you reach the rocky shore of Napeague Bay you will see that the sands carried westward by the prevailing current have formed a spit, a protective arm embracing Napeague Harbor. The end of this spit is Goff Point, allegedly named

A Nature Walk at Napeague: The Salt Marsh, Fresh Pond, and the "Walking" Dunes

after William Goff. In the summer of 1660, shortly after the English Restoration, Goff, a Regicide Judge who had condemned Charles I to be beheaded and who was himself forced to flee for his life, is supposed to have landed here. According to oral tradition, the people of East Hampton would not give Goff refuge, nor would they turn him over to the authorities in Connecticut. Eventually he found safety in Massachusetts.

Today oyster catchers with their crisp black-and-white markings and large coral-colored bills often congregate at Goff Point. If you are a scuba or skindiver, the shallows off Goff Point offer an excellent variety of marine life to inspect. You may return to your starting point by walking south along the quiet waters of the harbor, noticing the varieties of sea-

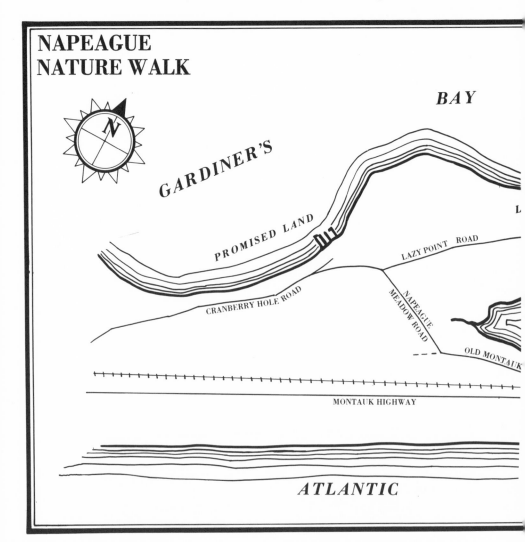

NAPEAGUE
NATURE WALK

BAY

GARDINER'S

PROMISED LAND

LAZY POINT ROAD

CRANBERRY HOLE ROAD

NAPEAGUE MEADOW ROAD

OLD MONTAUK

MONTAUK HIGHWAY

ATLANTIC

weed that have been washed ashore.

Or you may head east and walk for about two miles along Napeague Bay. The shore here is rimmed by a string of gentle dunes. Beach plums (*Prunus maritimus*) grow in their lee. When you reach the end of a rough road leading south, just before you come to the first of a long line of bluffs stretching eastward, turn right. After a quarter of a mile another primitive road runs off to the right. It leads to Fresh Pond, a beautiful pool full of largemouth bass. Here, completely secluded from the man-made world, one experiences a primeval stillness. In this remote and virgin spot one gains an impression of the wealth of wildlife that existed on eastern Long Island before its invasion by European man. Hawks can sometimes be seen

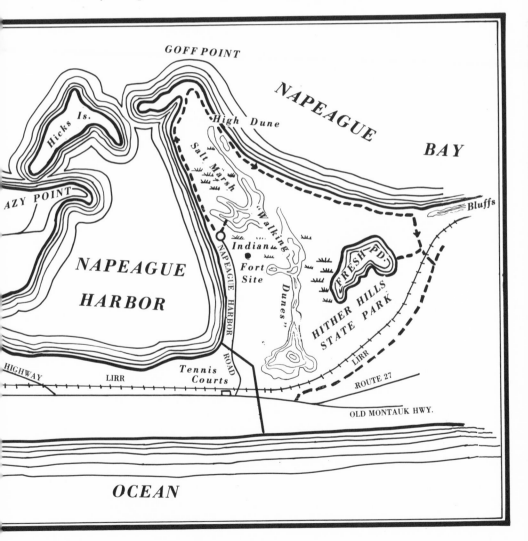

soaring overhead. A pair of bald eagles, a now endangered species, reportedly nested in the marsh near Fresh Pond in recent years. In winter, lovers of solitude will enjoy skating on this remote, lovely pond.

After visiting Fresh Pond, go back out to the road leading south from the beach, make another right, and cross the railroad tracks to turn right once more. Follow this road, paralleling the tracks, southwest until you reach Route 27 only a few hundred yards east of Napeague Harbor Road which will lead you back to your starting point. Or, if you are not too tired, climb the big dune just across the tracks when Route 27 is in sight and follow the tops of the "walking" dunes back to your car or bike.

The high wooded ground just north of the railroad tracks is the area the Indians referred to as Nominicks, meaning "the land to be seen from afar." In the old days travelers to Montauk were always glad when they had traversed the tedious heavy sands of Napeague and beheld Nominicks.

Cheerless Napeague! now bounds the heart to gain the hills that spring beyond thy weary plain.

Legends of Montauk (1849)

The "walking" dunes are so called because the heavily accreted sands which they represent are constantly migrating, burying even tall trees in their wake. They comprise a fantastical landscape (see page 83), and if you do not have time to explore them on this already lengthy tour, you should plan a subsequent visit. It is known that the Indians had a fort somewhere in or near the "walking" dunes. Some sources ascribe its location to Nominicks in the belief that it was a lookout or vantage point from which to spy enemies approaching. More probably it was in one of the boggy basins of the "walking" dunes, where the tangled undergrowth afforded a good hiding place until danger was past.

If you visit only the Napeague salt marsh and Goff Point, count on spending one and a half to two hours. If you make the long circuit around Napeague Bay and come through the "walking" dunes, take a lunch and plan on spending the better part of the day. If you eliminate the tour of the marsh and the circuit around Fresh Pond and head directly east into the "walking" dunes, you can spend an hour or more exploring as far as you wish and then turn back.

The "walking" dunes
at Napeague.

Montauk

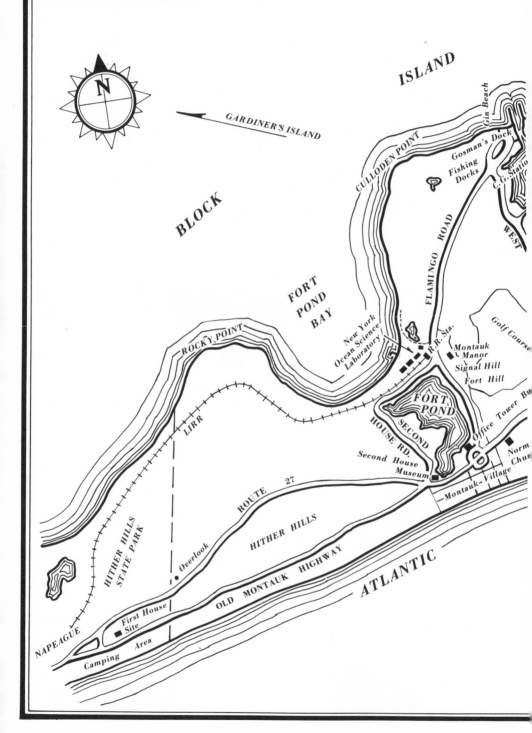

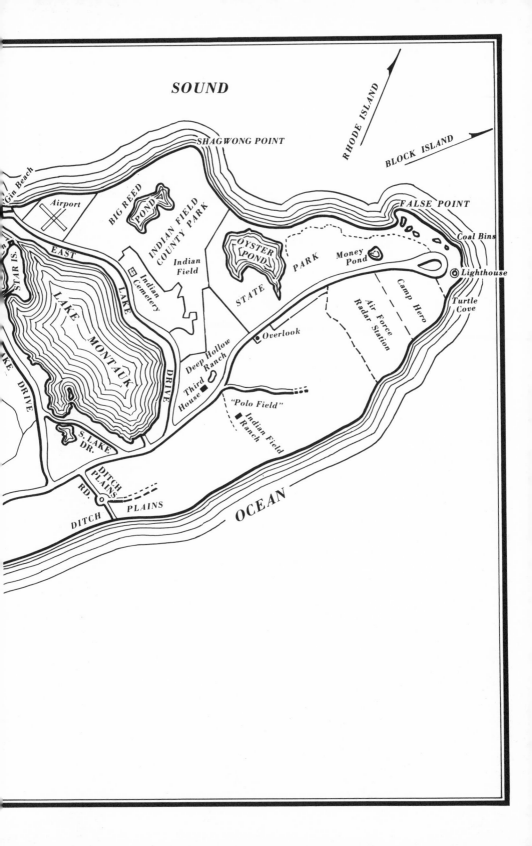

Montauk Tour

The lighthouse of Montauk.

Local people of long standing call it M'n-*tauk,* perhaps an echo of the time when everyone called it Montaukett; and they don't go to and from it but on and off it, as if it were still the island that it had been at the end of the last glacial age, some 15,000 years ago (see page 78). A much older geological formation than the rest of Long Island, Montauk is a crumpled mass of hills and boulder-strewn valleys, ten miles long by two miles wide, ringed by some thirty miles of beaches along its ocean and bays.

For years Montauk served as summer pasture for herds of sheep and cattle from as far west as Patchogue. "Its elevation in the midst of the ocean, its wonderful supply of fresh water from the springs, swamps and vast ponds, its luxuriant pastures, the refreshing sea breezes and the entire absence of flies and moschetoes which abound in the adjacent marshes, render it," according to the historian Nathaniel Prime, who wrote some 150 years ago, "one of the most delightful retreats for domestic animals where in the course of a few weeks they become fat and healthy." It was for this reason that the first settlers lost no time in acquiring Montauk from the Indians. By 1686 they had bought its 10,000 acres for £100, but with the understanding that the Montauks were free "to sitte downe again uppon ye land," a reasonable provision since the Indians had been "sitting" on the hills between Fort Pond and Oyster Pond for centuries and had no other place to go.

As you approach Hither Hills, the western boundary of Montauk, once known as Nominicks, you can see how the former island rises from the low-lying Napeague beaches. Napeague, which means "water land," was formed, like the ocean beaches farther west, from the erosion at Montauk Point, which has worn back some four miles since the end of the last glacial age.

Perhaps the best way to get a sense of Montauk is to proceed directly to the Point, along the hilly Old Montauk

Highway that branches away to the right of Route 27 at the entrance to Hither Hills State Park. From this road you can see through the clearings between the ocean-front hotels the steeply eroded beaches that plunge down to the sea. As you descend to the village itself you will see to your left, at the foot of Fort Pond, the Second House Museum. It is the oldest building in Montauk, built in 1746 and enlarged in 1797. It served as the residence of one of the three keepers of the cattle and sheep that once summered on Montauk. The museum and the agreeable herb garden behind it are well worth a visit on your return from your trip to the Point. The incongruous office tower at the traffic circle is a relic of Carl Fisher's ill-fated attempt in the late 1920s to develop Montauk as "the Miami Beach of the North." Another such relic is the Norman church to the right of the highway just beyond the village.

Proceed along Montauk Point State Boulevard. About a mile before you reach the Point there is an overlook from which you can see the lighthouse, the United States Air Force radar station, and, on the other side of the highway, Oyster Pond, which lies in the state park just southeast of Indian Field County Park. Beyond Oyster Pond is False Point, and in the distance is the shoreline of Connecticut and Rhode Island. It was along these shores that the Pequots and the Narragansetts, the traditional enemies of the Montauks, lived.

From the parking lot at the Point you may walk up the path to the lighthouse, except on foggy days when the Coast Guard closes the gates to protect the visitors' ears from the vibrating fog horn. The lighthouse stands on the remains of Turtle Hill, some sixty-eight feet above sea level. In 1790 President Washington signed a congressional order to build a lighthouse at the Point, and in 1792 the site was acquired from the town of East Hampton with the understanding that the government would erect no buildings other than those required by the keeper of the light so that poachers, posing as fishermen, might not move onto the Point and help themselves to the valuable animals pastured there.

The tower was built in 1795 of red sandstone imported from Connecticut. It was put in operation in 1796. The tower itself is 100 feet high. Originally it stood 297 feet from the shore. By 1938 the ocean had eaten to within 140 feet of its base. Today, with more than half of Turtle Cove worn away, the lighthouse stands nearly at the edge of a cliff. When Washington first saw the site he predicted that the lighthouse would stand for 200 years. Give or take a few years, he will probably have been correct.

From midsummer till late fall the sea between Coal Bins, just north of the lighthouse, and Turtle Bay to the south is dotted with small boats fishing for striped bass and bluefish. At the peak of the bass season during the October full moon the beach beneath the lighthouse is lined with surf casters. Farther out, between Block Island and Point Judith, Rhode Island, there are giant tuna, swordfish, mako shark, and marlin. In the summer of 1974 two Montauk fishermen hoping for a swordfish twenty-five miles south of the Point found themselves hooked to a giant white shark, the most ferocious of all sea animals and a rarity in these waters. The monster weighed nearly 4,000 pounds when it was landed after a fifteen-hour struggle.

Before the First World War the lighthouse keepers welcomed boarders and a part of everyone's tour of the Point was the climb to the top of the tower. Today the Coast Guard forbids visitors to enter the lighthouse.

A walk along the beach beneath the lighthouse will reveal the layers of rock and sediment in the exposed face of Turtle Hill, a formation quite unlike anything else to be found on Long Island. If you have an hour to spend you might walk a mile or so north along the beach beyond False Point where the outer beach forms a thin barrier between Oyster Pond and the ocean. Indian Field behind Oyster Pond was prime grazing land, and though it is now mostly overgrown you will still find a few rotting fence posts that separated the common pasture from the bull pasture and Fatting Fields where beef cattle and cows with new calves were sent after the annual roundup on June 20. The white house on the hilltop was built during World War II as an army observation post disguised as a summer cottage. It has since become a private residence and is one of only two such dwellings within the county park.

Oyster Pond itself, comprising some twenty acres, is uncommonly beautiful, ringed with shadbush and holly, sumac and marshmallow. A flock of swans shares the pond with quantities of Canada geese, mallard, coot, and black ducks; an occasional osprey passes overhead: pheasant, grouse, and deer abound in the surrounding woods, and the baymen seed and harvest oysters as they have done for years.

From the southwest corner of the pond you may follow a path through the woods which will take you back to the Point. The path is lined with blackberry and dwarf goldenrod bushes and passes within a few hundred feet of Money Pond, which is said to be bottomless and the repository of pirate treasure.

Third House at
Montauk as it ap-
peared in the 1890s.

As you leave the Point you will pass the entrance to the
radar station and the border of Camp Hero, an abandoned
army post, now part of the state park system. About a mile
farther on you will pass a group of buildings to the north
of the highway. Until 1974 these buildings had been operated
as a resort hotel but now they belong to the county park. The
original building on this site was erected in 1747 and replaced
in 1804. It was known as Third House, the easternmost of the
three houses occupied by the overseers of Montauk's livestock.
First House, which stood on the site of the present Hither
Hills campground on the Old Montauk Highway, was built
in 1744 and replaced in 1798. It burned in 1909. For years First
House, Second House, and Third House were the only buildings on Montauk except for the lighthouse. The keepers of the
herds were appointed annually by the town trustees and the
arduous service was considered an honor.

When the herds were brought onto Montauk, usually in
mid-April, it was the task of the keeper of First House to
enter the sheep and cattle, together with their earmarks, on
the common pasture list. Pasture rights were divided into thirty
shares among the East Hampton proprietors of the Montauk
commonage, and each of the shares was divided into eighths.
Each eighth entitled its owner to pasture seven cattle or
forty-nine sheep. Later these shares were enlarged to permit
forty-eight cattle in the common pasture and twelve or fourteen in the Fatting Fields. In the early nineteenth century
some 6,000 animals were grazing on Montauk each summer.

The keeper at Second House looked after the sheep, while the keeper at Third House had over-all responsibility for the entire pasture and particular responsibility for the animals that were rounded up on June 20 for the Fatting Fields. The sheep were driven off at midsummer to be sheared, and on a date in November chosen by the trustees according to the weather, the cattle were driven off. The autumn cattle drive was a major event. The road through Amagansett was barred and served as a holding pen for the night. Houses along the way were opened to the cowboys, and the revelry concluded the following day with the celebration of Thanksgiving, which traditionally followed the return of the herds from their summer pasture.

In the summer of 1898 the pasture at Indian Field was dotted not with cattle but with the white tents of the United States Army. After the Spanish American War 29,500 soldiers were quarantined here together with their hero, Colonel Theodore Roosevelt. It was on the porch of Third House that Roosevelt learned of his nomination for the governorship of New York. It was here too that William McKinley visited his future successor and was heard to say as he gazed at the Montauk hillsides, "This is beautiful."

The stables across the highway to the south were built adjacent to a polo field and trotting track by Carl Fisher as part of his grand scheme to turn Montauk into an expensive resort.

To the north is East Lake Drive, which skirts the eastern edge of Lake Montauk and passes several roads leading into Indian Field, where the Indian burying ground is. Inquire of the park rangers at the end of East Lake Drive for directions to Stephen Talkhouse's grave. Proceed past the airport to the end of the drive where you will find the county park rangers. They will suggest the best ways to enter the park. At the end

Second House as it appeared at the turn of the century.

of the drive is the eastern half of Gin Beach, separated from the western half by the entrance to Lake Montauk. Before Carl Fisher opened Lake Montauk in 1927 Gin Beach extended from Shagwong Point to the east to Culloden Point to the west. Gin was the settler's word for corral, and it was along this beach that East Hampton's livestock were penned before being distributed to the various pastures. Culloden Point takes its name from a British warship wrecked on Shagwong Reef in 1781. It sank off the Point that bears its name as it sought refuge in Fort Pond Bay.

If you return along East Lake Drive to the highway and turn west you will soon come to Ditch Plains on your right. Follow Ditch Plains Road to the east. You will come to a group of handsome buildings built in the 1880s by Arthur Benson, the developer of Brooklyn's Bensonhurst. In 1879 Benson bought most of the Montauk pasture lands from the East Hampton trustees for $151,000 with the idea of turning the area into a hunting and fishing resort for sports-minded tycoons. Most likely he was speculating on the prospect that Montauk would become a deepwater port for transatlantic steamers. Benson died, but not before he had engaged Frederick Law Olmsted, the great landscape designer and the architect of Central Park, to lay out the grounds for his Montauk Association. He then hired the distinguished firm of McKim, Mead and White to build eight cottages for his friends. Seven of these handsome houses still stand at the end of Ditch Plains Road.

In 1895 Benson's heirs sold 5,500 acres at Montauk to a group of promoters led by Austin Corbin, president of the Long Island Railroad. Corbin had extended his tracks to Montauk that year in the hope that Fort Pond Bay would become a port of entry for transatlantic shipping as Benson had anti-' cipated, saving passengers a day at sea and providing the railroad with a new source of revenue. The scheme came to nothing and Corbin died a year later. But the dream of a transatlantic port at Montauk persisted. In 1911 there were rumors that a new White Star liner, the *Titanic,* would dock at Montauk. Fate had other plans, and World War I soon put an end to all such speculation. In 1928, as Carl Fisher was building his Tudor resort, a new company was formed to revive the scheme, but the depression intervened and Montauk slumbered on. Fort Pond Bay, which was to have seen the arrival of dozens of great liners, saw nothing but the scurrying of bootleggers' speedboats until Repeal removed even this prop from under Montauk's economy.

Carl Fisher died of alcoholism in the mid-Thirties, but the monuments to his spiraling ambitions are Montauk's most prominent landmarks after the lighthouse itself. Fisher was what his contemporaries called a "live wire." He began as a bicycle salesman in Indiana, switched to motor cars, became a racing driver, and built the Indianapolis Speedway. He promoted the Lincoln Highway, which crossed the country from east to west, and the Dixie Highway, which crossed it from north to south. In the early Twenties he developed an avocado grove on a forlorn Florida sandbar into Miami Beach, and in 1926 arrived at Montauk, his energies unimpaired. He built the seven-story tower at the traffic circle as his headquarters, and from its penthouse he would show prospective buyers the golf courses he had built behind Signal Hill where his million-dollar Montauk Manor stood. On the ocean directly south of Fort Pond he built an elaborate bathing pavilion and boardwalk, and he projected two more hotels as costly as the Manor itself. In 1931 he went bankrupt.

If you proceed north around the traffic circle you will soon pass the terminus of the Long Island Railroad. The road to the left passes the New York Ocean Science Laboratory, a project sponsored by several New York State universities. In World War I the navy had an air station near here, and in World War II it maintained a torpedo testing range. From 1882 an old fishing village had stood here. For years the area had been the center of Montauk's commercial activity, and it was here that the troopships landed after the Spanish American War. The hurricane of 1938 and the arrival of the navy three years later destroyed the village. Thereafter Montauk's commercial fishermen moved to the northwest corner of Lake Montauk.

Early in the American Revolution three British men-of-war and nine transports carrying 600 men arrived in Fort Pond Bay from Boston. Fearful that their livestock would be taken, the townsmen removed some 2,000 head of cattle from Montauk, but 3,000 sheep remained behind. Captain John Hulbert of Bridgehampton and Sag Harbor assembled a force of just over 100 men and marched them to the hills west of Fort Pond, in full view of the British fleet. As soon as his small force had passed out of sight of the British, Hulbert ordered the men to turn their coats inside out. Then he marched them back again. The British observers concluded that there were probably more men than sheep on Montauk and decided to plunder Fishers Island instead. The hillside on which Hulbert's men are said to have marched may be seen on the opposite shore from the old fishing village.

The road past the old fishing village rejoins Flamingo Road. To the south of Signal Hill where Montauk Manor

From the penthouse of his office tower Carl Fisher would show prospective buyers their future homesites in the Miami of the North.

stands is Fort Hill, where the Indians are said to have built their palisades. According to legend this was the site of Ninigret's attack on Quashawam's wedding night (see page 33). The land between Fort Hill and Signal Hill was once called Massacre Valley. The theater at the foot of Signal Hill originally housed indoor tennis courts.

From Flamingo Road, before you descend to the new harbor, you can see the Connecticut shore, an easy trip by canoe for the Montauks as well as for their mainland enemies.

The new fishing village at the foot of Flamingo Road is now the center of Montauk's commercial and tourist activity, with a large fleet of charter and party boats as well as commercial fishing and lobster vessels. Gosman's Dock, with its restaurant, fish market, and shops, attracts as many as 4,000 visitors daily in summer. Along the docks, when the charter boats come in each afternoon, you are likely to see catches of shark, swordfish, tuna, bluefish, and striped bass. The markets are filled with fresh fish, clams, and lobsters, and even in winter the party boats set out before dawn for cod and pollock. The Coast Guard Station is on Star Island, connected to the mainland by a causeway. Fisher built a yacht club here and held nightly gambling parties.

As you leave Montauk you will pass Second House at the foot of Fort Pond. Take the new highway out of the village. From an overlook atop Hither Hills about a mile outside the village you can see Gardiners Island to the north, with Napeague Bay to the west, and Accabonac and Fireplace in the distance.

A History of Gardiners Island

Gardiners Island, about six miles long and three miles wide at its broadest point, sits in Napeague Bay about three and a half miles from the East Hampton mainland. It can best be seen from the Hither Hills overlook on the new Montauk Highway or from the shore at Fireplace where the old windmill is clearly visible. Gardiners Island is private property and may not be visited except by invitation, which is rarely given. A result of its seclusion is that the island has remained in nearly pristine condition, its great forests of white oak, swamp maple, wild cherry, and birch much the same as when Lion Gardiner and his wife Mary first saw them in 1639; its woods still a nesting place for wild turkeys, pheasant, woodcock, and plover; its skies still punctuated after each March 21 by the great ospreys returned from their Amazonian wintering grounds.

Lion Gardiner, the island's first proprietor, served as an engineer with the army of William of Orange during the Low Country campaigns of the early seventeenth century. Toward the end of his long life he wrote a memoir which began, "In the year of our lord 1635—July the 10—Came I Lion Gardiner and Mary my wife from Woerden a town in Holland . . . and from thence to New England and dwelt at Saybrook Fort four years of which I was commander . . . and then went to an island of my own which I bought of the Indian Called by them Manchonake by us the Isle of Wight." The Indian name means island of the dead and for them it must have been a battleground or perhaps simply a burial place. For the English settlers of East Hampton the island became, under Gardiner's able proprietorship, something quite different: a source of wealth and leadership, and something more as well, for the inaccessible island has remained throughout the changing years a changeless part of the past, as stubborn as a pyramid, a monument to the intransigence of its successive proprietors and to their capacity for making or marrying enough money to keep it in their possession.

Lion Gardiner (see page 25) was a redheaded giant of a man who stood some six feet tall at a time when the kings of England seldom reached five feet. In 1635, as his memoirs reveal, he crossed the Atlantic in the *Batchelor*, a Norsey (or North Sea) bark of twenty-five tons. He built his fort at Saybrook in a wilderness of hostile Pequots and querulous Dutch traders, and managed to prosper despite the calculated provocations of the Massachusetts Englishmen whose deliberate injustices turned the Pequots into murderers and thus led to their eventual extermination.

He bought his island from Wyandanch, the Montauk

sachem (see pages 26-34), and on March 10, 1639, was granted the right to possess it now and forever by James Farrett, deputy to the Earl of Sterling, secretary for the Kingdom of Scotland; in other words the agent for Charles I. The property remains the oldest continuous royal grant in the New World.

On April 27, 1650, Gardiner wrote to John Winthrop, Jr., the Connecticut governor, thanking him for some hayseed that he sent and offering to sell him some cows for "fiftie pound in good marchantabl wampem, bever or silver; but if you will have them now, before the hefers have calvid, then I will keep the first five calves, and their price is 55 pounds. If my ocations were not great," he continued, "I would not sell them for 8 pounds a peece." He then went on to a different subject.

> *As consarning this yong man yow writ of . . . at present we ar willing to give this man . . . 20 pounds a year, with such diat as I myself eat, til we see what the Lord will do with us; and being he is but a young man, hapily he hath not manie books, therefore let him know what I have. First, the 3 Books of Martters, Erasmus, moste of Perkins, Wilsons Dixtionare, a large Concordance, Mayor on the New Testament; some of theas, with other that I have, may be ucefull to him. I pray you for the Lord's sake, do what you can to get him hither, and as I am ingagid to you allredie, so shall I be more.*
> *Yours to command in the Lord,*
> *Lion Gardiner*
> *I pray you send me word speedily about the cows, for else I must dispoes of them othar ways.*

What became of the cows is unknown, but the young man turned out to be Thomas James, East Hampton's first pastor and Lion Gardiner's lifelong friend. Together they gave direction to the young settlement, revealing in their deportment the combination of moral earnestness and commercial dedication which was already apparent in Gardiner's letter to Governor Winthrop. It was at James's suggestion that Gardiner built a house in East Hampton and for the rest of their lives they remained neighbors on the south side of Town Pond.

Gardiner's happiness was marred by the death of his daughter Elizabeth (see page 38) and the foolishness of his son David whom he dispossessed for fear that he would ruin the island as he had already squandered his own fortune. He left the property to his wife Mary with a warning to beware of David, but when Mary died in 1655, two years after her husband, she ignored his warning and left the island to David nevertheless. Little remains of David's memory except the recollection of Selah Pike, a hired man on the island, that "it was his habit to sit top of studdy Hill and drink a bottle of rum a day."

His son John was a different matter, a redheaded farmer in the mold of his grandfather, though crafty where the older man had been prudent, and somewhat reclusive, as the town itself was becoming, some fifty years after its settlement. John was a man of large appetites and rustic manners. He fathered innumerable Indian half-breeds, spoke the Montauk language, and according to John Lyon, his great-great-grandson, "came to their wigwams to eat fresh fish and liked the young squaws of the old sachem breed." He called himself Lord John and "thought that if he did not sleep with Royal Family . . . he should make a poor nobleman." He married his fourth wife when he was over seventy and complained of his third wife, whom he married when she was forty-one, that he "would as lief lie with a bag of carpenter's tools." It was during this third marriage that a band of Spanish pirates came ashore, ransacked the manor house, and before they left tied old John, who was sixty-seven at the time, to a mulberry tree.

But John's most controversial encounter with piracy occurred twenty-nine years earlier when Captain Kidd landed on the island and buried a part of his treasure there. William Kidd had been a substantial citizen of New York, a founder of Trinity Church and an investor in Manhattan real estate, who lived with his wife, Sarah, at 56 Wall Street. He was born about 1645 in Greenock, Scotland, became a sea captain and commanded British privateers in the war between England and France in the reign of William III; that is, he sailed under letters of marque issued by the Crown which were, in effect, licenses that allowed him to attack and seize French shipping, as well as pirate vessels, and divide the spoils among the investors in his voyages.

His difficulties began in the Indian Ocean when his ship, the *Adventure Galley*, captured the *Quedah Merchant*, a ship that belonged to the Great Mogul. Since the Mogul's ship was sailing under French letters of marque, Kidd had done nothing illegal. In fact, Lord Bellomont, the British governor of Massachusetts, New Hampshire, and New York who had recently replaced a predecessor charged with abetting piracy in the colonies, was an investor in the *Adventure Galley*, as were Lord Orford, Lord High Admiral of England, and Robert Livingston of Livingston Manor, perhaps the leading, and surely one of the richest, citizens of New York at the time. The Mogul, however, was furious, the more so since a British pirate named Avery had, a few years earlier, captured another of his ships which had been carrying his daughter and her dowry to Madagascar, where she was about to marry the Sultan. Inevitably, the Mogul directed his wrath at the employees of the British East India Company. To placate him the authorities in London disowned Kidd and declared him a pirate.

Kidd learned of these charges when he reached the West Indies. He left the *Quedah Merchant* in Hispaniola (Santo Domingo), abandoned the *Adventure Galley*, which was no longer seaworthy, and bought a sloop, the *San Antonio*, to which he transferred a portion of the Mogul's treasure, leaving the rest behind. He then sailed north and landed at Oyster Bay. There he discussed his problems with his wife and his attorney, James Emmott, a vestryman of Trinity Church.

A map drawn in 1722 of the Isle of Wight later known as Gardiners Island.

Through Emmott Kídd sent a message to Bellomont, enclosing the French papers that he had taken from the *Quedah Merchant*, and demanded a pardon before proceeding to Boston. Bellomont replied that "I have never granted (a pardon) yet," but he acknowledged receipt of "the French passes," and added that he had discussed the matter with His Majesty's Council "who are of the opinion that if you can be so clear as you have said that you may safely come hither . . . and I you." Thereupon, Kidd put his wife aboard the *San Antonio* and withdrew to Block Island to think things over.

A few days later Emmott visited John Gardiner on his island, told him that Kidd was anchored nearby, and explained the difficulties that had befallen his client. Soon thereafter Kidd himself arrived at the island and invited its proprietor aboard the *San Antonio*. Gardiner returned to shore with four black slaves and two bales of Indian muslin. The next day Gardiner boarded the sloop again and Kidd asked him for six sheep and a barrel of cider. Gardiner delivered these and Kidd sailed away, presumably for Boston. Three days later, however, he returned, evidently having decided that Gardiner could be trusted to guard his treasure. Kidd's men buried a quantity of gold, silver, and precious stones in a swamp near Cherry Harbor, gave Gardiner a present of a sash and pair of worsted stockings, and sailed to Boston where Kidd and his wife arrived toward the middle of June, 1699. They stayed at the home of Duncan Campbell, Boston's postmaster.

On July 6 Bellomont, under orders from London, seized Kidd and put him in jail. He then summoned Gardiner to Boston and demanded that he deliver Kidd's treasure. Gardiner complied, except for the presents that Kidd had given him and a large, dull, uncut diamond which Mrs. Gardiner seems to have decided to keep for herself.

Kidd remained imprisoned in Boston until the following February when he was sent to London. There he languished in chains for nearly a year before he was at last put on trial. Meanwhile Bellomont died in Boston.

Kidd throughout his imprisonment insisted on his innocence and appealed for the return of the French letters of marque. These, however, had disappeared and were not to turn up until the present century when an American maritime scholar discovered them in the Public Records Office in London. Kidd was put on trial on May 8, 1701. Fearful that the evidence would not support charges of piracy against Kidd, the Crown charged him with "an assault in and upon one William Moore (on board the *Adventure Galley*) and that the said William Kidd with a certain wooden bucket

The present manor
house on Gardiners
Island which re-
placed the house
that burned in 1947.

bound with iron hoops, of the value of eight pence, did feloni-
ously and of malice aforethought beat and strike the said William Moore on the head a little above the right ear, one mortal
bruise."

Kidd protested his innocence. He said that Moore, a gun-
ner, had urged the crew to attack a Dutch ship. Since such an
attack would have been piracy indeed, Kidd told Moore to
desist, and when he refused Kidd "took up a bucket and just
throwed it at him. I had all the provocation in the world . . . ,"
Kidd testified. "I had no design to kill him. . . . It was not
designedly done, but in passion, for which I am heartily
sorry." However, on the testimony of two convicted pirates
who had been offered pardons by the Crown, the jury convicted Kidd and he was sentenced to hang. Then, on May 9,
Kidd was tried for piracy and again one of the convicted
pirates testified against him. Once more he was found guilty,
and on May 23 he was taken to Execution Dock and killed.

Of the treasure, little is known. What was left on Hispaniola has never been found. Of the portion that Gardiner
returned to Bellomont, a part was sent to London and auc-
tioned off. The proceeds, £6,571, were given by Queen Anne
to Greenwich Hospital. But the total worth of the treasure
left at Gardiners Island was estimated at £20,000. What happened to the rest is unknown.

In 1765 John's great-grandson David inherited the island
and became its sixth proprietor. He raised the roof on the
fourth manor house, which was destroyed by fire in 1947. In

1774 he died and left the island in trust to his three-year-old son John Lyon, whose diaries supply much of the island's history. Among his recollections is a visit, while still a boy, to the British ship *Royal Oak*, Admiral Arbuthnot's flagship, which was anchored in Gardiners Bay during the Revolution. The occasion was a feast given by the admiral in honor of John Lyon's uncle, Colonel Abraham Gardiner, and his grandfather Samuel Buell. It was on this occasion that Dr. Buell, who was East Hampton's minister at the time and an uncertain patriot, read a poem to the admiral and his guests whose concluding lines were, "The foe in vain shall heaven invoke,/Triumphant sails the *Royal Oak*."

In 1803 John Lyon, a solemn young man, married Sarah Griswold, whose father was the son of a governor of Connecticut and whose mother, Sarah Diodati, was descended from an Italian noble family. Upon John Lyon's death in 1816 the island was leased to a cousin, David Gardiner, a grandson of Colonel Abraham. Three of his four children were born on the island and two of them, David Lyon and Julia, were to figure significantly in the fortunes of the Gardiner family and its increasingly legendary island. David Lyon married his cousin Sarah Gardiner Thompson, the granddaughter of John Lyon and the daughter of David Thompson, a rich New York banker. It was their daughter, Sarah Diodati Gardiner, who used the Thompson fortune to rescue the island from bankruptcy in 1937. She became its fifteenth proprietor and left it in trust to its present occupants, her nephew Robert David Lion Gardiner and his sister Alexandra Creel.

At the age of twenty-four Julia Gardiner married President John Tyler, a widower thirty years her senior. Her mother was the daughter of a rich New York brewer. Her father, David, had served briefly as a New York State Senator. Julia herself was an extraordinary beauty and aware of it. In New York the family had an imposing house near Astor Place, and when Julia was fifteen she attended her first ball. She wrote to her mother in East Hampton, "I suppose you would like to know how I was dressed. Pearl ear-rings, your buckle and a beautiful boquet of flowers in my bosom; it was composed of minunet, lily of the valley, lovers' wreath, a geranium flower and a leaf. There was also a rosebud. It was beautiful. My dress looked very well indeed among white satins, silks and lace dresses." Soon Julia was known as the Rose of Long Island, and added notoriety to her other distinctions when she appeared in a lithograph, strolling along Ninth Avenue, wearing a sun bonnet and a fur-hemmed winter coat, and carrying instead of a handbag a scalloped sign that said, "I'll purchase at Bogert & Mecalmy's, No. 86 Ninth Avenue. Their goods are Beautiful and Astonishingly Cheap."

The family made the grand tour of Europe, where Julia predictably broke the usual hearts, and returned to take up residence in Washington. It was the winter of William Henry Harrison's death. Julia promptly fell in love with his handsome successor. Tyler reciprocated the affection, despite the difference in their ages, and inevitably Julia and her father were among the notables asked aboard the new warship *Princeton* during the last week of February, 1844. Invited to the wardroom by the President, she and her father drank champagne. Later her father withdrew to the deck where the crew had been firing the "Peacemaker," a huge gun, for the amusement of the dignitaries aboard. Senator Gardiner was accompanied on deck by the secretaries of state and the navy as well as by Senator Thomas Hart Benton. As they gathered to watch the firing, the gun exploded, killing Senator Gardiner, the two secretaries, and several other bystanders. In the confusion that followed, the President carried his distraught young guest ashore, and the following June they were married. Throughout the remainder of Tyler's term Julia reigned as the most glamorous hostess that Washington had so far seen. Occasionally she and her husband visited East Hampton. She introduced dancing to the White House and was the first to insist that the band play "Hail to the Chief" whenever the President appeared. She enjoyed politics and seems to have been of some help to her husband in his successful effort to annex Texas. Upon Tyler's death she retired to his Virginia estate, remained loyal to his memory, and died on July 10, 1889, in the same Richmond hotel where Tyler himself had died.

After 1910 the island was leased to Clarence Mackay, head of the Postal Telegraph Company, a now defunct competitor to Western Union. Mackay, who was later to become the father-in-law of Irving Berlin, was an immensely rich man who seldom used the island himself but invited his friends to use it as a shooting preserve. His major-domo was Baron Blixen, the husband of the distinguished author Isak Dinesen. Blixen lived on the island with a succession of mistresses and a Turkish butler who occasionally disrupted the proceedings with his observances of Mohammedan festivals. By 1937 the island had fallen into receivership and was rescued by Sarah Diodati Gardiner, Julia Tyler's niece.

Today the island is maintained by her estate and is protected from unwelcome visitors by the East Hampton police as well as by its own caretakers.

Three Bicycle Tours

by Marvin Kuhn

AMAGANSETT TOUR

Begin at the flagpole on the village green at the east end of Main Street. Just east of the green is the Amagansett Railroad Station parking lot where you can park your car if you are coming from some distance. If you are waiting for someone to join you, you might wander through the old cemetery across the street. There you will find the headstones of persons prominent in the history of the village (see pages 156-162).

This tour consists of two loops. The first loop is approximately 3.6 miles with an optional side trip to the bay of 1.5 miles. The second loop is approximately 5 miles, or a total of 6.5 miles with the same optional side trip. Both loops are mostly in the woods, protected from the wind, and therefore ideal for beginners.

Leaving the flagpole, head east and bear left across the railroad tracks turning immediately left on Springs Amagansett Road, also known as "Old Stone Highway." For a short distance you will travel in the open along a small rolling golf course on your right. You then enter a wooded area as you curve to the right downhill. Coast while you enjoy the white tunnel of dogwood blossoms around you in the spring or the brilliant color in the fall.

As you near the bottom of the hill look for a sign on the right indicating an intersecting road to the right. Make this turn onto Albert's Landing Road and continue downhill on a road which is now a little narrower and winding, with small ups and downs which seem like a shady miniature roller coaster as you penetrate farther into the woods.

Soon you will come to a fork which is Cross Highway. Here you have an option of taking a side trip to Gardiners Bay, adding 1.5 miles to your ride. If you decide to visit the bay, continue straight on Albert's Landing Road. Notice how the woods give way gradually to occasional marsh areas and streams. This is the head of Fresh Pond where spring-fed water mixes with salt flow from the bay. You may see an osprey or marsh hawk sitting in the gnarled branches of the trees beyond the feathery sea oats and tall cattails. To see Fresh Pond, take the fork to the right, winding along its north shore. The pond is bordered on three sides by woods, and by the low dunes and beach grasses of the bay beach on the fourth. It is open to the bay through a small "cut" on its southeast corner and usually abounds in wildlife.

Beyond the pond you will arrive at a parking lot and beach picnic area. If you do not take the fork that goes along

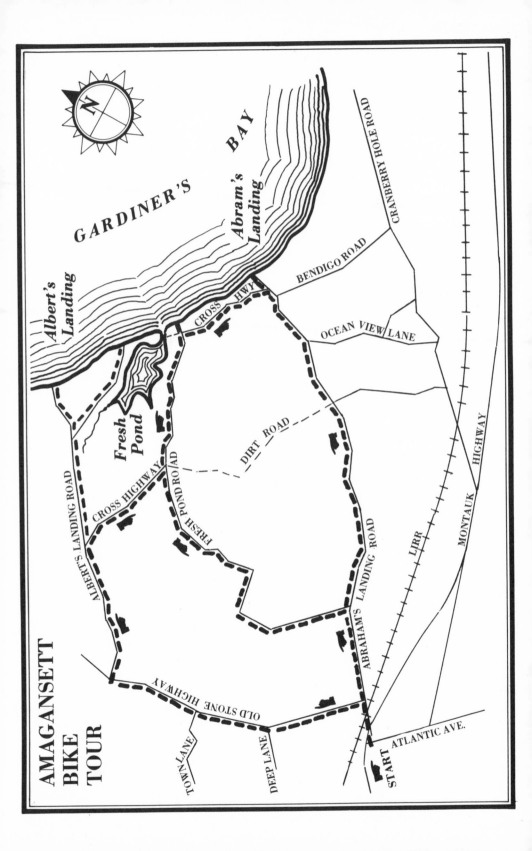

Fresh Pond, but continue straight, you will also reach the parking lot, a larger, sandier section of the beach, and a restroom. You can see Gardiners Island to the left (the manor house and windmill are visible with binoculars) and the South Fork of Long Island stretching to Montauk Point on the right.

Stop and swim if you like, then return the way you came to the first fork and turn left to get back on the loop.

Look for scattered holly and clumps of laurel among the tall oaks on each side as you begin your ascent up a small hill. At the bottom of the other side of this hill is the next intersection which is Fresh Pond Road. Here you may decide whether to take the shorter loop by turning right or the longer by turning left.

Loop 1: The shorter way back to Amagansett.

By turning right you will start another gradual climb through woods filled with wild flowers, birds, and occasional deer. After you reach the high point of the road (a mile or so) you will start the descent toward the home stretch, rounding a curve to your left and rolling out into the open along the east side of the same golf course you passed at the beginning of the tour. Continue past a few houses on either side to the next intersection at Abraham's Landing Road (also known as Devon Road). Turn right for the last short stretch back to the railroad tracks and the starting point of this tour.

Loop 2: The longer way back to Amagansett.

If you turn left at the Fresh Pond Road intersection you will pass along the south side of Fresh Pond. If you have not previously stopped at the beach you will eventually reach another of the town-maintained parking, picnic, and recreation areas on the bay front. There is a restroom here as well as a nature trail along the pond, beginning at the west side of the picnic area.

You may reach the entrance to the pond from the bay by walking north to the little footbridge that crosses the "cut" to the beach. Here you may hunt for shells and wade in the tidal current under the bridge.

To resume your tour, bear south, following the shore road —another Cross Highway—along a row of shore-front houses to the next beach access and the intersection with Abraham's Landing Road. This is Devon Landing or Abraham's Landing. Turn left into the parking area and pause to imagine the sloop *Endeavor* standing in against the prevailing summer westerly wind with a load of cattle or lumber to be landed at this spot. You will probably see sail of a contemporary sort if it is summer and the Devon Yacht Club sailboat races are in progress. The club is just to the right of the Abraham's Landing parking area.

As you leave the parking area continue straight ahead and follow Abraham's Landing Road through the trees, passing three roads which turn off to the left. If you want to walk into the woods there are a number of small dirt roads along the way where you can walk your bicycle.

Eventually you will start down out of the woods into the open where you can see the ocean stretching along the horizon to your left beyond the fields sloping down to Amagansett.

At the bottom of the hill on your right is the intersection with loop 1 at Fresh Pond Road. Continue straight for the last short section of the tour, past the houses beside the golf course on the right and along the railroad on the left, to the flagpole and the end of loop 2.

You may explore any of the previously mentioned roads to the left off Abraham's Landing Road if you care to. They all meet with Cranberry Hole Road, where a right turn will bring you up some little hills to a railroad bridge (good view of the ocean to left) before joining the Montauk Highway. This will increase your distance to about ten miles and includes a mile or so of main highway riding.

MONTAUK TOUR

Starting at the Amagansett flagpole, head east along the Montauk Highway, traveling with traffic flow. In a few minutes you will leave Amagansett behind and roll downhill onto the Napeague flat where the road is straight, the shoulder wide, and the road surface smooth.

You are beginning a 30-mile-plus round trip if you go all the way to the lighthouse at Montauk Point so it is advisable to plan the time and check the weather before leaving. An experienced cyclist can complete the ride comfortably in under three hours with a couple of rest stops but a leisurely touring pace may take double that time in which case you will want to include a lunch stop.

The first seven miles or so are flat as you cross the narrow strip of land connecting Amagansett to Montauk. Napeague Harbor will be visible on your left and the ocean on your right across the low-lying sand dunes. Enjoy the salt air and the beautiful black pines and beach grasses. Some of the small ponds behind the dunes contain the moundlike homes of muskrats. You will see osprey nests in the lower structure of the radio towers on the bay side of the road.

Just before you reach Hither Hills State Park Boundary at the end of the flat stretch you will pass some tennis courts and the road to Napeague Harbor. This road leads to Goff Point and the "walking" dunes mentioned on page 83.

Now the route will start uphill at the forked intersection where the Old Montauk Highway meets the main highway. Either route will bring you to the village of Montauk, the old road being narrower and hillier but affording a more continuous view of the ocean.

A short distance past the fork on the north side of the old or lower highway is a small Indian burial ground on a knoll facing the sea. A visit here makes a good first rest stop. If you are traveling the main or upper road there is a right turn at the top of the first hill which connects with the lower road just west of the burial ground.

The main road now dips and then rises in a fairly steep climb to the first overlook, a parking area at the top of the hill. Here the view of the ocean and bay to the west is magnificent. You look back over the Napeague strip with the bay visible beyond the unspoiled wooded and rolling landscape to the north, and the Atlantic Ocean stretching away to the south and west as far as you can see.

Continuing along the highway to the east the woods close in to the edges of the road. You will see deer-crossing signs along the way. You may also see deer in the shadows of the trees or even crossing the road in this section.

After three miles or so the road descends into the village of Montauk. At the bottom of the hill where the old road rejoins the main highway is the intersection with Second House Road. On the northeast corner of this intersection is Second House (see pages 169-171), and just beyond to the east is Kirk Memorial Park on Fort Pond Bay. Both of these places are pleasant rest stops.

As you pass through the village, or perhaps stop for lunch in one of the local shops, notice the only "skyscraper" on eastern Long Island, a legacy of Carl Fisher's dream to make Montauk the Miami of the North (see page 174).

As it leaves the village the highway continues east. You will pass West Lake Drive on your left; this is the way to the fishing docks and the entrance to Lake Montauk. A little farther on, Ditch Plains Road intersects to the right; it leads to the site of the old lifesaving station on the ocean, a favorite spot for surfing.

Next on the left is a short road allowing access to the

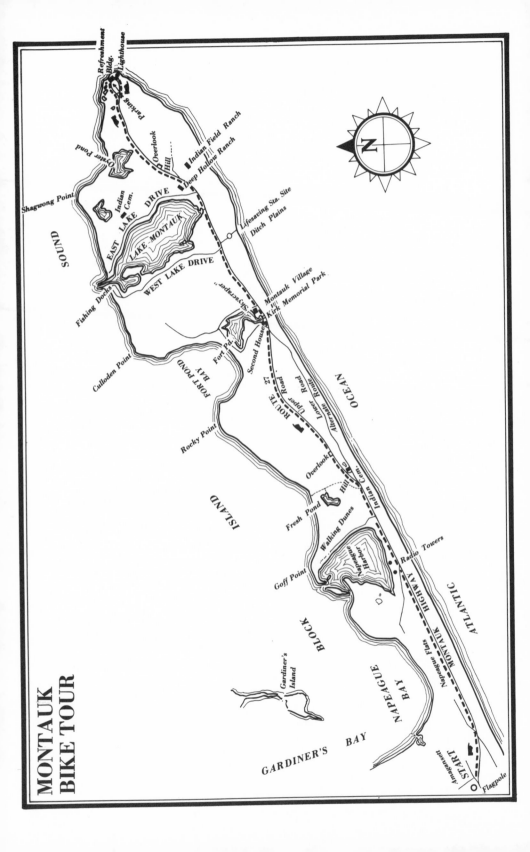

south shore of Lake Montauk. Beyond is the intersection with East Lake Drive, the route to the Indian cemetery (see page 172).

The road dips again to another fork before climbing to the left. Here is the site of Deep Hollow Ranch and Indian Field Ranch, two of the largest horse ranches on Long Island. The building to the north on the hill at Deep Hollow Ranch is Third House (see page 171) and to the south, in the pastures of Indian Field Ranch, you will see horses grazing.

Back in the bicycle saddle you now have a fairly steep hill to climb but another overlook awaits you at the top with a view to match that of the first. Here you are looking out to the north over open rolling grassland mixed with pockets of woodland, across Oyster Pond to Block Island Sound. On a good day the shore of Connecticut is a blue line in the distance. To the west the eye travels across Lake Montauk to the Sound. Because of the elevation here, almost the entire eastern tip of Long Island is laid out like a panorama before you.

It is only a few miles to the Point now, and again the woods border both sides of the road; holly abounds among the trees as you near the loop at the lighthouse. Follow the circle to the right up to the parking lot entrance opposite the park refreshment building. In front of this pleasant stone and glass building is a large patio with tables overlooking the sea to the east. This is another beautiful stopping place, especially for a cyclist who has just ridden approximately seventeen miles.

Fishing boats are usually working offshore, and sea birds wheel overhead in their wakes. On a clear day, you can see Block Island looming on the eastern horizon.

The return trip is by the same route. If you choose to go by the Old Montauk Highway, take the fork to the left just west of the village. There are some very nice views of the ocean from the tops of the small hills along this route.

Often in summer the wind is from the west, and you may be facing into it on your return. The rest stops you have taken will stand you in good stead for the return across Napeague if this is the case. Try taking turns with others in your group riding single file. You will find a "drafting" effect against the wind most helpful as you ride in the wind-breaking protection of the riders in front of you.

This tour can, of course, be broken into segments by driving to various points by car before starting your ride. Refer to map and section on Montauk for planning.

SAG HARBOR-WAINSCOTT TOUR

This ride in loop form is approximately thirty miles and is ideal for a day's outing including a lunch stop. It covers a variety of scenery through areas on both sides of the Montauk Highway. During the first half, the wind will usually be against you, but you will have the protection of wooded roads most of the way, while the return half is in the open with the wind behind you.

This time the flagpole in East Hampton at the south end of Main Street is the starting point. While waiting, you will find many points of interest close by (see section on East Hampton Village and map).

The first leg of the ride is along Route 114 north to Sag Harbor. The shoulder is wide and the road surface smooth for this first eight miles or so.

As you roll down the slight grade into the village of Sag Harbor (Hampton Street as well as Route 114) you will see the old houses that line both sides of the street. Turn left at Clinton Street where the brick school building stands on the northwest corner. Follow Clinton to Jermain Avenue, turn right and then bear left past Pierson High School to Division Street. Cross Division Street to Madison Street. Turn right past Cap Amundsen's studio and marinescape art gallery, then immediately left to remain on Jermain Avenue, and continue across Suffolk Street, past Palmer Terrace and Oakland Avenue to Oakland Cemetery. This section of the village is part of the walking tour found on page 98 and makes an excellent place to stop and rest. A little farther past the cemetery is Otter Pond, a good place for watching ducks and geese.

Continue across Main Street, a projection of Jermain Avenue, now North Sea Road, following a straight line to the next intersection at Brickiln Road. At this point, from late spring through late fall, you should see yellow marks painted on the road surface: circles with arrows indicating the route of the New York Cycle Club's semi-annual tour of eastern Long Island. You may follow these marks and not have to worry about the map until the point where you turn back to the east. The route has been carefully plotted by experienced cyclists for least traffic and maximum scenery.

After a climb through the woods the road dips to a fork intersection where you follow Brickiln Road off to the left (two yellow marks repeated for advance warning before turn). Now the road surface is blacktop and narrower as you climb into quiet wooded glades through patches of light and shade. A series of small hills makes occasional coasting possible, and since the bicycle is silent, your chances of observing wild-life are excellent. Listen, too, to the sounds around you as you wind through the slow turns of this beautiful woods road.

As you come out of the woods after a mile or so the scene changes to open farm land looking south over the fields behind Bridgehampton to the ocean in the distance. Turn right at the intersection with Scuttlehole Road.

A note here about the marks at the occasional intersecting roads: a single circle with arrow pointing straight ahead means just that. Continue in a straight line.

One of the loveliest stops on this tour is coming up now on the right, a small pond in a hollow off the road. It is part of the Sayre Baldwin farm near by. Stop in the shade of a roadside tree and watch the cattle graze along the road's edges.

Follow Scuttlehole Road to Head of Ponds Road and eventually you will come to County Road No. 39. Follow either the yellow marks or the accompanying map and you have come to the halfway point of your tour. You are now on a main highway for a little distance, and the marks turn west (right) at the intersection. Do not follow them, but instead turn left, following the highway (with traffic) across the rail-road tracks to the intersection with Montauk Highway. On the right just before this left turn onto Montauk Highway you will see a delicatessen among a group of small stores. After the turn there are two restaurants, the second of which has counter and booth accommodations.

Heading east along the highway you pass through the little village of Water Mill with its windmill on the green and then you are again in open farm land. In late summer or fall the farm trucks and stands along the road offer an abundance of produce.

The next turn is at Mecox Road and here you may find an open yellow circle with arrow. This mark, along with some similar to those you have been following, has been placed by a local group and the American Youth Hostel Association. You may follow these marks if you like; when in doubt, consult the accompanying map.

Make a left turn at Atlantic Avenue. Continue to the intersection with Bridge Lane, then turn right down Bridge Lane and go over the little bridge across Sagaponack Pond. This brings you to another stop. The pond runs almost to the ocean on the south. You may see a great blue heron wading the shallows in search of food.

Bridge Lane meets Sag Main Street at roughly right angles. Here you turn left and go up to the fork at the old

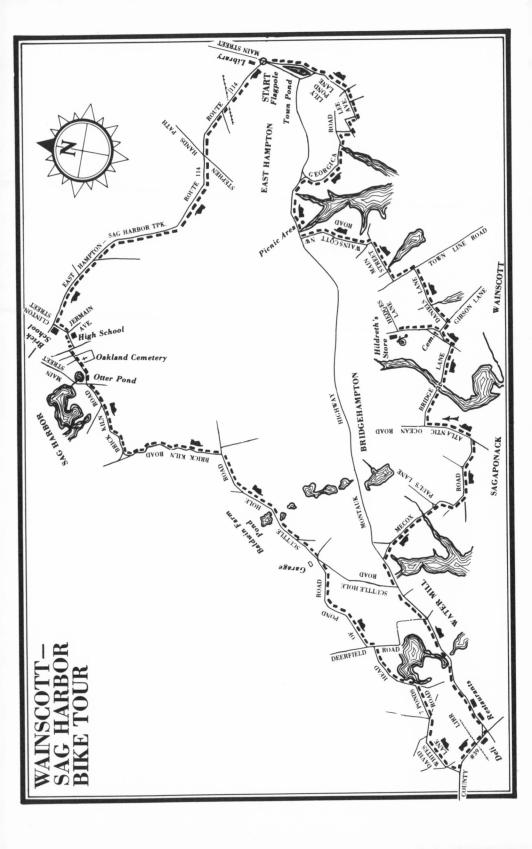

WAINSCOTT—
SAG HARBOR
BIKE TOUR

cemetery. If you like, take a short side trip up Sag Main Street to Hildreth's General Store and the Sagaponack Post Office. To do this you continue past the cemetery to the intersection of Hedges Lane. The companion store and post office is on the west side of Main Street. The store is a relic of the last century as is the five-foot highwheel "Ordinary" bicycle in the post office window which was rebuilt by Mr. Hildreth.

To continue your tour, return south on Sag Main Street to the fork at the cemetery, bear left on Gibson Lane, then turn left at Daniels Lane. At this intersection the fences enclose the Topping horse farm, and a friendly horse or two may greet you over the split rails as you ride past.

A right on Daniels Lane takes you due east again, and here the road travels through flat, open farm land along the ocean. If the wind is behind you, you will sail along Daniels Lane, catching a glimpse of the ocean to your right from time to time.

At the intersection with Town Line Road you leave Southampton Township and re-enter East Hampton Town at Wainscott. Refer to pages 146-153 for the next portion of the tour as you enter this pleasant rural village.

Follow Main Street through Wainscott to the left turn at Wainscott Stone Road, bear right at the immediate fork, and soon you will be back to the Montauk Highway. Turn right again and pedal along the shoulder for a little while to Georgica Road. Refer to the map for a stop at the head of Georgica Cove, then pass by Jericho Lane to Apaquogue Road, which runs into Lily Pond Lane. Follow Lily Pond Lane east to Ocean Avenue. Turn left and continue to the Town Pond. Follow the south side of the pond (right at the fork) past South End Cemetery to the point of beginning at the flagpole.

This rather arduous trip will have rewarded you with a great deal of beautiful scenery and historical detail.

A BIBLIOGRAPHY FOR BIKERS:

Cuthbertson, Tom. *Anybody's Bike Book*. Berkeley, California: Ten Speed Press, 1971.

DeLong, Fred. *DeLong's Guide to Bicycles and Bicycling*. Radnor, Pennsylvania: Chilton Book Company, 1974.

Sloan, Eugene. *The Complete Book of Bicycling*. New York: Simon & Schuster, 1970, 1974.

A Selective Guide to Living Well in East Hampton

Despite the upheavals that have taken place since the first settlers sailed from Kent, the South Fork of Long Island resists the efforts of those who would transform it into another suburbia and remains predominantly rural and agricultural. To the west the sprawling towns of Islip and Brookhaven, aggressively seeking new development and industry, account for Suffolk's standing as the fastest-growing county in the nation, but there are still fewer than 100,000 year-round residents living on the far side of the Shinnecock Canal in the East End towns which Suffolk secessionists hope may one day become Peconic County.

East Hampton Town stretches from Wainscott to Montauk Point, embracing the villages of Wainscott, East Hampton, Amagansett, the Springs, Montauk, and part of Sag Harbor. Only East Hampton and Sag Harbor are incorporated villages, with a tax structure and police force of their own. When East Hampton Village is spoken of it means the relatively small area surrounding Main Street, bounded roughly by Georgica Pond on the west and Two Mile Hollow Beach on the east, but East Hampton Town means the entire seventy-square-mile area.

All the telephone numbers given here have the Suffolk County area code 516 unless otherwise noted. For those who spend the entire year or a good part of it in East Hampton, we recommend getting a copy of the green **Handi-Guide**, which lists telephone numbers from Speonk to Montauk and is much less cumbersome than the Suffolk directory. It is published by Roberts Press (AT 9-1200), 380 Grove Avenue, Patchogue, N.Y. 11772, and is free.

Accommodations

Except for Montauk, which has more than seventy motels, there isn't as much transient space on the East End of Long Island as you might ex-

pect in a resort area. This is due in great part to the comparatively short high season, which makes owning a motel a risky business when you have to depend on three months' income to pay a year's maintenance and taxes. Also, East Hampton is very much a residential family community, and much of the visiting summer population either owns or rents houses.

Lists of motels and guest houses (a few with breakfast included) are readily available from the East Hampton and Montauk chambers of commerce (see "Tourist Information Centers"). If you are looking for more than just a closet to keep the beach towels in, the following places offer the most amenities. None of them is cheap.

MONTAUK (zip code 11954)

Driftwood (668–5744; winter phone 374–5114). A comfortable motel on the ocean. Rooms, suites, cottages. Swimming pool and tennis courts.

Gurney's Inn (668–2345). Long-established. This is the largest resort in the area. The Audubon Club takes birding weekends here in May and October. Gurney's has a vast private beach. All rooms and cottages M.A.P. Open year-round.

Panoramic (668–3000). An attractive new apartment-motel on the ocean. Rooms with kitchen facilities. Landscaped grounds and swimming pool.

AMAGANSETT (11930)

Mill-Garth (267–3757). Scenic location overlooking open farm land on Windmill Lane, a short walk to shops. Quaint, well-furnished cottages blend right in with the local architecture.

Ocean Colony and Tennis Club (267–3130). Ocean-front complex on the Napeague strip with cottages and studio apartments. Ultra-modern.

Ocean Dunes Apartments (267-3406). Amagansett's only ocean-front resort has a swimming pool and is within walking distance of town.

EAST HAMPTON (11937)

East Hampton House (324–4300; in New York, 895–6777). Despite its unattractive location on the Montauk Highway, this is a popular motel. The rooms face the back, so it's quiet. There are tennis courts, a swimming pool, a coffee shop for breakfast and lunch. Golf privileges at nearby South Fork Country Club.

Huntting Inn (324–0410). The historic hostelry in the heart of the village is open year-round, with its own restaurant.

1770 House (324–1770). Main Street near the library.

SAG HARBOR (11963)

American Hotel (725–9716). This handsomely restored Victorian hotel is on Main Street, with a restaurant serving fine French food. Open year-round.

Baron's Cove Inn (725–2100). A favorite of yachtsmen, with docking for boats up to 65 feet. Inn and restaurant open year-round.

SHELTER ISLAND (11964)

Dering Harbor (749–0900). Vast resort complex overlooking Peconic Bay. Efficiencies, suites, villas. Mooring area and dock. Open year-round.

Animal Hospitals and Kennels

A sick pet can turn a pleasant vacation into a family trauma. Here are some places that will help you cope:

East Hampton Animal Hospital (324–0282) on Montauk Highway half a mile west of the village. Open 9:00–12:00 A.M. and 2:00–4:00 P.M. year-round. Answering service for emergencies, 6:00 P.M. to 8:00 A.M. Some typical fees: cat spaying, $30; altering,

$15. To bathe an "average size" dog, $7; St. Bernards and similar, $10. A standard fee of $7 per visit, exclusive of medication, is charged.

For those who live further west, the **Southampton Animal Hospital** (AT 3–1094) on North Highway has similar hours and fees, as does the **Olde Towne Animal Hospital** (283–0611) on the Southampton bypass (County Road 39). The **Hampton Animal Shelter** (725–9730) on Brickiln Road, Sag Harbor, has pets for adoption and accepts strays. It also has boarding facilities, but a better place to board a pet is **Dick's Kennels** (324–1119), 116 Accabonac Highway, East Hampton, where personal attention and a high standard of cleanliness are the rule.

Antiques and Auctions

WATER MILL

Et Caet Er A (RA 6–4840), Main Street. Norman Shepherd travels to England twice a year to bring home some of the nicest furniture and accessories to be found in the Hamptons.

Baron's Antiques (726–4810), Montauk Highway between Water Mill and Bridgehampton. Arthur Baron is the engaging auctioneer who tempts your pocketbook with his pleasant banter at various country auctions throughout the summer. His own shop reflects his twenty-five years of experience in the trade. Many excellent English and American pieces.

BRIDGEHAMPTON

Blue Door Antiques (537–1555), Montauk Highway between Bridgehampton and Wainscott. Norma Dorfman has a particularly fine collection of scrimshaw and Americana. You'll also find old snuff boxes and other small objects in this pleasantly cluttered shop. Open year-round.

Collectibles (537–1273), Main Street. A potpourri with some unusual pieces. Open only on summer weekends.

Old Glory (537–3868), Main Street. Don Kelley and Warren Fitzsimmons are specialists in well-restored antique wicker furniture. Their shop is an interesting jumble of Victorian and turn-of-the-century bric-a-brac, boxes, and baskets (some fine old Indian ones included).

SAG HARBOR

The old whaling town is something of an antique hunter's heaven and a fine place to spend a rainy Saturday. When you're tired of browsing stop off at the bar of the American Hotel to recapture some of the flavor of early Sag Harbor.·

Antiquities (725–0490), Main Street. Svend Rasmussen has one of the finest collections of early iron tools in the country. The accent in this small shop is on American primitive furniture and accessories.

Richard Camp (725–3765), Division and Henry streets. A shop specializing in English and American furniture, plus their own designs in wire/rope étagères.

Cobble Hill Antiques (725–1688), Main Street. Old historic prints are the main feature here.

The Glad Hand (725-2330), Madison Street. Lovelady Powell and Peggy White advertise their wares as old and not-so-old. You'll find some interesting small items here.

The Little Barn on Sage Street (725–3034), Madison and Sage streets. When you smell the fragrance of burning cedar follow your nose to Hal and Diana McKusick's wood-burning stove and charming primitive American shop of country furniture and folk art. Their small but choice collection includes a number of gold and gold-filled watches. Open year-round.

Old Acquaintance (725–3725), Madison Street. Late Victorian and early twentieth-century memorabilia. American and European accessory furniture.

The Pheasant (725–1234), Main Street. A small shop of turn-of-the-century attic finds. Oak, pine, and walnut country furniture.

Sag Harbor Antiques (725–1732), Madison Street. John Krug and Otto Fenn are the proprietors of this country-style shop. You'll find a lot of stripped furniture here, some quilts, and a number of kitchen utensils and old crocks. Chat with Mr. Fenn about Sag Harbor's history, a subject on which he's very knowledgeable.

EAST HAMPTON

Clipper Cargo Ltd. (324–5656), 33 A Main Street. This delightful little shop is hidden away down the alley between the Bike Shop and Candles 'N Things. The owners are anthropologists, and their travels to far-off places such as New Guinea have produced a wide assortment of carefully chosen items, many with a nautical motif. Some fine copper and brass accessories.

Richard V. Hare (324–2154), 23 Main Street. There is an elegant collection of old china, lamps, and bric-a-brac in this pretty shop. Mr. Hare is also a designer and decorator; several East Hampton estates bear witness to his style.

Village Antiques (324–2113), 11 Newtown Lane. Orientalists will enjoy browsing among the fine old urns and screens here. There is a well-displayed collection of Victorian jewelry, glassware, and furniture.

AMAGANSETT

Balasses House (267–3032), Main Street. George and Teda Balasses run a shop held in the highest regard by those who know antiques. They have an extensive collection of eighteenth- and nineteenth-century English, Irish, and French country furniture, accessories, and clocks. Before Bloomingdale's started sending its buyers abroad they used to stock up here, and almost cleaned the place out twice.

198

The Skylight (267–6565), Main Street. The Wallace G. Carrs have a splendid inventory of miniatures—dollhouses and furniture—in the tiny shop that's a part of their home. Glass and export china are also features. Ask to see the silver collection in the back.

AUCTIONS

Country auctions occur throughout the year, but most often in the summer when more people are around. Sometimes they're held on premises, sometimes at the Veterans of Foreign Wars Building in East Hampton on Main Street. Occasionally a really memorable auction comes along, like the one in 1969 when the contents of the Bell estate—a mansion set on 600 acres overlooking Napeague Bay—were sold, or the Irving Hotel auction in 1974, just before that famous old Southampton hostelry was demolished to make way for a motel.

Advertisements and descriptions of forthcoming auctions appear in the East Hampton **Star**'s "Coming Up" column the week of the sale. Once you've attended one of Arthur Baron's sales, he'll send you advance notice of future ones by mail.

Guild Hall holds a benefit auction annually, late in June. The Water Mill Community Club's yearly flea market and auction, held under tents in an open field on Nowedonah Avenue, takes place on the first Saturday in August. The Montauk Lions Club sponsors weekend art auctions throughout the summer on the village green there. And the Hampton Day School has one over Thanksgiving at the Bridgehampton Community House. Watch the **Star** for exact dates of these events.

Antique Restoration

If you have five period Queen Anne chairs, **George A. Schulte** (324–0188) will make you a sixth so perfectly that you won't be able to tell it apart, according to George Balasses, who uses Mr. Schulte's services for Balasses House's own restorations. Mr. Schulte is located on Spring Close Road in East Hampton, and he will be just as pleased to refinish or repair modern furniture as antiques.

Appliance Repairs

For washers, dryers, dishwashers, etc., on the fritz, call the manufacturer. For *General Electric* appliances: 727–6380. For *Westinghouse* appliances: (212) TW 8–5700. For *Sears Roebuck* appliances: 727–6320. Major appliances which have been purchased locally will normally be serviced by the store where you bought them.

South Fork Appliance Repair (283–3858), Noyac Road, Southampton, will also fix major appliances. Be sure to tell their answering service the make and model of yours.

For small-appliance repairs, we recommend **John Ketcham** (324–0547), **Ray's Appliances** (324–4022), and **Mike's TV Repair** (324–2780) in East Hampton; the **Repair Korner** (283–0633) in Southampton; and **TV Tech** (267–8492) in Amagansett.

Art Galleries

Art galleries have a way of arriving in town just before the season opens and departing, never to reappear, when it ends. Here are five that have been in the community long enough to have acquired reputations as showcases for good work. The Benson, which is the oldest and largest, is especially recommended.

Benson Gallery (537–0598), Montauk Highway, Bridgehampton.

Bittersweet Gallery (668–3099), Main Street, Montauk.

Steel Gallery (537–3713), Main Street, Bridgehampton.

Tower Gallery (283–3951), 3 South Main Street, Southampton.

Upstairs Gallery (324–1456), Newtown Lane, East Hampton.

Art Supplies

Serious artists will probably need to supplement their supplies in Riverhead or New York, but amateur painters should be able to find what they need at **The Golden Eagle** (324–0603), 14 Gingerbread Lane, East Hampton, just beyond the railroad station. The best selection of brushes, canvas, paints, tools, etc., in the area.

Baby Sitters

Cashiers in the local supermarkets are a remarkably good source of babysitter information. So are lifeguards at the town beaches. Several stores around town have community bulletin boards where teenagers advertise for baby-sitting jobs: check at Marley's in East Hampton; the Devon Pharmacy and IGA in Amagansett; White's in Montauk; and the Penny Candy Shop in Water Mill.

Also, **Dan's Papers** (the Montauk **Pioneer**, the East Hampton **Summer Sun**, the Southampton **Summer Day**) publish listings of baby-sitters, both male and female. **Dan's Papers** are free, published weekly, and available at almost any shop or bank.

Beaches and Beach Parking

In 1969, East Hampton Town and Village began issuing beach parking stickers in three categories—resident, renter, motel or hotel guest—at varying annual fees. The most important thing to know about beach stickers is that you *must* have one in order to park your car or motorcycle at any town- or village-maintained ocean or bay beach (except Fresh Pond, see page 201). Cars

without stickers will be ticketed for a first offense and towed away thereafter.

There are no restrictions of any kind, and no fees, for pedestrians and bicycles.

If you are staying at a motel, ask the owner for a temporary beach permit. It should be complimentary. If you are simply driving to East Hampton for a day at the ocean, you will either have to park your car far from the beach and lug the beer and blankets down, or go to Main Beach (see "Village Beaches"). If you own or rent a house, you may buy a permanent sticker.

Stickers for town beaches are available at Town Hall (324–4143), the redbrick building set back from the north side of Montauk Highway about midway between East Hampton and Amagansett. Proof of ownership or rental is required.

TOWN BEACHES

AMAGANSETT

Coast Guard Beach (267–3100). Also known as Asparagus beach because its popularity as a singles' scene has given it a standing room only reputation. Located at the foot of Atlantic Avenue, it has an immense parking lot, refreshment stand, sanitary facilities. Lifeguard-protected.

Albert's Landing A broad bay beach popular with families, at the foot of Albert's Landing Road off the Springs-Amagansett Road. Adjacent picnic area. Comfort station. Lifeguard-protected.

Little Albert's or Albert's Landing, Jr. A smaller area just south of Big Albert's; same parking lot. Unprotected.

Lazy Point A bay beach and boat-launching ramp (see "Marinas") at the end of Lazy Point Road on Napeague Harbor. Fishermen's shacks. Quiet, sandy beach. Unprotected.

Indian Wells Parking at this ocean beach at the end of Indian Wells Highway off Route 27 is restricted to town residents with cars displaying "resident" stickers. Lifeguard-protected.

THE SPRINGS

Barnes Landing Bay beach, space for about fifty cars. Watch out for jellyfish in August; seaweed all summer. Many small children. Roped-off swimming area. Off Barnes Hole Road on Napeague Bay. Unprotected.

Maidstone Park (324–2510) Gardiners Bay beach; a favorite of local residents. Large parking area. Fishing. Picnic and sanitary facilities. Softball field. East of Three Mile Harbor Inlet, off Flaggy Hole Road. Lifeguard-protected.

Sammys Beach Also favored by year-rounders. Beautiful bay beach north of Three Mile Harbor, off Sammys Beach Road. Unprotected.

Louse Point Swimming on both sides of this sandy spit. Accabonac Harbor to the west; Napeague Bay to the east. Stony, narrow beaches, shallow water, but one of the most scenic spots in town. Foot of Louse Point Road off Springs-Amagansett Road. Unprotected.

Gerard Park Across Accabonac Inlet from Louse Point. Used mostly by summer residents of Gerard Drive, off Fireplace Road. There can be heavy marine traffic at both Louse Point and Gerard Park beaches. Unprotected.

WAINSCOTT

Beach Lane Ocean beach, south of Wainscott Main Street. Small parking lot. Unprotected.

MONTAUK

Ditch Plains Watch the wipe-outs while you tan. Surfers' paradise, from about mid-May to mid-October. Former site of the Ditch Plains Coast Guard Station. Lifeguard-protected.

South Lake Drive At the foot of the drive, on the shore of Lake Montauk. Comfort station, picnic area. Unprotected.

East Jetty Foot of East Lake Drive. Beautiful Gardiners Bay beach opposite the West Lake town dock, at the entrance to Montauk Harbor. Swim, watch the fishing boats. Sanitary facilities, picnic area, fishing. Lifeguard-protected.

Fresh Pond Beach is the single exception that proves the sticker rule. None is required at this little known, out of the way, bay-front beach in Amagansett. To get there, cross the railroad tracks about a tenth of a mile past the Amagansett flagpole; turn sharp right on Abraham's Landing Road, take first left (it comes up fast) to end of Fresh Pond Road. No lifeguard, but plenty of other amenities: parking lot, picnic tables, comfort station, nature trail. The favorite retreat for cub scout sleep-overs, senior citizens' picnics, covered-dish church suppers.

VILLAGE BEACHES

There are five ocean beaches in East Hampton Village, which has its own sticker system apart from the town's. Parking permits for these beaches are available only at Village Hall (324–4150), 27 Main Street. After June 21 they may also be obtained from the manager of the Main Beach, at the foot of Ocean Avenue.

Stickers for **Two Mile Hollow, Egypt,** and **Wiborg's** beaches, at the dead ends respectively of Two Mile Hollow Road, Old Beach Lane, and Highway Behind the Pond, are free to village residents and renters. Others, whether or not they live in town, may buy parking permits for these three beaches for $15 inclusive.

Two Mile Hollow is a "double-dune" beach, so called because two lines of sand dunes, one behind the other, protect the valuable acreage adjoining it from the enroachment of the sea. This unprotected beach is a favorite with young men, and some older ones who go there to meet them.

Wiborg's is nicknamed "Pink Beach." The sand is no pinker than elsewhere, but some say that the Maidstone Club to the east casts a rosy glow across everything around it. Unprotected.

The beach at **Old Beach Lane** is as scenic an ocean beach as any, but is usually so deserted, even on weekends, that you'd never know it was a public beach. No facilities, no lifeguards (no people).

Georgica Beach, at the foot of Apaquogue Road, used to be the ocean-front outpost of the artists' colony until nearby residents protested that the outlanders from the Springs were taking up all the parking places. Georgica is now restricted to village residents and renters only, at no charge.

Main Beach (324–0074) is the largest in town with the most facilities. Lifeguards, lockers, indoor refreshment stand, sanitary facilities, ample parking area. The only beach in East Hampton where you can park your car on a daily basis: $2 Monday-Thursday, $3.50 on weekends and holidays, less for village residents.

Main Beach stickers, which are also good at Two Mile Hollow, Egypt, and Wiborg's, cost $10 for residents. Nonvillage residents can buy them too, for $30. All these fees are subject to change.

Bookstores

Keene's (283–1612) on Hampton Road (Route 27 A) in Southampton is one of the best-stocked general bookstores in America. Robert Keene is a bibliophile who offers a number of antique and out-of-print volumes on a variety of subjects, particularly Long Island and American history.

Job's Lane Bookstore and Conservatory (283–6467) in the Complex. A brand-new store which carries house plants as well as a wide stock of books.

Bookhampton (324–4939), on Newtown Lane in East Hampton, is a well-stocked shop with everything that's current and a large collection of paperbacks.

LVIS Bargain Bookshop (324–0158 for pickups and information) is a secondhand bookstore run by and for the benefit of the Ladies Village Improvement Society. It's on Newtown Lane, East Hampton, behind De Bracieux. Open summers only, daily except Wednesdays.

Old Barn (324–0783), down the alley next to the 5 & 10¢ store on Main Street, East Hampton, is more of a gift shop than a bookstore, but it has the usual best sellers and coffee-table books.

The Bookshop (267–8077), Amagansett Square near the Royale Fish. A new bookshop with a good general selection.

Bowling

Starlanes Bowling Alley on the Montauk Highway about a mile west of East Hampton has the bowling monopoly in town. Ball and shoe rentals, and the usual candy and soda machines. A good place for birthday parties, but don't bring the kids after 6:00 P.M. In winter, Starlanes is home of the local Tuesday, Thursday, Friday, and Saturday evening bowling leagues.

Caterers

Besart Food Shop (267–3140), Montauk Highway, Amagansett. Fine homemade cakes and other specialties, but if they don't see you arriving in a chauffeur-driven car it may be a while before they'll let you buy something. Located next to the IGA.

Dreesen's Market (324–0465), 33 Newtown Lane, East Hampton. Dreesen's, the long-established purveyors of fine meats and produce, also runs a popular catering service. Among the specialties are whole roast beefs, spare ribs, and creative salads. In winter when things are slow they'll cook your own recipes for you.

Loaves and Fishes (537–0555), Sagg Main Street, Sagaponack. The first white house just south of the flashing light on Montauk Highway, between Bridgehampton and Wainscott. Devon Fredericks and Susan Costner have taken over what used to be Tillotson's and inherited all of the Tillotsons' recipes, so those wonderful barbecued ducks, homemade breads and casserole dishes are not lost to posterity. The new partnership will cater for two to 200 people, from the most formal dinner party to a picnic on the beach.

The Store in Amagansett (267–3650), Main Street. Some people wouldn't think of having a party in the winter because The Store is closed, and what would they do for whole baked hams, ziti and string bean salads, raspberry, lemon, fig, and chocolate mousse? Maybe pick up a copy of **The Store Cookbook** and do it themselves, but probably not with the spectacular results of this dependable shop.

The Seafood Shoppe (537–0633), Montauk Highway, Wainscott. In the short time it's been around the Seafood Shoppe has acquired an enviable reputation for fine seafood catering. We recommend the poached salmon and crabmeat quiche especially.

Children's Camps

If your kids are happiest within an organized framework of games and activities, consider sending them to camp. The East End has several, both residential and day.

Pathfinder Country Day Camp (668–2080), Second House Road, Montauk, takes 100 boys and girls, aged four to twelve. Eight-week summer session, but arrangements may be made for shorter periods. Transportation to and from camp by school bus. Noncompetitive. Red Cross swimming instruction. A warm, happy atmosphere with concerned supervision. Owners, Dr. and Mrs. Leon Lefkowitz. Winter phone: 333–7907.

East Hampton Boy's Club (324–2452), run by East Hampton High School swimming coach Francis Kiernan, is a comparatively inexpensive half-day program for boys aged six to thirteen. Transportation provided within limited area. Highly competitive; organized team games. Swimming in Coach Kiernan's pool and at nearby bay beaches. This camp is popular with sons of year-round and summer residents alike. Enrollment is usually closed by May.

Meadow Way Girls' Club (324–2677) is run by Robert Budd, assistant football coach at the high school, and Frederic Yardley, a teacher at the Springs School. Half-days with transportation to and from Legion Hall in Amagansett, opposite Brent's Store on the Montauk Highway. Swimming at local beaches and private pools. Noncompetitive, relaxed atmosphere for girls aged six to thirteen.

Blue Bay (324–9862), at Maidstone Park, East Hampton, may be just the ticket if you have a daughter who's a girl scout. Residential; two-week sessions. Write to: Great South Bay Girl Scout Council, Lindenhurst, N.Y. 11757, for information.

Southampton College has in the past run a half-day summer program for boys and girls aged six to eleven, with emphasis on trips to local places of interest. Some use is made of college facilities. Call 283–4000 for information after June 15.

Camp St. Regis (212–863–2630) is a co-ed residential camp for children aged five to sixteen. Located on Shelter Island Sound, this long-established camp offers all sports including riding, with an emphasis on waterfront activities.

Another well-regarded day camp which has been in operation for a few years is the one run by Suzy Prudden at the **Bridgehampton Racquet and Surf Club.** The camp is open to children of nonmembers and makes use of all the club's facilities. For information, call 537–1180.

There are usually at least half a dozen more day camps for very young children run by local residents and/or college students on a part-time basis in the summer. These change from year to year. Consult the classified pages of the East Hampton **Star** for details.

Churches and Synagogues

All of these churches are open year-round, except in one or two cases as noted. Call for times of services.

BAPTIST

Calvary Baptist Church (324–5313), Springs Road, East Hampton.

Cooper Memorial Baptist Church (537–1087), Sag Harbor Turnpike, Bridgehampton.

Living Gospel Church (324–0295), Cedar Street, East Hampton.

CATHOLIC (Roman)

Most Holy Trinity R.C. Church (324–0134), 57 Buell Lane, East Hampton.

Queen of the Most Holy Rosary (537–0156), Montauk Highway, Bridgehampton.

St. Andrew's R.C. Church (725–0123), Division Street, Sag Harbor.

St. Therese of Lisieux (Little Flower Church) (668–2200), Montauk Highway, Montauk.

CHRISTIAN SCIENCE

First Church of Christ, Scientist (283–5772), Pine and Cameron streets, Southampton.

COMMUNITY

Community Bible Church (725–2342), Noyac Road, Sag Harbor.

Montauk Community Church (668–9786; 668–2022), Montauk Highway.

EPISCOPAL

St. Luke's Church (324–0048), 18 James Lane, East Hampton.

St. Peter's Chapel (324–0048), Old Stone Highway, the Springs.

St. Thomas' Church (267–3080), Montauk Highway, Amagansett. Summers only.

FUNDAMENTALIST

Hamptons Alliance Church (726–4889), Montauk Highway, Water Mill.

JEWISH

Jewish Center of the Hamptons (324–9858; 324–0526), 44 Woods Lane, East Hampton.

Temple Adas Israel (725–0054), Elizabeth and Atlantic streets, Sag Harbor.

LUTHERAN

Incarnation Lutheran Church (537–1187), Hayground Road, Bridgehampton.

St. Michael's Church (267–6351), Montauk Highway, Amagansett.

METHODIST

Methodist Church of Sag Harbor (725–2310), Madison Street.

United Methodist Church of East Hampton (324–0794; 324–4258), 26 Pantigo Road.

PRESBYTERIAN

Amagansett First (267–3454; 267–6404), Main Street.

East Hampton First (324–0711), Main Street.

Sag Harbor First (Old Whaler's Church), (725–0894) Union Street.

Springs Community (324–4791; 267–6404), Fireplace Road, the Springs.

UNITARIAN UNIVERSALIST

East End Unitarian Universalist Fellowship (283-6799), Bridgehampton Community Center.

Fishing(see also "Marinas")

FISHING STATIONS

These are located directly on the water and can supply most of the basic equipment you will need. For complete tackle, repairs, etc., see "Fishing Supplies."

Bayview (725-0740), Bay Street, Sag Harbor. Bait, tackle. Dories for rent.

Merrill's Irish Mist (267-8186), Old Lazy Point Road, Amagansett. Rowboat rentals. Bait, tackle. Head. Restaurant. Beverages. Rooms for rent.

Overton's (324-9795), Northwest Landing Road, East Hampton. Rowboat rentals. Bait, tackle.

Promised Land (267-8751), Old Lazy Point, Amagansett. Rowboat rentals. Bait, tackle for sale or rent.

Remkus Marine (725-9224), Old Ridge Road, Sag Harbor. Boat rentals.

Three Mile Harbor (324-1977), Maidstone Park, East Hampton. Boat rentals; motors. Gas. Bait, tackle.

There are town-owned docks and launching ramps at the ends of East Lake and West Lake (Flamingo Road extension) drives in Montauk, and a county-owned dock and ramp at the end of Alewive Brook Road in Cedar Point Park, East Hampton. Fishing is also good at Louse Point and Gerard Park in the Springs (see "Beaches"). Town beach permits are needed in summer for parking at most launching ramps.

Both Big Reed Pond and Fort Pond, Montauk, are popular spots for fresh-water fishing. Panfish, bass, and pickerel abound. A license is required for fresh-water fishing; it may be obtained at the Town Clerk's office (324-

4143) in Town Hall, or at Tony's Sport Shop, Newtown Lane, East Hampton (324-0969).

Shellfish licenses covering the taking of clams, crabs, mussels, oysters (if you can find them), and scallops are also available from the Town Clerk.

FISHING SUPPLIES

Captain Teddy's Tackle Shop (668-2462), West Lake Drive, Montauk. Handmade diamond jigs. Rod repairs.

Freddie's Bait & Tackle (668-5520), Main Street, Montauk.

Johnny's Tackle Shop (668-2940), Main Street, Montauk.

Tony's Sport Shop (324-0969), Newtown Lane, East Hampton. Complete tackle. Fresh-water fishing licenses.

BAIT

Babin's (668-2107), West Lake Drive, Montauk.

Stuart's (267-3563), Oak Lane, Amagansett.

In addition to these two, most fish markets will be glad to sell bait at a nominal cost. (Fish heads, by the way, have a deadly attraction for the delicious blue claw crabs found in fresh water in late summer and fall.)

Food

One of the principal benefits of vacationing or living on Long Island is the incredibly good quality of fresh fish, poultry, and produce near at hand. It is not merely fortuitous that cooking professionals like Craig Claiborne and Pierre Franey have settled here.

In certain fields in Water Mill and Wainscott you can pick your own fragrant ripe strawberries. Look for directions along the Montauk Highway in late June and early July. Tender delicate snow peas make their appearance around this time at our favorite farm stand, the Green Thumb in Water Mill, and a wonderful variety of beans: sweet purple beans, green beans, yellow wax beans, fat lima beans. Later on at the Green Thumb theres okra for southerners and other gumbo fanciers, and several varieties of succulent worm-free corn. Best of all, we think, is Silver Queen.

Throughout the season all the local farm stands are laden with that supermarket rarity, the vine-ripened tomato. There are zucchini and other summer squashes to combine with the tomatoes in vegetable casseroles. In the fall cabbage, broccoli, Brussels sprouts, and the root vegetables—turnips, parsnips, celeriac, rutabagas and potatoes—appear. Taking a vegetarian vow under these circumstances would not be difficult.

However, you don't have to stop with vegetables, for there are always hard and soft shell clams. These you can dig for yourself, if you are so inclined and have a town permit, or you can fish for your dinner (see page 205). Most people will probably prefer to buy their lobster, flounder, bluefish, and striped bass from a local fishmonger.

Local clamdiggers will often pile their surplus wares into the back of a pickup truck and park along the Montauk Highway to sell them, usually at prices lower than in the fish stores. Potato farmers do this too, and so do cauliflower, corn, tomato, squash, and muskmelon growers. Farmers normally park right in front of their fields, and if you don't like what you see on the truck they'll go out and pick some more, or let you do it yourself if you prefer.

At Iacono's Farm north of the East Hampton High School on Long Lane you can also find fresh chickens that have been raised organically—pecking on the ground instead of growing fat in cages—and country eggs still warm from the nest. Suffolk County is home of the Long Island duckling, the Pekin duck that is featured on restaurant menus across the country. At Iacono's you can also find Muscovy duck, capon, and goose.

Following is a list of our favorite places to buy fresh food:

WATER MILL

The Green Thumb, half a mile east of the village on Montauk Highway. Outstanding for its several varieties of delicate salad greens and its many kinds of fresh vegetables not ordinarily obtainable in a supermarket or grocery store.

The Milk Pail, Montauk Highway between Water Mill and Bridgehampton. In the summer fresh locally grown peaches are the specialty of this popular stand. In the fall and winter there are local apples and apples from the Hudson River Valley and Vermont—apples like McCouns and Northern Spys that are hard to find elsewhere. Vermont cheese, maple syrup, and the smell of raw pine enhance the Milk Pail's image as a bit of New England in the Hamptons. The cider is excellent, and so are the homemade cider donuts.

BRIDGEHAMPTON

A good place to buy fresh eggs is at **Hendrickson's** farm just north of the railroad tracks on Lumber Lane. It is simply marked "Eggs," and you leave your money on the farmer's back porch if he doesn't happen to be around. Good eggs from up-island bearing the label of Broad Hollow Farms are sold at some supermarkets and grocery stores.

WAINSCOTT

Seafood Shoppe (537–0633), Montauk Highway. This outlet is open only during the summer. In the winter its pleasant, helpful proprietors are busy teaching school. Fresh local fish as well as some cooked seafood and seafood salad.

EAST HAMPTON

Iacono Farm (324–1107), Long Lane. East Hampton used to have a number of poultry farmers. Refrigerated trucking and mass poultry breeding killed off the bulk of this thriving enterprise and at the moment Sal Iacono is something of a one-man institution. His product, the natural chicken, is almost as different from the store-bought variety as the vine-ripened tomato is from its cellophane-wrapped cousin. Iacono's also carries fresh eggs.

Taber Lobster & Fish Co. (324–5410), 104 N. Main Street. Taber's has fresh oysters, which aren't so easy to find, and succulent smoked eels along with the fresh local fish. Their prices are often a little lower than elsewhere.

AMAGANSETT

Farmer's Market (267–3894), Main Street, east of the village. Pat Struk, with the enthusiastic help of her own and other people's teenagers, grows vegetables and flowers in the fields behind the stand and also imports some fancy fruits at fancy prices. Stick to the local produce, breads, and pies, and homemade peanut butter, and look for the housewares from the Promised Land Supply Company.

Fishermen's Cooperative, Cross Highway off Montauk Highway, near Brent's Store. A group of commercial fishermen have gotten together to form a coop, and this is their retail outlet. A new venture which deserves encouragement.

Stuart's Seafood (267–3563), Oak Lane opposite the Texaco station on Montauk Highway. Craig Claiborne has told the world that he buys his fish here, and so do a whole lot of other good cooks. If you want them to open three dozen clams or save a five-pound lobster for you, call the day before.

THE SPRINGS (Three Mile Harbor)

Howard Seafood Company (324–0662), Three Mile Harbor Road near Maidstone Park (follow signs). Lee Dion specializes in lobsters, big and small. Springs residents who've found their way to Howard's buy fresh fish here too. Unfortunately, it's a long way from any place else.

MONTAUK

Gosman's (668–2447), Gosman's Dock, end of West Lake Drive. The larger the

lobster the lower the price per pound at this well-regarded market right on the water. Gosman's has lobsters when nobody else does, and why not? They're practically selling them right off the boat. There are several smaller fish and lobster markets near Gosman's Dock. Walk around and compare.

OTHER DELICACIES

While the area is deficient in the smorgasbord of good things found in New York City's delicatessens and foreign food markets, it does possess Crutchley's donuts.

Crutchley's (AT 3–0058), Hampton Street (Route 27 A), Southampton, used to turn out both donuts and "hearts"— the round centers that are left after the donuts are cut. Now, for some reason, it produces hearts exclusively. They are very good. You can also buy them in Southampton at **Herbert's** on Main Street or, in Bridgehampton, at **Muller's.**

Cheese Shed (537–1019), Main Street, Bridgehampton. This shop carries a good selection of the more usual varieties of imported and domestic cheeses.

Cheese Cupboard (324–2688), 23 Newtown Lane, East Hampton, behind the police station. Besides the cheese there are fancy jams, soups, accessories such as cutting boards which make nice gifts, and a pretty good cheesecake.

Garbage Disposal

East Hampton does not have a public garbage pickup service, but it does have two free dumps, one on Springs-Fireplace Road, East Hampton, and the other near Montauk, off the Montauk Highway about two miles west of the village. (Follow signs for "sanitary landfill.") There used to be a third on Bull Path, East Hampton, but it was closed in 1975. The East Hampton dump can also be entered from Accabonac Road.

No permit is needed to use these facilities, just a little muscle and a talent for holding your breath. The dumps are open daily except Sunday, 8:00 A.M. to 4:00 P.M.

There are several reliable private services in town which will make collections three times a week. Consult the classified pages of the Suffolk directory or the business classifieds in the East Hampton **Star**, and call to compare rates.

Gardening

East Hampton's generally excellent soil, good moisture, and moderate climate make it a hospitable spot for gardeners. The town, in fact, boasts several showcase gardens which are periodically featured in various magazines.

If you live in the dunes your gardening opportunities are more limited than if you are situated on the Bridgehampton loam, but there are plants which do beautifully in a seaside location. **The Salty Thumb**, published by the Montauk Village Association and available at Keene's in Southampton and Whimsey's in East Hampton, will help if you are a dune gardener.

The following garden centers all carry complete basic supplies. Unless you're looking for something special, go to the one nearest you.

WATER MILL

Warren's Garden Center (726–4767), a quarter of a mile east of the village on Montauk Highway. Friendly service and a fine selection of trees, bushes, shrubs, herbs.

BRIDGEHAMPTON

Agway (537–0007), the farmers' cooperative on Railroad Avenue (follow Corwith Avenue and turn right after the railroad underpass), is headquarters for commercial growers and home gardeners alike. Tools, fertilizer (both organic and chemical), lawn mowers, bulbs, seeds—it's all here and reasonably priced. Open daily year-round to 5:00 P.M. Open Saturdays to 3:00 P.M. in season; to noon in winter.

Bridgehampton Garden Center (537–0888), Montauk Highway just east of the traffic light. Enthusiastic and well-run new center. They have some small supplies, like waterproof marking sticks, that are hard to find elsewhere.

EAST HAMPTON

Buckley's (324–0966), Montauk Highway west of the village. A family-run nursery with helpful advice on care and maintenance. A good place to buy tomato plants and annuals.

Vetault's Flowers (324–2323), 89 Newtown Lane. Specialists in hanging baskets, cachepots, and elaborate holiday arrangements. These nice people are really florists rather than nurserymen.

AMAGANSETT

Bayberry House and Garden Center (267–3000), Montauk Highway west of the village. Many handsome planters to choose from and a fine selection of herbs.

Hren's (324–0640), Montauk Highway between East Hampton and Amagansett. Many of their shrubs and trees are home-grown, so you know they are varieties that will thrive in East End soil. A stroll through Hren's extensive nurseries, behind the garden center, makes a pleasant morning's occupation.

McConnell's Nursery (324–1055), Montauk Highway between East Hampton and Amagansett. Pleasant, friendly advice on which perennials, shrubs, rock garden plants, and ground covers will be best for your soil.

LAWN AND TREE MAINTENANCE

Tree pruning, root feeding, and spraying for insects (in recent years the gypsy moth has been the number one leaf predator) usually require the services of a specialist. As for spraying, do it only if you must and be sure one of the "environmentally safe" compounds is used. Before engaging any contractor for this type of work, obtain a written estimate.

For tree work we recommend:

Bartlett Tree Service (283–0028), North Sea Road, Southampton.

Davey Tree Experts (727–4278), 40 W. Main, Riverhead.

Ed Durka Tree and Landscape, Inc. (324–1110), 525 Springs-Fireplace Road, East Hampton.

Whitmore-Worsley (267–3756), Montauk Highway, Amagansett.

Golf Courses

Most of the golf on the East End is played on private courses such as those at the Bridgehampton, Sag Harbor Golf, and Maidstone clubs, but there are a few places open to the public.

The **Poxabogue Golf Club** (537–9862) on the Montauk Highway east of Bridgehampton has a nine-hole course and driving range.

The **South Fork Country Club** (267–3575) on Springs Road in Amagansett is semiprivate but will allow visitors to use its course if no tournaments are scheduled. Nine-hole course.

In Montauk, the **Golf and Racquet Club** (668–5000) has an award-winning 18-hole course laid out by Robert Trent Jones. It is open to guests of selected member motels (ask the manager if yours is one) and extends reciprocal playing privileges to members of some other private clubs.

Call for greens fees and schedules.

Government

All meetings of local government bodies are open to the public and advance notice of their agenda is published in the **Star**, the town's official newspaper. Residents and taxpayers are encouraged to attend these meetings, especially the twice monthly sessions of the East Hampton and Southampton town boards, where a delegation of a dozen concerned citizens can be enough to sway official opinion for or against a proposed new marina or housing development.

Regular meetings are held on schedule.

FIRST WEEK OF THE MONTH:

Tuesday: Southampton Town Board, Town Hall, 11:00 A.M. Sag Harbor Village Board, Municipal Building, 8:00 P.M.

Thursday: East Hampton Village Planning Board, Village Hall, 8:15 P.M.

Friday: East Hampton Town Board, Town Hall, 10:00 A.M.

SECOND WEEK OF THE MONTH:

Monday: Amagansett School Board, at the school, 8:00 P.M. Bridgehampton School Board, at the school, 8:00 P.M.

Tuesday: East Hampton Town Trustees, Town Hall, 8:00 P.M. East Hampton School Board, Middle School, 8:00 P.M.

Wednesday: East Hampton Town Planning Board, Town Hall, 8:00 P.M.

THIRD WEEK OF THE MONTH:

Monday: Sag Harbor School Board, Elementary School, 8:00 P.M. Springs School Board, at the school, 7:30 P.M.

Tuesday: Southampton Town Board, Town Hall, 7:30 P.M.

Friday: East Hampton Town Board, Town Hall, 10:00 A.M. East Hampton Village Board, Village Hall or Annex, 7:00 P.M.

Saturday: Concerned Citizens of Montauk, Montauk Fire House, 8:00 P.M.

FOURTH WEEK OF THE MONTH:

Wednesday: Sag Harbor Planning Board, American Legion Building, 7:30 P.M. East Hampton Town Planning Board, Town Hall, 8:00 P.M.

Thursday: Montauk School Board, at the school, 7:00 P.M. (in a month of five Thursdays, held on the fifth one.)

In addition, the East Hampton Town Board often meets in open executive session at 3:00 P.M. on the Wednesday preceding a Friday meeting. Call Town Hall for confirmation.

Watch the **Star** for monthly meetings of the Springs Improvement Society and the Amagansett Residents Association. In recent years these groups, together with the Concerned Citizens of Montauk and the Bridgehampton-based Group for America's South Fork, have spearheaded the acquisition of parkland, upzoning for residential and recreational use, and the preservation of wetlands. They actively seek new members.

Hairdressers

Warren Hairdresser (324-0083), 100 Newtown Lane, East Hampton. For women accustomed to simple New York City hair styling, Mr. Warren's, whose winter headquarters is the Regency Hotel in Manhattan, is the place to go.

Elizabeth Arden (283-0871), Main Street, Southampton. For those who desire the security of this famous "brand name," the competently-staffed Southampton salon is recommended.

Laundries and Cleaners

In all of East Hampton there is exactly one self-service laundromat: the **East Hampton Launderette** (324-9899), on the Montauk Highway about two miles east of the village. You shouldn't have any trouble finding it; just look for the line of cars parked on the shoulder (and watch out for parking tickets).

If you are renting a house for the season, be sure to ask if it has a washing machine. If not, prepare to spend a lot of time on line at the laundromat, or to pay a premium to have them do the laundry for you.

For the more affluent there's the **East Hampton Laundry** (324-0501), which will pick up and deliver. It does an adequate job on sheets and shirts, and is dependable. In Sag Harbor try the equally good **Sag Harbor Launderet** (725-9765). In season, both of these will need at least a week to do the job.

There are several dry cleaning establishments in the area. We recommend **East Hampton Cleaners** (324-0036) and **Star Cleaners** (324-0032) in East Hampton, and **Whalers Cleaners** (725-0342) in Sag Harbor.

Libraries

EAST HAMPTON

East Hampton Free Library (324-0222), Main Street opposite the pond.

Summer hours (June 15-September 15): Daily except Sunday, 10–5. Tuesday and Thursday, 10–9 P.M. Children's room open daily except Sunday, 10–5.

Winter hours (September 16-June 14): Monday, Wednesday, Friday, Saturday, 11–5. Tuesday and Thursday, 1–9 P.M. Children's room open 1–5 daily except Wednesday.

The East Hampton Free Library is a major town resource for education and entertainment. The Long Island Collection is, together with the library of the Long Island Historical Society in Brooklyn, the most extensive archive of local and Long Island history in existence. The new Jeannette Edwards Rattray wing, named for the late marine historian, author, and publisher of the East Hampton **Star**, will serve among other uses to house documents from the collection.

The library has a large, cheerful children's room, where storytelling sessions and short films are presented throughout the year. Check with the librarian for dates and times.

Borrowing privileges are free to residents and renters within the boundaries of East Hampton Village, and to residents of East Hampton Town. Annual or summer memberships are available to others at a fee.

AMAGANSETT

Amagansett Free Library (267-3810), Main Street.

Year-round hours: Monday and Friday, 1–5. Tuesday and Thursday, 1–5 and 7–9 P.M. Saturday, 10–12 and 1–5. Closed Wednesday.

The excellence of this small library is due in no small measure to the helpful presence of Carleton Kelsey, its librarian and a knowledgeable antiquarian.

SAG HARBOR

John Jermain Library (725-0049), Main Street, Sag Harbor.

Year-round hours: Monday through Friday, noon–5; Saturday, 9:30–12:30.

BRIDGEHAMPTON

Hampton Library (537-0015), Main Street, Bridgehampton.

Summer hours: Monday through Saturday, 10–12; 1–5.

Winter hours: Monday through Friday, 1–5; Saturday, 10–12 and 1–5.

This is quite a good library for its size. It has a modest collection of local history and a fine selection of fiction for adults and children.

Marinas

These are all public marinas, many with space for transient dockage. Boat owners, remember that it's strictly illegal to dump "oil, refuse, garbage or waste," or to discharge toilets, into the water.

EAST HAMPTON

East Hampton Marina (324-4042), off Three Mile Harbor Road, Springs. 65 dockside slips. Ramp. Wet/dry storage. Gas. New, used boats for sale. Repairs. Head.

Gardiners Marina (324-9894). Three Mile Harbor Road. 35 dockside slips. Transients. Water, gas, diesel. Head, showers.

Halsey's Marina (324-9847), Three Mile Harbor Road. 40 dockside slips. Transients. Water, gas, diesel. Head, showers. Ice, beverages, restaurant.

Harbor Marina (324-9869), Three Mile Harbor Road. 70 dockside slips. Wet storage. Boat rentals and sales. Head. Beverages, ice. Engine/hull repairs.

Harbor Marina of East Hampton (324-5666), Three Mile Harbor Road.

Maidstone Boat Yard (324-4830), Three Mile Harbor Road. Dockside moorings 12. Travelift 15 tons; hoist for large boats. In-out storage. Sales. Gas, diesel, bottled gas. Engine/hull repairs; hardware. Head. Ice, beverages, ships' store.

Maidstone Marina (324-1650), Three Mile Harbor Road. Dockage by day, week, month, season. 125 deep water slips (to 5½' draft). Wet storage. Head, showers. Groceries, laundry, car rentals arranged. Restaurant and cocktail lounge. Swimming pool. Mail port.

Shagwong Marina (324-9882), Three Mile Harbor Road. 40 dockside slips. Gas. Head, showers. Ice, beverages. Laundry and cottages.

Three Mile Harbor Boat Yard (324-1320). 54 dockside slips; RR 2, 20–40 tons. Ramp. Wet/dry storage. Gas, propane. Boat sales; outboards. Engine/hull repairs, hardware. Ice.

Three Mile Marina (324-5500), off Three Mile Harbor Road, Springs.

MONTAUK

Anchor Marina (668-9809), West Lake Drive.

Bridgeford Marina (668-2273), East Lake Drive. Boat sales, rentals, repairs. Cottages.

Captain's Marina (668-5705), East Lake Drive. Inn, cocktail lounge, restaurant.

Cove Marina (668-5995), West Lake Drive. Charter boat **Montauk** based here, for all fishing, especially sharks.

Deep Sea Marina (668–2166), Star Island Road. Transient slips dockside. Gas, diesel. Restaurant, cocktails.

Duryea's Dock (668–2822), West Lake Drive. Gas, diesel. Bait, tackle. Charter boats: 4 D's, Frances Anne II, Leatherneck, others, for inshore, offshore, big-game fishing. Ice, beverages, groceries.

Gone Fishing Marina (668–3252), East Lake Drive.

Gosman's Dock (668–9837), end of West Lake Drive. Seafood restaurant, clam bar, shopping plaza (see "Restaurants").

Inlet Marina (668–2569), East Lake Drive.

Joe's Dock (668–9869), Flamingo Road. Transient space dockside. Gas, diesel. Fishing station. Head. Restaurant. Ice, beverages, groceries.

Keeler's Anchor Marina (668–9809), West Lake Drive.

Lake Montauk Marina (668–2111). East Lake Drive. 15 dockside slips. Seasonal, transients. Fishing station. Beverages.

Montauk Marine Basin (668–5900). West Lake Drive. 180 dockside slips; transient, seasonal. Travelift 20 tons; travelift 50 tons. Wet/dry storage. Gas, diesel, propane. Tackle, bait. Charter boats: Blue Water, Fortenate, Seacon III, others, for inshore-offshore fishing; trolling. Boat sales, rentals. Engine, hull repairs. Head, showers. Ice, beverages, groceries, snack bar.

Montauk Sportsman's Dock (668–2824), West Lake Drive.

Salivar's Dock (668–2555), West Lake Drive. Charter boats: Blue Fin, Hel-Cat, Helen II, Marlin III, Jigger III, for inshore-offshore sport fishing, fluke. Head. Bar, restaurant.

Sea & Sky Portel (668–2151), East Lake Drive. 23 dockside slips. Transients. Water, gas, electricity A and C. Head, showers. Ice, beverages. Laundry. Restaurant-cocktail lounge. Motel and cottages. Airport. Sailboat rentals.

Shay's Dock (668–5520), East Lake Drive. 30 dockside slips. Gas. Fishing station; bait, tackle, skiffs. Head. Ice, beverages, groceries. Charter boats: Flying Cloud, Little Bear, Viking Skipper, for bottom fishing; fluke, sea bass; Block Island for cod.

Star Island Yacht Club and Marina (668–5052), Star Island Road.

Tuma's Dock (668–2490), West Lake Drive. Three open fishing boats; 10 charter boats, including Gannett III, Jean III, North Star, Sportfisher, for big bass; inshore-offshore, sport fishing. Split charters arranged. Head. Ice, beverages. Electricity A. Sport and foul weather gear. Fish mounting. Fishermen's general store.

Uihlein's Dock (668–2545), Wells Avenue. Private dock. Boat rentals. Oil, gas. Fishing station.

Viking Dock (668–9896), West Lake Drive. Transient space dockside. Four open fishing boats, 10 charter boats, including Viking Star, Viking Starlight, Capt. Spider, Triton II, Easy Rider, for local fishing off Cox's Ledge; fluke, bottom fishing, and trolling; tuna, sharks, bass, blues. Head. Restaurant. Beverages, groceries.

NOTE: In season, the Rockaway Coach Corp. runs buses direct from New York City and Nassau County to the Montauk docks. For reservations call (212) 835–0616, after 6:00 P.M.

SAG HARBOR

Baron's Cove Marina (725–2100), West Water Street. 150 dockside slips. Outside storage. Gas, diesel. Sail and power boat rentals.

Mill Creek Marina (725–1351), Noyac Road. Dockage, storage. Repairs. Cabins.

Peerless Marine Center (725–0400), Bay Street.

Redwood Boat Basin (725–0138), Redwood Road.

Remkus Marine (725–9724), Old Bridge Road. Dockside space; ramp;

small boats. Gas. Sales new-used boats; inboard and outboard. Head. Ice, beverages. Restaurant. Rowboat rentals. Fishing station.

Ship Ashore Marina (725–3755), Redwood Road.

Whaler's Cove (725–9767; 725–1605), West Water Street. 80 dockside slips. Gas. Floating docks. Repairs.

Medical Services

Ambulance: 324–0024 (East Hampton)
            725–0058 (Sag Harbor)
            537–0004 (Southampton)
Southampton Hospital 283–2600
East Hampton Medical Group 324–1300
Montauk Medical Group 668–3200
Poison Information 542–2323

Ambulances Should an emergency requiring an ambulance arise, call the East Hampton Town Police (324–0024). West of Wainscott, call the Southampton Town Police (537–0004). An ambulance will be dispatched immediately from the jurisdiction nearest you.

Volunteer firemen man most ambulances. The fire departments of Montauk, Amagansett, East Hampton, Sag Harbor, Bridgehampton and Southampton all have well-equipped ambulance companies with trained drivers and attendants. The South Fork Volunteer Ambulance Association, in cooperation with Southampton Hospital, gives regular brush-up courses in emergency medical procedures to its more than fifty members.

Southampton Hospital (283–2600), on Herrick and Old Town Roads (take Old Town at the traffic light on Hampton Road just west of the high school), is the major medical facility serving the South Fork of Long Island. It is a modern, cheerful institution with skilled operating room personnel and a well-staffed, round-the-clock emergency service. It cares for an average of 125 patients a day (excluding newborn), and is expanding its acute care bed comple-

ment to 207, in part to offset crowded conditions during the resort season. Thirty-one member dental staff.

If you suffer an accident or injury severe enough to warrant hospitalization, a police or fire department ambulance will speed you to Southampton. If you sustain minor bruises from a fall off a bicycle, you will be taken instead to the **East Hampton Medical Group** (324–1300), on the Montauk Highway about a tenth of a mile east of the Egypt Lane traffic light, for prompt emergency treatment by one of a half-dozen attending physicians.

The Medical Group, with nurses on duty from 8:00 A.M. to midnight (answering service midnight to 8:00 A.M.), is equipped to treat a host of complaints ranging from stomach aches to fractures. X-ray service, blood tests, cardiograms, urinalysis, etc. Warning: if your ailment is not too serious, and especially if it strikes on a summer weekend, it may be a long time before you are seen. An hour's wait is not uncommon. Call in advance if possible.

The village of Montauk, thanks to determined efforts by local people, summer residents, and merchants, now has a medical service of its own. The **Montauk Medical Group** is housed at the west end of town in the brick building next to the diner. It is staffed on a part-time basis off-season. In summer months, a physician and/or surgeon is almost sure to be there daily; a podiatrist, once a week. Call ahead to be sure.

Other Medical Services Specialists and general practitioners alike are lumped together under "Physicians" in the yellow pages of the Suffolk telephone directory, which isn't much help. To secure the services of a dentist, psychiatrist, pediatrician, acupuncturist (yes), or any other medical specialist, call the East Hampton Medical Group for referral. Or ask your real estate agent, motel manager, or plumber.

Tick Fever A Word to the Wise: A persistent high-grade temperature accompanied by headache and rash on the palms of the hands or soles of the feet might turn out to be Rocky Mountain spotted fever. Suffolk County recorded some twenty cases of this generally rare disease in 1974. It is caused by the bite of an infected tick, and can be dangerous if not recognized and treated at an early stage.

Local physicians will usually spot "tick fever" symptoms easily enough, but doctors in other areas may not. Precautions: Keep children and pets away from tall grass and underbrush if possible, especially in late spring and early summer. Wear long pants in the woods. Check head and neck area at night for ticks, and use tweezers or cotton to remove them.

Very few ticks are carriers of Rocky Mountain spotted fever. Be careful, but don't be unduly alarmed about every tick you see.

Movie Theaters

Movies in the Hamptons are elusive. All too often a film which has been advertised in the papers and on the radio arrives a week or two later than promised. Sometimes it never arrives at all, or if it does, it leaves three days earlier than it was supposed to. The only way to be certain of what's playing where, and when, is to call the theater the day you go.

The East Hampton, Southampton, and Sag Harbor Cinemas show children's matinees at 2:00 P.M. on rainy-day weekends, and regular weekend matinees if the weather is fine. The Southampton theater sometimes shows "midnight specials" on Friday nights after a regular feature.

Here is the roster of local movie houses:

Montauk Manor Playhouse (668–5953), Edgemere Road. The audience sits in deck chairs set up in the former ballroom of the old Manor. The Playhouse opens around June 20 and closes the day after Labor Day.

East Hampton Cinema (324–0448), 30 Main Street. Open year-round.

Old Post Office Cinema (324–4820), Newtown Lane, East Hampton. Year-round.

Sag Harbor Theater (725–0010), Main Street. Year-round.

Hampton Drive-In (537–0770), Montauk Highway at Grant City shopping center, Bridgehampton. The Drive-In is open in season only, to around October 1. Movies begin at dusk, and in high summer they often last till past midnight.

Southampton Theatre (AT 3-1300), Hill Street. Year-round.

Museums

EAST HAMPTON

Guild Hall (324–0806), the large white building on Main Street opposite the East Hampton Library, is the community center and the focus of East Hampton's cultural activities. It contains the 444-seat air-conditioned John Drew Theater (box office: 324–4050); several galleries housing rotating art exhibitions; and a tranquil garden in back where sculpture is displayed. Galleries and garden are open daily 10–5 and Sunday afternoons, May through September. Closed Sunday and Monday off-season. No admission charge.

Guild Hall's summer theater season begins in late June and continues through August. A resident company (one year it was New York's Phoenix Theater; another, the Yale Repertory) performs Tuesday through Friday evenings at 8:40 P.M., Saturdays at 9. Matinees Thursday and Saturday at 2:40 P.M.

Sunday night "specials," benefits for Guild Hall, are one-shot galas which often star theatrical luminaries who make their summer homes in East Hampton. Call for tickets well in advance; these evenings are usually sell-outs.

More Guild Hall attractions: children's matinee theater; films, including the end-of-season Film Festival of the Hamptons; concert and dance programs;

crafts and photography exhibits; off-season classes in everything from pottery to bridge. Stop in for a free schedule of events.

On the opposite side of Main Street a few doors from the library is **Clinton Academy,** the first chartered Academy in New York State (see page 44), now a museum of local artifacts, old silver coins, antique dolls and clothes. Open from around June 20 to September 10, 1:30–5. Adults 50¢, children 25¢.

The Clinton Academy admission fee will also gain the visitor entry to the **Old Town House** just next door. It dates from 1731 and was the village school-house until 1895. Some original desks and the schoolroom stove remain.

In good weather the American flag waves proudly from **"Home Sweet Home"** (324–0713), a short walk east of Guild Hall on James Lane. This ancient cedar-shingled building is said to have been the inspiration for composer John Howard Payne's song (see page 131).

"Home Sweet Home" is furnished with period antiques. Open year-round, 10–12:30; 1:30–5, Sundays 2–5. Closed Tuesdays off-season. Admission $1, children 50¢. Maintained by the village of East Hampton.

Next door can be seen the sloping roof of the **Old Mulford Farmhouse,** built in 1680 and furnished appropriately. The broad lawn of this landmark is the site of the annual East Hampton Ladies Village Improvement Society fair (see "Special Events"). The farmhouse is open 1:30–5, in season only. Admission 50¢, children 25¢. The East Hampton Historical Society maintains the Mulford house as well as Clinton Academy and the Old Town House.

Hook Mill, symbol of the village, stands on the green at the head of Main Street. It was a working mill, grinding wheat flour and cornmeal, until East Hampton's last miller, Maurice Lester, died in 1955. Lester was the successor to Charles Dominy, whose great-grandfather built the mill in 1806. The mill is open daily in season, 10–5; Sundays

2–5. Admission 25¢. New sails were fitted in 1974; you may see them turn if you're lucky.

The East Hampton **Town Marine Museum,** on Bluff Road just west of Atlantic Avenue, Amagansett, contains, among other mementos of this old sea-faring community, full-scale murals of whaling life, photographs, scrimshaw, and the very boat from which Cap'n "Josh" Edwards and his crew took Amagansett's last right whale in 1909. Operated by the East Hampton Historical Society. Open daily, late June to September, 1:30–5. Admission 50¢, children 25¢.

Miss Amelia's Cottage (267–3020), at the entrance to Amagansett on Montauk Highway, is a 240-year-old Cape Cod house now maintained as a museum by the Amagansett Historical Association. Its broad back lawn facing Windmill Lane is the site of summer musicales and concerts sponsored by the Association. Open in season only. Adults $1, children 25¢.

THE SPRINGS

Ashawagh Hall (324–9802), in the center of the Springs, is really a meeting house and community center, but it does double duty as a museum during the first two weeks of August, when the annual "Artists of the Springs" invitational show and sale takes place. If you're in town then, don't miss it, or the Fisherman's Fair on Ashawagh Green, a gourmet's delight and bargain hunter's playground (see "Special Events").

MONTAUK

Second House Museum (668–2759) stands high on a bluff at the entrance to Montauk, just before the Old Montauk Highway joins the new bypass into the village. It was the second house you reached on Montauk and is the oldest still standing. Once the home of herdsmen when Montauk served as a giant pasture for the town's livestock, it is now maintained by the Montauk Historical Society and houses a collection of

Indian artifacts, local relics, and furniture of the Victorian period.

Military historians of all ages will like the "Rough Rider" room, with photographs of Colonel Teddy Roosevelt and his troops taken when they were stationed in the area after the Spanish-American War. Second House is open daily except Tuesdays in season, 11–5; Sundays 1–5, and on weekends in June and September. Adults 50¢, children 25¢.

Sampson Occum Day, honoring a Mohegan Indian who was a missionary to the Montauks and was instrumental in the founding of Dartmouth College (see page 29), is held in mid-June at Second House, with appropriate Indian ritual dancing and storytelling under the supervision of Chief Red Thunder Cloud of East Hampton. The Chief, who is a Catawba, with his wife, Princess Pretty Pony, a member of the Blackfeet tribe, operates the **Montauk Indian Museum** on East Main Street at the Atlantic Shopping Center. A full-scale model of a Montauk wigwam is among the attractions there. Arrangements may be made here for guided tours to historical Indian locations in the area. Open Memorial Day to Labor Day, 10:00 A.M.–evening. Free.

The grounds of the **Montauk Lighthouse** (668–2544) in Montauk State Park are open on summer weekends from 12:30–3:30 P.M. (parking facilities, refreshment stand). The lighthouse itself is not open to the public, though special arrangements for groups to visit it may occasionally be made through the Coast Guard. Written permission is needed. Write: Group Commander, Shinnecock C.G. Station, Hampton Bays, N.Y., 11946.

There are 136 spiral steps to the top of the lighthouse.

SAG HARBOR

The **Customs House** (941–9444), at Garden Street near Main in Sag Harbor, dates from about 1770 (see page 113). It originally contained the village post office, the customs office, and was the home of the Henry P. Dering family. It is furnished with many of the family's belongings, and is maintained by the Society for the Preservation of Long Island Antiquities. Open June 15 through September, Monday, Wednesday, Friday, Saturday 10–5; Sunday 1–5. Admission 50¢; children 7 to 14, 25¢, under 6, free.

The **Suffolk County Whaling Museum** (725–0700), in Sag Harbor at the corner of Garden and Main streets, is an imposing Greek revival edifice dating from the mid-nineteenth century (see page 112). Whaling equipment, scrimshaw, logbooks, ship models. Open daily 10–5, Sundays 2–5, from May 15 to September 30. Adults 50¢, children 6–16, 25¢. Under 6, free.

BRIDGEHAMPTON

The **Bridgehampton Historical Society Museum** (537–1088), at the corner of Main Street and Corwith Road, is a well-preserved eighteenth-century house containing colonial and Victorian period furniture. Open in summer only, from 1:30–5 on Monday, Wednesday, and weekends. Adults 50¢, children 25¢.

Sayrelands (941–9444), on Route 27 east of Bridgehampton, is a center-hall colonial home built in 1734 of Long Island white oak. Fine furniture, including some Duncan Phyfe pieces. Original hand-decorated walls. Open in season only; call for hours.

SOUTHAMPTON

Southampton has the **Parrish Art Museum** (283–2118), located at 25 Job's Lane. The Parrish is one of the nation's most respected smaller museums. Its permanent collection, ranging from ancient Chinese tomb figures to abstract expressionist art, includes some fine examples of works by nineteenth-century American painters; among them are paintings by Innes, Blakelock, Homer, Childe Hassam, and an extensive collection by William Merritt Chase, who, like Hassam, was a local resident.

The Parrish was founded to be

"chiefly educational," and its main emphasis is upon rotating exhibitions of high quality. A typical summer schedule might include a major retrospective; a group show of well-known artists of the region, and a mixed media competition open to all. In addition the museum sponsors concerts, films, workshops, and lectures throughout the year.

The Parrish is open year-round from 10–5 daily except Mondays and legal holidays; from 2–5 on Sundays. Its delightfully landscaped grounds contain some unusual specimen trees and are an oasis after a morning's shopping in Southampton—but please, no picnics here.

Nature Walks and Camping

SANCTUARIES

The federal government, the state, and the county all preserve large areas of woods and wetlands in Suffolk as nature sanctuaries, where birders may spot unfamiliar shore birds and migratory geese, where wild flowers grow abundantly and fish spawn, and where a visitor bent upon a day's hike or an hour's stroll may be alone with his camera and his thoughts.

In addition, the privately sponsored Nature Conservancy, through its South Fork-Shelter Island chapter, maintains several hundred acres in the area, ranging in size from isolated pockets of dune land to the sixty-seven-acre Kaplan Meadow and Merrill Lake Sanctuary on Accabonac Harbor, East Hampton. Permission to enter should be obtained well in advance.

Here's a list of major sanctuaries and parks. At the parks, boating, camping, swimming, etc., are permitted; details will be found under "Camping." The crowded parks will probably not be as agreeable to dedicated nature-lovers as the quiet sanctuaries.

Morton Wildlife Refuge Southampton (725–2270): From County Road 39 (the Southampton bypass) take North Sea Road to Noyac Road and follow signs. The sanctuary, at Jessups Neck in Little Peconic Bay, is a link in the chain of migratory waterfowl refuges along the Atlantic flyway. It is managed by the Fish and Wildlife Service of the US Department of the Interior. Picnicking permitted. No dogs.

Cedar Point County Park See "Camping."

Hither Hills State Park See "Camping."

Indian Field County Park See "Camping."

Quogue Wildlife Refuge Quogue (OL 3-4771): Follow signs off Montauk Highway, west of the village. About an hour's drive from East Hampton, but worth it for its miles of nature trails, ponds, marshes, and rare local flora. A small zoo houses foxes, raccoons, and other wildlife. Managed by the New York State Department of Environmental Conservation.

SANCTUARIES OF THE NATURE CONSERVANCY

Kaplan Meadow-Merrill Lake Sanctuary Springs: Springs-Fireplace Road and Hog Creek Road, on Accabonac Harbor. Two large and several smaller parcels of open plains and wetlands fronting the harbor. Typical of tidal marshes of the area. Deer are common here; osprey, less frequently seen, have been staging a minor comeback in recent years.

Atlantic Double Dunes on the ocean between East Hampton and Amagansett: A complex of widely spaced ocean-front acres, the largest parcel being **Sheppard's Dunes** in Amagansett, at the foot of Indian Wells Highway. Large stands of American dune grass, false heather, and beach pea. The Conservancy, which has recommended R. W. Miner's *Field Book of Seashore Life* as a useful companion here, asks visitors to avoid walking over the crest of the dunes.

Sagg Swamp Sagaponack: From the Montauk Highway, take Sagg Main Street (at the flashing light) south; sharp right on Sagg Road and follow signs.

The preserve contains more than seventy-five acres of the largest surviving fresh-water marsh on the South Fork.

Moffet's Pond East Hampton: Foot of Dunemere Lane, adjacent to the Maidstone Club golf course. A small fresh-water pond surrounded by cattails and rushes. As many as 500 coot have been seen at rest here at one time. Many other birds may be found at and near the pond, as well as the swans and mallards which are perennial tenants.

Note: Calls for permission to enter sanctuaries of the Nature Conservancy should be made to 267–3748. The chapter's office is located at the Town Marine Museum on Bluff Road, Amagansett.

Nature Trail, East Hampton: The trail and sanctuary lie between Huntting and David's Lane, and may be approached either from Main Street or Egypt Lane, just east of the post office. Signs mark the entrance. Maintained by the East Hampton Ladies Village Improvement Society, it is open year-round (no permit required). The Nature Trail is home to several fat mallard families which thrive on the stale bread they get from visitors. Skunk cabbage and ferns abound.

CAMPING

Gone are the days when the cyclist or back-packer could spread a blanket in the shelter of some solitary dune and settle down to a night's rest under the stars. East Hampton has strict laws forbidding sleeping out at night on public lands, which include beaches, woods, potato fields, the main street of Amagansett, and just about everything else that isn't private property. Dozens of young people persist in breaking the law every week during the summer, and all they get for their pains is a sleepless night and a $25 fine. Even the most deserted beaches are patrolled nightly by town police.

There are three public campgrounds in the area.

Cedar Point and **Montauk Park** (Indian Field Park) are maintained by Suffolk County, and are open only to county residents and their guests upon payment of a one-dollar fee. Proof of residency required; payment may be made at the entrance.

Cedar Point (324–2195), 608 acres at Northwest Woods, East Hampton, has 190 general campsites with facilities for trailer and tent camping (no hookups). Woods, wetlands, bay beaches. Swimming when lifeguard is on duty. Rowboats available for hire; fishing at no charge. Sanitary facilities nearby. Campsites at Cedar Point are available on a first-come, first-served basis; call ahead to be safe.

Indian Field Park (668–5111), east of East Lake Drive, was acquired by the county in 1974. Ambitious plans for it, including public tennis courts and an 18-hole golf course, have been contemplated, but for the moment its 865 acres facing Gardiners Bay are undeveloped and a naturalist's paradise.

No roads here yet, but four-wheel drive vehicles will be allowed by special permit; call the County Department of Parks at 567–1700. Excellent salt-water fishing. Bring a sleeping bag if you plan to stay overnight.

Hither Hills State Park (668–2554), Robert Moses's dream-come-true, is a vast, enormously popular campground about three miles west of Montauk on Route 27 (Old Montauk Highway). Its 1,775 acres front directly on the ocean, making it one of the most scenic public facilities in the state. Tent and trailer sites, central shower building and bathhouse, playing fields, refreshment stand and general store.

Hither Hills is open from April 15 to October 15, with a two-week limit on camping. It is absolutely necessary to reserve space as much as six months to a year in advance. Write or call: Long Island State Park Commission, Belmont Avenue, Babylon, N.Y. 11702 (516-669–1000).

There are no camping facilities at **Montauk Point State Park** (668–9867), the easternmost extremity of Long Island, but it's a nice place to picnic and the surf fishing is good. 724 acres, refreshments available. See "Museums: Montauk Lighthouse."

Newspapers

If you'd like to have it known that you've given a party or gone to visit your daughter in California call or write the **East Hampton Star** (324–0002, –0477), 153 Main Street, the town's official newspaper. Read the **Star** for its no-nonsense editorials, hard news, features, Kuhn cartoon, classified ads, calendar, obituaries, or tart letters to the editor, but read it, or you won't know the half of what's going on. The **Star** is published Thursdays, a bargain for a quarter.

Dan's Papers (537–0500) originate in Dan's Publishing Tower, a Victorian house in Bridgehampton. There's a paper for almost every East End town (a North Fork edition too), and they are free. Dan himself, according to rumor, works out of a small room in Central Islip, dreaming up front-page stories about how to harness sea gulls for gas-free driving on the beach. There's some fact among the fancy and a valuable list of baby-sitters in the back.

Permits

State or town permits are required for various pursuits. The place to get them is the East Hampton Town Hall, on the north side of Montauk Highway opposite Amy's Lane, about midway between East Hampton and Amagansett. Town Hall is also where to go to pay a parking ticket, complain about taxes, or file notice that you are about to build a garage two feet from your neighbor's property line. In other words, for any official business. The Town Hall staff is unfailingly pleasant and patient, even on a Memorial Day weekend when 200 people want beach stickers at once.

Town Hall is open from 9:00 A.M. to 4:00 P.M. daily year-round, and from 9:00 A.M. to noon on Saturday. It is closed Sunday.

The following permits are available (prices are subject to change):

Shellfish licenses	$ 2
Fresh-water fishing (resident)	$ 4.25
Fresh-water fishing (nonresident)	$11
Fresh-water fishing (seven-day nonresident)	$ 6.50

(Fishing permits are also available at Tony's Sport Shop, Newtown Lane, East Hampton.)

Hunting (resident)	$ 4.25
Hunting (nonresident)	$18
Big game (resident)	$ 4.25
Big game (nonresident)	$18
Trapping (resident only)	$ 4.25
Archery	$ 3.25
Parking stickers for town beaches	See "Beaches"

Duck-hunting licenses are issued by the federal government and may be obtained at any post office.

Photo Supplies

John Reed's Lighthouse (324–1067) on Newtown Lane, East Hampton, will sell you film, cameras, and a number of accessories. It will also send your film out to be processed or, if you wish, do it for you in its custom lab.

Photo Works (324–6882), Newtown Lane, East Hampton. Located over the Old Post Office Cinema. Processing on premises; photographers available for portrait and candid work.

Picture Framing

SOUTHAMPTON

Morris Studio (AT 3–0085) Main Street, has a fairly good selection of frames for photographs and art. It also carries some art and photo supplies.

BRIDGEHAMPTON

The **Gillan Gallery** (537–3775), next to Bobby Van's on Main Street, does custom picture framing and has some interesting framed prints as well.

AMAGANSETT

Gallery East Hampton (267–8654), Amagansett Square. Albert Sharp's art gallery and framing shop is straight ahead as you enter the main building. Creative custom work.

Pizzerias

Pizza is pizza, in some people's opinion, and will never be anything else no matter how you slice it. The true aficionado knows, however, that every pizza has a personality of its own. We venture to recommend the personable pizzas at:

Pizza Village (668–2232), Main Street, Montauk. Crunchy crusts and lots of cheese.

Felix Astro Pizza (267–8300), Main Street, Amagansett. Try the Sicilian on for size. Beer and wine.

Brothers Four (324–5821), 39 Newtown Lane, East Hampton. Thin crust, done to a flip.

Sam's (324–5900), 36 Newtown Lane, East Hampton. A different taste. Those who like it, love it. Beer and wine.

Ma Bergman's (324–0590), 136 N. Main Street, East Hampton. Distinctive cheese crust. Indoor-outdoor seating. Beer and wine.

Peri's (324–9800), Montauk Highway at Cove Hollow Road, East Hampton. Don't be put off by the outside. Some say this is the best of all.

Restaurants

If your expectations are modest there are several restaurants in the Hamptons that may please you. The problem is not that there aren't good cooks in the area. There are plenty, but most of them know better than to try to run a seasonal restaurant.

As a rule, the longer a place has been operating under its original owners, the more dependable it tends to be. Usually the simplest menus produce the best results.

Ten to fifteen dollars a person will generally buy you a drink and dinner with a modest wine in most of the places listed here. Dress is mostly casual, with a few exceptions as noted.

Restaurant schedules are subject to seasonal change, and a phone call is always wise. In season, reservations are advisable.

MONTAUK RESTAURANTS

Flying Fish (668–2920). Overlooks Lake Montauk. A pleasant place to spend an afternoon. Lunch, dinner. Fresh fish is the specialty. East Lake Drive opposite the airport. Open daily, May–October, lunch, noon–3; dinner, 6–10. Diner's Club, American Express. Moderate-expensive.

Foxy's (668–9478). Breakfast, lunch, dinner in an informal village restaurant on the main street. "Old-fashioned ice-cream creations." Open 7:00 A.M.–midnight, May 30–Labor Day; to 7:00 P.M. September and May. Closed October–April. Inexpensive.

Gosman's Restaurant (668–5330). A tourist landmark for fresh fish, lobsters. Indoor-outdoor dining rooms. The view of the harbor is its best feature. The crowds and the cooking are less agreeable, but the service is usually friendly. Watch the boats pull in with the day's catch at 5:00 P.M. Gosman's Dock, off West Lake Drive. Open daily, noon–10, April–October. Closed Monday out of season. No credit cards. Moderate-expensive.

Gurney's Inn (668–2345), Old Montauk Highway about two miles west of the village. Montauk's most elaborate year-round resort and convention hotel, with a huge dining room. Restaurant and cocktail lounge, overlooking the ocean, open to public. Caters to weddings, parties, conventions. Landscaped grounds for after-dinner strolls. Entertainment. Dress: "according to the rules of good taste." Lunch noon–3; dinner 6–10; Sundays 1–10. Reservations a must. American Express. Moderate-expensive.

Montauk Golf and Racquet Club (668–5000), South Fairview Avenue off West Lake Drive. Modern clubhouse open to the public for dining, dancing, entertainment. Sunday brunch (11–2:30) buffet-style includes omelets, roast filet, creamed chicken, fresh Montauk blueberries. Open for dinner from 7:00 P.M., Tuesday–Sunday, June–September. Reservations and appropriate dress appreciated. No credit cards. Moderate-expensive. See "Golf Courses."

Ruschmeyer's (668–2912 or 2877), Second House Road, off Montauk Highway at the west end of town. Montauk's oldest restaurant. Box lunches prepared for fishermen. Banquet and party facilities. Open daily, April 15–December 1. Informal. Credit cards accepted. Moderate-expensive.

NAPEAGUE RESTAURANTS

"Napeague," an Indian word meaning "land overflowed by water," is the narrow stretch of mostly undeveloped land, about five miles long, between Amagansett and Montauk. The Montauk Highway runs down the center of the strip.

The Inn at Napeague (267–8103). A long-established restaurant with a good local menu. Open daily for lunch in season, noon–3; dinner, 5–10. Weekends only, 5–10, November–May. Closed February–March 15. Moderate-expensive.

AMAGANSETT RESTAURANTS

Fromm's (267–3553), Main Street in the center of town. Homemade breads and pastries. Sunday morning breakfast mecca. New York papers on sale. Open twenty-four hours a day in July and August, except 2–5 P.M. Off season, 6:00 A.M.–2:00 P.M.; closed Monday and

Tuesday (and for winter vacation). Try their Amagansett clam chowder. Moderate.

Gordon's (267–8190), Main Street. Gordon's takes itself too seriously, but the food is good. So is the wine list. Sittings at 7:00 and 9:00 P.M. Jackets required for gentlemen; skirts for ladies. Reservations necessary. Closed off-season. Expensive.

Martell's (267–6363), Montauk Highway, east of Amagansett business district. A very popular singles bar and restaurant. If you haven't found a date at Asparagus Beach try here. Cover charge in season. Dining and dancing. Open year-round. Moderate.

Royale Fish (267–3459), Amagansett Square. Indoor-outdoor restaurant with cheerful service and good local menu. Everything is fresh. Open daily in season, 11:00 A.M.–1:00 A.M. Weekends only September–Thanksgiving and March–June. Reservations suggested. American Express. Moderate.

EAST HAMPTON RESTAURANTS

Chez Labbat (324–4120), 20 Main Street. A local landmark. Next to the East Hampton Cinema. Under new management. Open year-round except Tuesday, noon–2:30; 5:30–10, later on Saturday. Sunday: dinner only. Reservations suggested. Credit cards honored. Moderate-expensive.

East Boondock (324–9845), 128 Springs-Fireplace Road. Soul food—ham hocks, chitlins, fresh fish, corn bread. Late-night entertainment and dancing to rock combo. Dinner served 6:00 P.M.–3:00 A.M. Open daily except Monday, year-round. Moderate.

The Fat Flounder (324–0725), 28 Maidstone Park Road, off Three Mile Harbor Road in the Springs. A dependable family restaurant. Fresh local fish. Make-your-own-salad bar. Children's menu. Small, friendly, informal. Open daily 5–10 in season. Closed Tuesday off-season. Closed January–February. Reservations a must. Moderate.

The Hedges (324–6300), across from Town Pond at the entrance to the village. This elegant establishment has undergone several changes of ownership since the late Henri Soulé ran it as a summer extension of Le Pavillon. John Eyre, the new proprietor, is determined to restore it to former glories. He's an ambitious and skillful cook and deserves all the encouragement he can get. *Prix fixe* dinner with wine. Open daily except Tuesday in season, for lunch and dinner. Off-season, daily for lunch; Friday–Monday for dinner. Reservations suggested. Expensive.

Huntting Inn (324–0410), 94 Main Street, corner of Huntting Lane. Dining in an early American landmark. Traditional cooking featuring Long Island duckling and local seafood. Open daily in season; weekends only October–June. Sunday brunch noon–3. "Suitable casual attire." Reservations suggested. Moderate-expensive.

Moon (324–5512), Montauk Highway one mile west of East Hampton. Popular discotheque downstairs; restaurant upstairs. Food is commendable. Open year-round. In season daily, 6:00 P.M.–3:00 A.M. Off-season, Thursday–Sunday, 8:00 P.M. on. No credit cards. Moderate-expensive.

1770 House (324–1770), Main Street near the library. Hearty American cuisine. Complete dinners served in an historic inn. Open daily from 5:00 P.M. year-round, except Monday off-season. American Express. Moderate-expensive.

Shazam (324–2400), 128 N. Main Street. Restaurant and discotheque. Late-night dancing. Silvered, mirrored dining rooms; glass bar glows in the dark. The food is somewhat better than the decor would suggest. Open daily except Monday, from 6:00 P.M., in season; weekends only April–June and September–December. Reservations suggested. Credit cards honored. Expensive.

Spring Close House (324–0233), Montauk Highway at Spring Close Highway, opposite Gertz's. Well-run, long-established restaurant with food as good as you'll get in East Hampton. Reasonable prices, professional service. Indoor-outdoor dining in agreeable surroundings. Open March–Thanksgiving. Lunch, noon–3; dinner, 6:00 P.M. on. Men should wear jackets at dinner. Reservations necessary on weekends. Credit cards honored. Moderate-expensive.

SAG HARBOR RESTAURANTS

American Hotel (725–9716), Main Street. Ambitious French menu in a mid-Victorian landmark hotel painstakingly and intelligently restored. Open daily in summer, noon–2:00 A.M. Closed Monday and Tuesday off-season, and January–February. Reservations imperative. Mastercharge, Diner's Club, American Express. Moderate-expensive.

Baron's Cove Inn (725–3332), West Water Street at the foot of the bridge. Docking for boats. Harbor view. Pleasant dining room with a standard menu; food adequately prepared and served. Open daily year-round, noon–10:00 P.M., later on weekends. Entertainment and dancing Saturday night. Reservations suggested. Credit cards honored. Moderate-expensive.

WAINSCOTT AND BRIDGE-HAMPTON RESTAURANTS

The following establishments, unless otherwise noted, are located along the Montauk Highway between Bridgehampton and East Hampton.

Bobby Van's (537–0590), Main Street, Bridgehampton. Where to go to discuss the price of potatoes, the op ed page of the *Times*, and the curriculum at the Hampton Day School. One of the most popular bars in the Hamptons, mostly for Bobby's piano. Open daily, noon–11:00 P.M., year-round. Bar stays open till the last customer goes home to bed.

Bridgehampton Candy Kitchen (537–9885), Main Street. Homemade ice cream, made with fresh local strawberries, peaches, blueberries, etc. Good big sandwiches too. New York newspapers on sale. Open daily 7:00 A.M. to around 8:00 P.M. year-round; later in summer. Closed February.

Old Stove Pub (537–9895). A pleasant restaurant in a former private house next to the Poxabogue golf course. A few homemade Greek dishes. Greek wines. Open year-round, 6–11. Occasionally closed off-season (never on weekends); call to be sure. Moderate.

Sherri's (537–9877), School Street, Bridgehampton. Popular local restaurant. Good food at moderate prices. Steak sandwiches, local bay scallops in season. Open daily, 11:00 A.M.–11:00 P.M., year-round.

The Sugarplum (537–1055), opposite Grant City shopping center. Nice surroundings, continental cuisine. Dinner from 6:00 P.M. daily in season. Closed Monday–Tuesday off-season. Informal. American Express, Diner's Club. Moderate.

WEST OF BRIDGEHAMPTON

Herb McCarthy's Bowden Square (283–2800), North Sea Road, Southampton. A fashionable cocktail lounge and restaurant for people who miss 21 and El Morocco. Good wine cellar in this Southampton institution. Entertainment and dancing on weekends. Open daily year-round, noon–2:00 A.M. Reservations necessary. Informal, but don't wear blue jeans. Credit cards honored. Moderate-expensive.

John Duck Jr. (283–0311), Prospect Street off N. Main Street, Southampton. John Duck is a local favorite. German-American cooking in a vast family restaurant. The duckling is crisp and stuffed with a bread and apple dressing. Don't be discouraged by the full parking lot; there'll be room inside. Meeting place for Rotary, Kiwanis, Lions clubs. No reservations. Open daily from 11:00 A.M. year-round; closed Monday off-season. Informal. Credit cards honored. Moderate.

The Lobster Inn (283–9828), Inlet Avenue, about six miles west of Southampton, where the Southampton bypass (County Road 39) meets the Sunrise Highway Extension. The Inn serves steamed lobsters in all sizes up to about five pounds, at prices that are not exorbitant for what you get. Potato, vegetable, salad included with dinner. Very crowded in summer, and on Sunday nights in spring and fall with city-bound weekenders, so if you arrive at dinner time be prepared to wait. It's much less busy at lunch: a pleasant place to spend a rainy afternoon. No reservations. Open noon–10:00 P.M. April–November; closed off-season. Informal. American Express.

Old Mill Restaurant (283–2488), 56 Nugent Street, Southampton. Good home cooking prepared by a local woman who deserves her loyal following. Pleasant service. Open in season only. Informal. American Express. Moderate.

Shippy's (283–0007), 36 Windmill Lane, Southampton. Southampton's version of Bobby Van's, but without the piano. A lively bar with a straightforward menu. Not a place to go for peace and quiet. Open year-round, 4:30 P.M. to 4:00 A.M. Closed Tuesday. No credit cards.

Riding Stables

Deep Hollow Ranch (668–3113; 668–2744), Montauk Highway, Montauk. About three miles east of Montauk Village. Horses for hire. Ring and trail riding. English and Western saddles. Trail rides wind through some of Montauk's most beautiful wooded terrain; you may even spot a fox or two.

Indian Wells Ranch (267–3212), Windmill Lane, Amagansett. Horses for hire by the hour or half-day. Trail riding with guide. English and Western saddles.

Jan-Su Stables (324–9791), Oak View Highway, East Hampton. Full-size indoor arena. Full boarding facilities. Private and group lessons. English saddles.

Spring Close Stables (324–9838). Spring Close Highway, East Hampton. Group and private lessons. Ring or trail riding. English and Western saddles.

Stony Hill Stables (267–3203), Town Lane, Amagansett. Private or group lessons. Experienced instructors. Group lessons given by the series only; early registration recommended in season. English saddles. Boarding and stabling facilities.

Swan Creek Farms (537–0662), Halsey Lane, Bridgehampton. Private and group lessons. English saddles. Boarding and stabling facilities. Group lessons in season by series only.

Topping Riding School (537–0948), Gibson's Lane, Sagaponack. Private riding club. Recommendations necessary. All facilities.

Sailing

Small-boat enthusiasts will find superb sailing in East Hampton. Three Mile Harbor, Lake Montauk, and Fort Pond offer calm, protected waters; Gardiners and Napeague bays will delight the experienced sailor.

Sailboats may be rented at several places around town. In Sag Harbor, **Baron's Cove Marina** (725–2100) and **Ned's** (725–0560). In East Hampton, **Tradewind Sailboat Rentals** (324–4013). In Montauk, **Sea & Sky Portel** (668–2151); also at the miniature golf course on the Montauk Highway at the entrance to the village.

If you're thinking of buying a boat check the boat ads in the East Hampton **Star** and call a few of the larger marinas to see what's available. The **Hampton Marine Center** (537–0914) on the Montauk Highway near Wainscott and the **Peerless Marine Center** (725–0400) in Sag Harbor are authorized small-boat dealers.

For free sailing instruction, sponsored by the town and the Red Cross, see "Special Events."

Special Events

Fireworks! Fish fries! Fairs! Here's a checklist of the not-to-be-missed happenings that go on all year long in East Hampton, and almost every day in the summer. Some take place annually on the same day; others are ad hoc and unpredictable.

Watch the "Coming Up" calendar on page two of the East Hampton **Star** for advance notice of church rummage sales and auctions. Also for clambakes, bake sales, and Chicken 'n Rib dinners (especially the savory one at the Calvary Baptist Church). If you've never seen a thousand people feasting together outdoors on barbecued chicken, corn, and watermelon, go to the East Hampton Lions Club benefit in early July at Dune Alpin Farm, west of the village.

Look out for signs in stores around town for exact dates and times of all events sponsored by local organizations. The East Hampton Baymen cook up a monster fish fry in August at Legion Hall, Amagansett. The Police Benevolent Association and the American Legion sponsor a round of cocktail parties and roast beef dinners, year-round, where the food is good, the price is right, and new faces are always welcome. The Amagansett Fire Department gives two big barbecues at the fire house during the summer: beer, clams, apple pie, and shiny fire trucks for the kids to climb on. Buy tickets early.

Music to the ears: the Choral Society of the Hamptons, accompanied by the South Fork Chamber Orchestra, performs a few times a year at the Bridgehampton Presbyterian Church, usually on Sunday afternoons. (Singers interested should call Mrs. Hildreth Rogers, RA 6–4609.) They are good enough to have earned the support of the New York State Council on the Arts. Go hear them, and also try to catch SPEBSQUA, if they do a concert at Guild Hall. (That's the Society for the Preservation and Encouragement of Barber Shop Quartet Singing in America.) SPEBSQUA sometimes sings with the Sweet Adelines; two great groups for the price of one.

For no money at all, a summer Sunday in Montauk might be topped off by an outdoor jazz concert on the big stage at Gosman's Dock. Bring a blanket or cushion to sit on. The concerts start around 5:00 P.M. Also free are the East Hampton Summer Band open-air concerts at the Middle School lawn on Newtown Lane; watch the **Star** for dates and times.

The band holds tryouts, by the way, in mid-June, and welcomes applications from summer people as well as locals, as long as you'll show up for evening rehearsals. Call the high school if you're interested and ask for Stafford Ezzard. They also play at the big Fourth of July fireworks exhibit (which is sometimes held on July 3) at Main Beach, and at the Ladies Village Improvement Society Fair on the last Friday in July.

Of all the fairs in East Hampton, and there are plenty, the LVIS's is the largest, the longest (10:00 A.M. to 10:00 P.M.), and the most ambitious. Planning for next year's fair begins the day after this year's ends. Besides the food booths, with their vast selection of homemade goodies, there are flowers, books, needlepoint, toys, "white elephants," etc., for sale, a playland for the kids, raffles, door prizes, lunch, tea, supper, and square dancing.

Amagansett Presbyterian Church Fair is another good one, especially for small children. It's held on the afternoon of the second Wednesday in July, at the church grounds on Meeting House Lane.

In the Springs, the Fisherman's Fair has become an annual eating orgy, with clam pies, raw clams, and chowder prepared by Craig Claiborne and Pierre Franey, who are on hand to ladle it all out. For some reason the temperature is always around 90 on the day of the Fisherman's Fair—the second Saturday in August—and the absence of trees on Ashawagh Hall lawn makes it feel even hotter. Get there early, before the *moules marinières* are all gone, and leave by noon or the kids will be trampled in the crush.

In Montauk, the entire fishing fleet —charter, sports, party, commercial, and private boats—turns out on a day in mid-June for the Blessing of the Fleet. The boats pass in review, flags flying and crews at attention, to receive the ancient benediction: success on the sea

and safe return to shore. Call St. Therese's Church (668–2200) for date and time of the ceremony.

Second House Museum in Montauk is the site of Sampson Occum Day, also held in the middle of June, when the birthday of the great Mohegan Indian preacher is marked with ritual dancing, singing, and storytelling. Sassafras tea and samp are for sale. Chief Red Thunder Cloud will tell you how to prepare both. (You can sometimes buy samp at the Amagansett IGA.)

There's no tea at the Montauk Village Association's annual "Greenery-Scenery" celebrity party, but plenty of other liquids are available. Don't be surprised if the fellow who mixes your drink looks like an image from your television screen or a face on a book jacket. A host of celebrities donate their bartending talents every year to this event, which started as a simple cocktail-and-cheese-dip affair and has become a five- or six-course outdoor banquet with hundreds in attendance. Proceeds benefit the MVA, which uses the money to beautify and maintain the streets of Montauk. Usually held the last weekend in July.

Another Montauk special: every Thursday night in season the New York Ocean Science Laboratory holds its "Ecologically Yours" series, a program of lectures and/or filmed documentaries presented by distinguished marine scientists, historians, and conservationists. The series is free. See the **Star** for times.

Art sales and shows go on in and out of season. In August look for Guild Hall's one-day outdoor Clothesline Art Sale. BAM, the Bridgehampton Association of Merchants, sponsors sidewalk art sales from time to time in that village, and in Sag Harbor, MASH (Merchants Association of) does the same. The Water Mill Community Club's open-air benefit sale and auction in mid-August is another good bet, with old furniture and new (clean, anyway) pots and pans for sale besides the art.

Bridgehampton is home to the summer's biggest strawberry festival, held at the Community House in or around the third week of June. There is a festival in Wainscott, too, at the Wainscott Chapel. Berries from the nearby. Osborn farm and other local sources are at their ripest then and the shortcake is unbeatable. When you've eaten your fill, honor your corner partner and square dance till midnight. The local chapter of the Order of the Eastern Star sponsors the Bridgehampton event.

Throughout the season the Red Cross, in cooperation with the town, gives free swimming and sailing instruction to residents of Sag Harbor, East Hampton, Amagansett-Springs, and Montauk. Each village gets its own two-week program at a nearby bay beach. Free round-trip bus transportation, too. Summer renters may also be eligible for the course, depending on length of stay. Call Town Hall at the end of June for information.

August is the month for house tours. Six or seven private homes and a local landmark or two generally make up an afternoon's tour. These events attract day-trippers from Connecticut and Nassau County in almost as large numbers as year-round people who've always wondered what the inside of that attractive house down the road looks like, so buy tickets early. There are tours in Montauk, Sag Harbor, Bridgehampton, Amagansett, and East Hampton, sponsored by the local historical societies and Guild Hall.

Wealthy and/or prominent summer residents often give benefit parties in their homes for worthy causes. It's an old East Hampton tradition and a popular way to meet new people, maybe see a notable art collection or garden that you wouldn't have otherwise, and support a foundation or charity as well. These parties are costly ($10 to $25 per couple), tax-deductible, dressy. The **Star** will note them about a week in advance.

On or about Labor Day, go see the artists-writers softball game at the field off Newtown Lane. Such talents as Jimmy Ernst and George Plimpton are rumored to sweat out secret batting practices all summer in preparation for this annual classic. In recent years a house-painter or two has been added to

beef up the artists' roster. They won for the first time in 1974.

Also held over Labor Day weekend is the Shinnecock Indian Powwow, at the Reservation off Montauk Highway west of Southampton. Members of tribes from several states join in the three-day song and dance festival. Refreshments, Indian headdresses, tomahawks, etc. for sale. Some of the white man's commercialism has crept under the tent, but the kids will love it anyway.

Maybe you'd rather read about happenings than go to them. The East Hampton Free Library holds an annual book sale early in June, and the Amagansett Library has one in August. Discarded volumes from the libraries' own collections, ranging from duplicates of best sellers to musty old denizens of the back stacks, as well as hundreds of books donated by the public, all marked down by the helpful members of the library committee to ridiculously low prices.

Finally, if you're still around in the fall, go see the East Hampton High School football team's Saturday afternoon home games. The Bonackers, despite the school's small size, consistently field one of the strongest teams in the A2 league. The band plays, the cheerleaders leap and twirl, the autumn sun shines, and the city people down for the weekend yell almost as loud as the quarterback's mother.

Surfing

Surfboards are available for rent at the **Albatross Beach Shop** (668-5833) on South Elmwood Avenue, Montauk. From there, ride the highway or the waves east to the Ditch Plains ocean beach, where you'll find lots of friends.

Tennis

An informal survey made in 1974 found that there are about 170 tennis courts, give or take a couple, in East Hampton. That sounds like a lot but isn't really, because nearly half belong to private clubs or motels.

The following are either public or semiprivate courts. Semiprivate courts are those which charge a fee, usually between $300 and $500 for a seasonal family membership. When not in use by members, these courts can be rented by the public on an hourly basis. If you have trouble finding one that's free, remember that a few motels (see "Accommodations") will rent out their courts when not in use by guests.

EAST HAMPTON TOWN COURTS

(All town-owned courts are assigned on a first-come, first-served sign-up system, so it's a good idea to go early in the morning. A small charge is made.)

Abraham's Path Amagansett. Four hard-surface courts about half a mile north of Montauk Highway.

East Hampton High School Long Lane. Six all-weather courts.

Herrick Playground Newtown Lane, East Hampton. Three hard-surface courts in dubious condition, behind the A & P.

John Marshall Elementary School Church Street off Dayton Lane, East Hampton. Two hard-surface courts.

SEMIPRIVATE COURTS

Green Hollow Tennis Club (324–0927), Green Hollow Road, East Hampton. They will rent open courts during the week, but there rarely are any on weekends.

Racquet Club of East Hampton (324–5155), Buckskill Road. Same restrictions as at Green Hollow.

Dunes Racquet Club (267–8508), Town Lane, Amagansett. Same restrictions as at Green Hollow.

Mashashimuet Park (725–9777), Sag Harbor. Six courts (four clay, two all-weather) maintained by Sag Harbor Village. Low annual fee. Will rent courts if not in use. Children's playground on premises.

Bayberry Tennis Club (267–3460), Abraham's Path, Amagansett. The charge for renting a court, if you can find one, is $15 an hour, typical in this category.

Bridgehampton Racquet and Surf Club (537–9840), Ocean Avenue. Non-members are welcome to take lessons; otherwise, the 13 courts are private.

Montauk Golf and Racquet Club (668–5000), South Fairview Avenue. Six clay courts, open to guests of member motels. See "Golf Courses."

Old Salt Racquet Club (267–8525), Montauk Highway between Amagansett and Montauk. Three clay courts open to the public by the hour.

Tourist Information Centers

The **East Hampton Chamber of Commerce** (324–0362), at 37B Newtown Lane (turn left off Main Street at the traffic light), can provide up-to-the-minute information for travelers. Maps of the village available at no charge.

The **Montauk Chamber of Commerce** (668–2428), Main Street at the Circle, will help you make your way through the maze of Montauk motels and marinas.

The **Suffolk County Department of Commerce and Industry** (979–2929) maintains a tourist information booth, in season, at Exit 66 (eastbound) of the Long Island Expressway. Extensive selection of free maps and folders.

The **Merchants Association of Sag Harbor** (MASH) distributes free maps of historic homes within walking distance at the Windmill on Main Street in Sag Harbor.

Transportation

The vast majority of people going to and from the South Fork travel by car. During the resort season, driving to Montauk, especially on weekends, can be a painfully slow process, since the Montauk Highway (Route 27) is also the main street of Water Mill, Bridgehampton, East Hampton, and Amagansett. A proposal by the state to construct a bypass road around these villages has met with strong support and equally strong opposition in the community.

There are a few detours which are longer but, in summer, probably faster ways of getting around by car. See "Automobile Services–Shortcuts."

As for train service to the Hamptons, it was actually faster in 1910 than it is today. Despite the best efforts of politicians and citizens' groups to improve service on the Long Island Railroad's Montauk branch, the prospect of truly efficient, rapid rail transportation on the South Fork is dim. From Penn Station, even the fastest train takes more than three hours to make the 95-mile trip to East Hampton.

In season, the LIRR nevertheless is a better bet for weekenders than the clogged Long Island Expressway, with its lines of stalled traffic stretching all the way from Manhattan to Moriches. And a round-trip by coach costs less than a tank of gas.

There are other ways—both more and less expensive—of getting to, from, and around the East End. The following guide to transportation facilities lists them all. Telephone for specific rates and schedules.

AIR SERVICE

East Hampton Airways (537–1010). Based at the East Hampton Airport, Daniel's Hole Road off Route 27, west of the village. Numerous daily scheduled flights in summer, between East Hampton and Flushing (N.Y.) Airport, next to LaGuardia. Winter charter flights anywhere; minimum two persons, weekends only. Services: minor repairs, aircraft rental to qualified pilots, flying lessons.

Montauk-Caribbean Airways Inc. (537–1010 or 668–9726): Based at Sea & Sky Portel, East Lake Drive, Montauk,

and at the East Hampton Airport. Daily scheduled flights to and from Flushing Airport and Montauk, East Hampton, and Block Island (summers only). Air taxi flights anywhere; charters.

Note: The nearest large airport to East Hampton is Islip-MacArthur (588–8062), about forty miles west in Ronkonkoma, which has scheduled service by American, Allegheny, and Altair Airlines.

Long Island Airways Inc. (JU 8–2344), at Islip-MacArthur, charters small planes. So do **Suffolk Aviation Inc.** (288–6250) at the Westhampton Beach County Airport; **Yankee Airways Inc.** (203–443–2297), a Connecticut-based company; and **Fishers Island Airways** (788–7249).

AUTOMOBILE SERVICES

How to get to East Hampton

The most direct route from New York to East Hampton is via Route 495 (the Long Island Expressway) east to Exit 70 (Manorville Road). Follow signs for Montauk to Route 27 (Sunrise Highway), east through Southampton, Water Mill, and Bridgehampton.

Alternate route: Southern State Parkway, following signs to Heckscher State Parkway, thence to Route 27 east.

Shortcuts around villages

The best way to avoid East Hampton and Amagansett traffic if you are driving to Montauk is this: instead of turning left at the traffic light at the entrance to East Hampton, continue across the road and make the left at the Hedges Restaurant on to James Lane. About a fourth of a mile along, turn right on Dunemere Lane, just before Guild Hall. Go left at the end of Dunemere, which will take you through the Maidstone Club's golf course, and follow the yellow line to Further Lane.

Further Lane ends at Indian Wells Highway. Turn right on Indian Wells, and left, after about 500 feet, to Bluff Road. Follow Bluff Road and admire the ocean view for about a mile, until it joins the Montauk Highway.

Coming west from Montauk, fork

left at Bluff Road, opposite DiSunno's Motors, and reverse the process.

To avoid the westbound build-up around Bridgehampton, which is very bad on weekends thanks to an improperly timed traffic light, turn right off the Montauk Highway at the Sagg Main Street overhead blinker, about a mile past Poxabogue Golf Course. Go left on Hildreth Lane, cross under a railroad trestle, turn left (Narrow Lane) and left again under another trestle, and continue on Narrow Lane across the Sag Harbor Turnpike to Lumber Lane.

Left on Lumber, sharp right on Railroad Avenue, to its end at Butter Lane. Go left for about half a mile and rejoin the Montauk Highway past Bridgehampton. **Don't** use this shortcut during or just after a heavy rainstorm, as the railroad underpasses may be flooded.

CAR RENTALS

Ford Rent-A-Car (324–0228), Plitt Ford, East Hampton

Hertz Rent-A-Car (324–2650), East Hampton, summer only

National Car Rental System (324–0100), East Hampton; (537–0704) Bridgehampton; (668–7507) Montauk.

CAR REPAIRS

Almost any gas station in town is equipped to make minor auto repairs. The following shops are repair specialists, and are recommended.

Alex's Garage (324–0140), East Hampton

Andy's Auto Body (725–0255), Sag Harbor

Daniel Tucker's Garage (267–3410), Amagansett

Maggrett Auto Body (537–0704), Bridgehampton

Sag Harbor Auto Body & Collision (725–3777)

BICYCLES

Biking becomes more popular every year in the Hamptons. Several gas stations and hardware stores add bike rental services in the summer. When biking on Montauk Highway, ride with the traffic—on the right shoulder.

Bicycle tours, in season, are run by Soporific East and meet at the Amagansett flagpole. For serious competitors there is an annual Fourth of July bike race from Amagansett to Montauk and back—about twenty-five miles. Call 267–8709 for information.

Cyclists should also know about the services of Hampton Jitney. See "Limousines and Taxis."

BIKE SALES AND RENTALS

Bike Barn (324–3998), 251 Pantigo Road, East Hampton

Bike Stop (267–8384), Montauk Highway, Amagansett

Chris Pfund Hardware (668–2456), Montauk Highway, Montauk

Gary's Cycles (725–3430), Main Street, Sag Harbor

Ideal Cash Store (725–1670), Main Street, Sag Harbor

Rent-A-Bike (267–6313), behind La-Carrubba's, Main Street, Amagansett

Soporific (537–3726), Montauk Highway, Bridgehampton

Soporific East (267–8709), Amagansett Square, Amagansett. (The two Soporific shops are headquarters for fine imported and racing bikes.)

South Fork Honda (537–0118), Montauk Highway, Wainscott

Strong Oil Co. (726–4700), Montauk Highway, Water Mill

Village Hardware (324–2456), 32 Newtown Lane, East Hampton

BUS SERVICES

East Hampton has no public bus service, except for a Saturday-only East

Hampton-Springs bus, though the question of starting one pops up occasionally at town board meetings. The answer is always the same: any profits buses might make in the summer would be more than offset by their losses off-season.

Hampton Jitney: See "Limousines and Taxis"

The **Long Island Railroad** (732–4300; in New York, 739–4200) has a scheduled bus service between Babylon and Montauk, Monday–Friday and on holidays, year-round. Buses run four or five times a day, stopping in Bridgehampton, East Hampton, and Amagansett, and connect with LIRR trains at Babylon for the ride to and from New York. Call for schedule, or pick up a copy of **Dan's Papers** and look on the back page.

Sunrise Coach Lines Inc. (477–1200 or 477–0823), based in Greenport on the North Fork, runs four scheduled buses daily, except Sundays and holidays, between that village and East Hampton. Buses stop at Sag Harbor, Bridgehampton, and a few places in between on signal. There is a connecting service to the Riverhead Shopping Plaza.

FERRIES

Ferries are a great way of avoiding the New York traffic if you are bound for southern Connecticut or New England, and are used much more by residents of waterbound Suffolk County than the casual tourist might realize.

North Haven, Sag Harbor, is the jumping-off point for the **Shelter Island South Ferry** (749–1200), which runs about every ten minutes between there and the island. Shelter Island's **North Ferry** (749–0139) connects it with Greenport on the north shore, and also runs continuously in season.

For Connecticut-bound travelers it's about an hour's ride from Greenport on east to Orient Point, where **New London Freight Lines** (323–2525 or 473–0294) runs an hourly ferry, in season, to New London, Connecticut. Service is cut down in fall and winter.

Further up the island, there's ferry service between Port Jefferson and Bridgeport, Connecticut (473–0286) from mid-May to mid-October. Special one-day round-trip fares are offered on both these lines.

From Montauk, the **Montauk-Block Island Ferry** (668–2141 or 668–2078) makes one round trip daily after July 1; and on weekends and Tuesdays from May 28-June 30. It leaves Montauk at 9:00 A.M. from Pier One. Service is sporadic, so be sure to call in advance.

LIMOUSINES AND TAXIS

All of these are reliable. Some are closed winters while their owners go south. Call a few to compare rates on long-distance trips.

Eames Taxi (324–1311). East Hampton and Amagansett. Also New York City trips. Twenty-four-hour telephone service.

Gansett Taxi (267–8080). Local and long-distance service. Based at the gas station on Atlantic Avenue, Amagansett.

Hamptons Custom Transit (537–3898; in New York, 628–0144). Long-distance limousine service to New York City or airports. Can accommodate eleven passengers. Closed off-season.

Hampton Jitney (726–9511; in New York, 679–5813). In summer, the jitney buses run hourly from Amagansett to Southampton College, with stops wherever you want along Montauk Highway. Look for the "Hampton Jitney—Stop" signs for boarding points. The brown Volkswagen buses carry trailers for bicycles, at no extra charge—a great way for bikers to cover more ground.

In winter, daily (Monday-Friday) trips to New York City from East Hampton and Amagansett, leaving about 8:00 A.M., returning 9:30 P.M. By reservation only.

Hampton Livery Service (212–866–1849). Air-conditioned shuttle service,

New York to all points in the Hamptons.

Jimmy's Taxi (537–0125). Serving the Bridgehampton area; also long-distance limousines. Twenty-four-hour telephone service.

Larry's Taxi (668–5232), Second House Road, Montauk.

Reggie's Montauk Taxi (668–5283).

Schaefer Taxi and Limousine (324–0334). A long-established East Hampton firm which goes anywhere, local or long-distance, between 7:00 A.M. and midnight. Schaefer's will also meet the early train by appointment. Open June 1 to October 1.

RAIL TRANSPORTATION

The **Long Island Railroad**'s East Hampton office (324–0967) is sometimes manned but more often not. If no one answers, call the general office at Selden (732–4300) for information.

From Penn Station, the LIRR runs three trains daily, year-round to the Hamptons: one at 8:10 A.M.; one at 4:20 P.M., and the third, the "Fisherman's Special," at 12:10 A.M. (arriving Montauk 4:00 A.M.). In season extra trains are added on Thursday and Friday afternoons. The most popular with weekend commuters is the 4:10 P.M. "Cannonball," which has parlor cars only and is normally a little faster than the other trains.

Write to TDI Publications Inc., 275 Madison Ave., New York, N.Y. 10010, for a complete schedule, or pick one up at Penn Station. In East Hampton, **Dan's Papers** carries it on the back page of the **Summer Sun**.

In addition to its regular service the LIRR runs inexpensive escorted rail tours of various scenic and historic Suffolk sites, in spring, summer, and fall. Several of these include lunch or dinner. Call 212–526–0900, ext. 498, for information.

Used Furniture

Many a summer cottage has been furnished from cellar to attic with finds from **Nilsson's** of Southampton. John Nilsson, the amiable proprietor, has several barns full of furniture, up to and including the kitchen sink. Beds, chests, chairs, paintings, old brassbound trunks, bird cages—plenty of dross, but more than enough gold among it to make the hunt worthwhile. Nilsson's (283–1434) is located on North Sea Road north of the Southampton bypass (County Road 39). Take Exit 9. They guarantee same- or next-day delivery.

M. Press (283–2110), on the Southampton bypass opposite the auto museum, also has a vast assortment of secondhand furniture, though not as vast as Nilsson's. You might find some good used garden furniture and statuary here.

The Warehouse (283–8962), North Sea Road south of the bypass (Exit 9), has a few pieces of furniture but is better for bric-a-brac, books, and clothing. Operated for the benefit of the Hampton Animal Shelter.

If you cannot find what you need try advertising on the radio. Every weekday morning at 10:05 A.M., station WLNG of Sag Harbor (725–2300; 1490 on the AM dial) presents "Swap 'n Shop," a folksy kind of trading post of the airwaves. Some listeners call in with items they'd like to sell; others with things they'd like to buy. You just might, as they say, hear of something to your advantage.

Index

Page numbers in italics refer to the Guide.

Index

Index

Index

A NOTE ABOUT THE BOOK

Jason Epstein is vice president and senior editor at Random House, a founder of *The New York Review of Books*, and the author of *The Great Conspiracy Trial: An Essay on Law, Liberty and the Constitution*.

Elizabeth Barlow is an author, journalist, and television screenwriter. Her previous books are *The Forests and Wetlands of New York City* (for which she was awarded the John Burroughs Medal in 1972) and *Frederick Law Olmsted's New York*.

Mr. Epstein lives in Sag Harbor, Mrs. Barlow in Wainscott. Each had independently begun writing a history of the town of East Hampton when they decided to collaborate upon the version that forms the first section of this book. Mr. Epstein also contributed the sections on Sag Harbor, Montauk, and Gardiners Island. Mrs. Barlow also wrote "A Landscape Left by Ice," "The Birds of East Hampton," "A Nature Walk at Napeague," and the histories of East Hampton Village, Wainscott, Amagansett, and the Springs.

Irene Silverman, the author of "A Selective Guide to Living Well in East Hampton," is a journalist and frequent contributor to the East Hampton *Star*. She has a home in Amagansett.

Ralph Carpentier is a painter, illustrator of several children's books, and sometime commercial fisherman. Working with the late Jeannette Edwards Rattray, he designed the exhibits at the Marine Museum in Amagansett and executed the drawings that accompany them.